Sources and Translation Series
of the Russian Institute
Columbia University

The Russian Institute of Columbia University sponsors the "Sources and Translation Series of the Russian Institute" in the belief that important works of Russian history, literature, and criticism as well as memoirs and other source materials not previously available in English in complete form should be made available to specialists and to a general reading audience. It is hoped that these publications will contribute to the knowledge and understanding of Russian history and culture, as well as to enhanced respect for the craft of translation.

V. V. GIPPIUS
GOGOL

Edited and translated by Robert A. Maguire

Ardis   Ann Arbor

Ardis Publishers
2901 Heatherway
Ann Arbor, Michigan 48104

Library of Congress Cataloging in Publication Data

Gippius, Vasilii Vasil'evich, 1890-
    Gogol.

        Translation of Gogol'.
        Titles of works by Gogol': p.
        1. Gogol', Nikolai Vasil'evich, 1809-1852.
    2. Authors, Russian—19th century—Biography.
    PG3335.G4913   891.78'309 [B]   80-21888
    ISBN 0-88233-612-6

TABLE OF CONTENTS

The Gippius family of St. Petersburg was prominent, well-connected and attuned to literature. Writers, among them Alexander Blok, were frequent visitors. The father, a high official of the Ministry of Internal Affairs, had dabbled in composition as a youth. The two older sons, Vladimir and Alexander, published verses in the various Symbolist journals; Vladimir was also a critic and scholar. But it was the youngest, Vasily Vasilievich, born in 1890, who became famous as a professional man of letters.[1]

He entered St. Petersburg University in 1907, and a year later began to publish poetry, criticism and translations. For a time it seemed that he might make his mark as a poet. But he stopped writing verse for publication around the time World War I broke out, apparently convinced that he possessed little original talent. Instead he pursued his interests in translating—Horace, Novalis, Molière, Tieck and Heine, among others—and honed his skills as a scholar and critic of Russian literature.

During World War I, Gippius served with the Russian Red Cross in the Ukraine. After the Bolsheviks came to power, he spent some time as head of a secondary school in Kiev Province. In 1922, he assumed the chair of modern Russian literature at Perm University, where he remained until 1930. Then came a brief stint as a professor at Irkutsk (1930-32). Finally, he was transferred to the Pushkin House of the Academy of Sciences in Leningrad, and appointed professor at the University. There he remained for the rest of his life. Death came in February, 1942, during the German blockade of the city.

Although Gippius wrote extensively on topics in nineteenth-century Russian literature, he is best known for his studies of Gogol. He was one of the initiators, and the first general editor, of the Academy of Sciences edition of the so-called "complete" works (fourteen volumes, 1937-52).[2] For many years he conducted a seminar on Gogol at Leningrad University. But it is the monograph offered here that ensures him an enduring place among students of Gogol. It was undertaken during World War I, and published in 1924. In later years, he supposedly came to look on it as "obsolete, both from a methodological as well as a factual viewpoint."[3] To be sure, much new "factual" work was done on Gogol in the Soviet Union after the book appeared, and it would have been natural for such a painstaking scholar to avail himself of that material. The reference to "methodological" obsolescence may be a way of reminding us that many Formalist studies of Gogol's works were published in the 1920s and that Gippius's book is not one of them. Undoubtedly it also hints at the increasing tendency among Soviet scholars, from the mid-1920s on, to regard Gogol almost exclusively as a "realist" and even a proto-revolutionary. The Gippius of 1924 could not have subscribed to those views without fundamental qualification; but there is evidence that in the 1930s he did try to make some accommodation to them.[4] At the time of his death, he was working on a monograph that was meant to supplant the 1924 book. The chapters he managed to complete (on the literary history of *Evenings on a Farm Near Dikanka*) were published in 1948.[5] In addition, he wrote a long essay entitled "The Development of Gogol's Art," as a kind of preliminary study for the projected longer work. Though intended as part of a new history of Russian literature under the auspices of the Academy of Sciences, it was published only in 1966, in a collection of his essays.[6] At first glance, it is almost unrecognizable as a product of Gippius's mind. It honors all the Soviet clichés about Gogol, as the "founder of critical realism in Russian literature," as "a banner of revolutionary Russia," as a man who could not "fully free himself from the ideas of the gentry class" nor "work out a clear program of struggle against social evil" because of the intrusions of his religious and moral ideas. Yet Gippius continues to emphasize, as he did in the 1924 monograph, the basic unity of all Gogol's work, both in fiction and non-fiction; and he reaffirms one of his major scholarly strategies by giving the reader a lively sense of the various literary and esthetic traditions that operated in Gogol's time, and showing how Gogol accounted for them in his work.

It is safe to say that Gippius never improved on his 1924 study. In fact, this book still stands, by general agreement, as the best single work ever written on Gogol. It should be known not only to specialists in Russian literature, but to anyone who is interested in one of the great and still enigmatic figures of world literature.

Gippius does not write a graceful or supple Russian. Often he falls short of what he intends to express. Generally I have shortened his sentences and broken up his paragraphs, and sometimes have resorted to paraphrase in the interest of clarity. By and large, however, I have resisted impulses to perform radical editorial surgery and have stuck to the letter of the text, often at the expense of smooth English; for I believe that translations should strive to convey the tone of the originals, even when sour notes are struck.

Gippius insists that he is aiming at the non-specialist as well as the specialist. By this he means, of course, the *Russian* non-specialist, who is bound to know Gogol better than do most foreign readers. Hence the need for annotations that amplify Gippius's rather meager apparatus. Here I have observed the following principles. (1) Any name that is mentioned in D. S. Mirsky's *A History of Russian Literature* (still the standard work) is not glossed. In most cases, I have followed Mirsky's spellings of the names so that readers will find it easier to use his index. Thus, I write Dahl (not Dal), Weltmann (not Veltman), and Küchelbecker (not Kyukhelbeker). All other names, with a few exceptions, are identified in my notes. (2) Gippius admits that his notes are spotty and often incomplete, because of the conditions under which he worked. (World war, revolution, civil war, and life in provincial Perm apparently were not conducive to careful checking.) One often has the impression that he is citing sources from memory; errors and lapses abound. I have rechecked his sources myself, wherever possible, and have made appropriate emendations and corrections. (3) Quotes from Gogol have been set against the originals, corrected when necessary, and identified when Gippius has failed to do so. (4) My own notes for the text proper are enclosed in square brackets. All others are Gippius's. (5) The titles of Gogol's works appear only in English in the text; an appendix lists all his works that are mentioned by Gippius, with both English and Russian titles. For all other titles, the Russian is supplied in the text at first mention. (6) Letters are dated according to "new style" (i.e., the Gregorian) unless specifically designated as "old style" (o.s., i.e., Julian). Russia did not officially adopt the Gregorian calendar until 1918, but Gogol spent much of his life abroad in countries that observed it. Hence the double system.

For generous help on problems of translation, I am indebted to Maurice Friedberg, Richard Gustafson, Eva Kagan-Kans, Marina Ledkovsky, Nicholas Ozerov, and Leon and Galina Stilman. Welcome editorial suggestions were made by F. W. Maguire. Richard Borden ably assisted in tracking down some of the materials that went into the notes. I owe special thanks to Rose Raskin. On this occasion, as so often in the past, she helped me to see what the sometimes recalcitrant Russian original was driving at, and suggested felicitous English equivalents. It is in acknowledgment of our long association as friends and colleagues that I am pleased to dedicate this translation to her.

New York, N. Y.   *Robert A. Maguire*
1978

V. V. GIPPIUS

GOGOL

Translated and annotated by

Robert A. Maguire

This translation is dedicated to ROSE RASKIN

AUTHOR'S PREFACE

Within the confines of a brief study that is accessible to specialist and non-specialist alike, it is no easy matter to present everything fundamental that bears on Gogol's development as man and artist. The literature on Gogol is vast. Much work has been done. But as of this writing, not all essential facts have been brought together, nor have all possible conclusions been drawn. The best studies treating Gogol as a whole have been made by Kotlyarevsky, Mandelshtam, Pereverzev and Zenkovsky. Yet they have only outlined problems, not resolved them.[1] Nor have they resolved the contradictions that exist between Gogol the realist and Gogol the romantic, Gogol the satirist and Gogol the reactionary, Gogol the humorist and Gogol the preacher.

Let me say that my study makes no claim to factual completeness or to definitive answers to the problems involved. I am raising problems, not solving them. My intention has been to add certain forgotten facts to the work already done by scholars, and to outline certain viewpoints of my own. I cannot hope to do more, because of the very nature of this book and because of the sometimes unfavorable conditions under which I have had to work.[2] For these same reasons, some chapters are more detailed than others. In particular, I go into less detail when I discuss the literary traditions out of which Gogol developed.

This book has been written with an eye to the reader who is not a specialist, but who is familiar with Gogol's works. For readers who are interested in the details, I have provided notes. Given the nature of this study, I have been able to furnish references and notes only in the most important instances. In the course of my work, I have naturally had occasion both to agree and disagree with what others have already written; but considering the scope of the book, I have not found it possible to mention every such occasion. Special problems which of necessity are only touched on here should of course be developed; but that is possible only in studies of a less general nature.

My work on Gogol has been facilitated by the kind assistance of B. L. Modzalevsky, A. S. Polyakov, I. I. Saitov, and V. I. Sreznevsky. I am also greatly indebted to personal contacts with P. I. Rulin, B. M. Eikhenbaum, and my brother, Vladimir Gippius.[3]

Vasily Gippius

CHAPTER I

THE FIRST INFLUENCES AND THE FIRST IDYLL

Gogol's native habitat was the old-fashioned Ukrainian farmstead, where he was brought up by parents who were old-fashioned landowners. We do not known much about his childhood. But it was spent in an atmosphere of relative affluence and parental indulgence. "The house was not large, but it was roomy; it had an extensive and picturesque park and pond, numerous servants, substantial meals. . . decent carriages and horses."[1] This is the way the Gogols lived. They owned an estate of only eighty souls, but of nearly three thousand acres, which yielded an income despite a measure of inefficiency on their part. Evidently "the blessed earth produced everything in such abundance that their house might have been a full cup,"[2] even if it could not compare with the fabulous "chemical laboratory" depicted in Gogol's own story "Old-Fashioned Landowners" (1835). This prosperity rested squarely on serf-labor; and the serf-owners of the "splendid beginnings of the days of Alexander I" did not give a moment's thought to the legitimacy of serf-owning itself, regarding it as "man's natural privilege."[3]

But then, in general they gave little thought to anything in their peaceful refuge, where "not a single desire winged its way over the fence that surrounded the small yard," and from where "you could ride three years and not come to any other country."[4] The reverberations of the Decembrist revolt of 1825, which were felt in the Ukraine as well as in Russia, apparently passed them by completely. For them, the living image of the unshakable solidity of the state and social structure was D. P. Troshchinsky, an important government official, a distant relative, and a "benefactor without parallel," who still clung to the ways of Catherine the Great's time. He was now taking his ease on his estate, Kibintsy, and serving as Marshal of the Nobility of Poltava Province. His palatial house attracted crowds of hangers-on, even buffoons, and even special "buffoon-hecklers." While not mingling with this crowd, his poorer relatives, the Gogols, were nonetheless guests in the "Athens of Poltava" more than once, and were accustomed to expecting certain favors, which their grand relative sometimes refused and sometimes dispensed. On occasion, however, even the Gogols were able to help him through a difficult moment with substantial sums of money (although in general they were finding it difficult to adjust to the changeover from a barter to a money economy). And at one point, the future writer's father, Vasily Afanasievich Gogol (who had once been a nominal employee of the Ukrainian postal service) worked as Troshchinsky's secretary until the latter was appointed Minister of Justice in 1814.[5]

Such was the atmosphere in which the first-born and favorite of the Gogol-Yanovskys grew up.[6]

When people speak of family influences on Gogol, they usually point first of all to the "deeply religious nature" of his mother, Maria Ivanovna. However, this is a very narrow way of looking at the whole matter. Certain facts have long been known: the family's church-going; the mother's purchase of an elaborate ceremonial shroud for the local church; fasting; pilgrimages to Dikanka, Bulishchi and Lubny; and readings in the church calendar.[7] All this bears eloquent witness to the atmosphere of religious ritual that prevailed in the Gogol household, but that is all. The family's belief in a prophetic dream (which in any event was dreamed by Gogol's father, not his mother) and in divine prophecies generally is also cited as further evidence of "patriarchal religiosity"—"lightly tinged with mysticism," one may venture to add, although with no certainty that the expression is accurate.[8] Of course it is tempting to try to find threads connecting these "light tinges" with the religious quests and experiences of Gogol's later life. But we must not forget that the forms of religion, as such, ceased to satisfy him very early in his life, if in fact they ever did. To his mind, they were devoid of content. In a letter to his mother in 1833, he wrote: "Instill in her [his sister] the principles of religion. They are the foundation of everything. . . . Even if she goes to church incessantly, that will not do much good either. Everything there is also incomprehensible to a child—the language, the rituals. She will develop the habit of looking on it as a comedy." (These lines are usually ignored by the biographers, either out of embarrassment or out of a desire not to detract from their picture of a religious Gogol.) He went on to recall his own upbringing: "Unfortunately, parents rarely do a good job of bringing up their children." His own mother was no exception, and he forgave her only because of her youth. "I looked on everything with indifferent eyes; I went to church only because I was told to go or was taken; but while I was standing there I saw nothing but the chasubles and the priest, and heard only the repulsive bellowing of the deacons. I crossed myself only because I saw everyone else crossing himself" (October 2 [o.s.], 1833).

In this same letter, Gogol also spoke about the debt he owed his mother. What left a mark on his mind was not those forms of religious ritual that Maria Ivanovna, with every good intention, had tried to implant in the family, but rather, something she perhaps did not foresee: an artless story she happened to tell about the Last Judgment, the rewards and punishments of the afterlife. (This story is all that biographers have extracted from the letter we have been discussing.) Actually, Gogol absorbed the religious mythology of the world around him, which was dualistic; his mother's stories merely provided confirmation. That he was influenced by certain aspects of his mother's and family's outlook on life cannot be denied; but this particular outlook did not play a definitive role in shaping his subsequent development. And that was even less true of the religious ritual that figured so importantly in the family circle. In his youth, Gogol took a critical attitude toward such ritual; in his later years, he arrived at it in his own way, and that way was not so direct as might appear to be the case.

On the whole, the influence of Gogol's mother could not have been great. Her son was only sixteen years younger, and he treated her with a mixture of condescension and deference. In this whole matter of maternal influence, a significant part has been played by the idealization of Maria Ivanovna. This originated with an off-hand remark by S. T. Aksakov, who scarcely knew her; it has been repeated by certain biographers and even overstated by others. He says: "She was a kind, tender, loving being, brimming with esthetic sensitivity and lightly touched with gentle humor."[9] But this does not fit in with what we know about her. To all appearances, it was precisely esthetic sensitivity and a feeling for poetry, humor, and, in general, spiritual refinement that were lacking in this naive and rather peculiar woman. She fearfully tried to shield her son from real and imaginary dangers, among them a passion for reading ("though it certainly is innocent, like a passion for cards, it too can bring ruin"). But at the same time, she was convinced that her son was a genius, and she credited him not only with writing all the novels she had read (whether anonymous or attributed), but even with inventing the steamship and the railroad![10]

However, Gogol could have derived his esthetic and, more specifically, his literary heritage from both his mother's and his father's side. One of his maternal ancestors was Vasily Tansky, "a splendid versifier in the plebeian manner," a writer of Ukrainian interludes who died in 1763. Gogol's maternal uncle, Ivan Kosyarovsky, was a Russian poet: in 1826 he published a long poem entitled "Nina," cast in very light verse, in the Pushkin manner. The Gogol family also had some literary acquaintances, albeit casual. Vasily Kapnist, a landowner who lived in the Mirgorod District, was Gogol's predecessor both as the author of a comedy about civil servants *(Chicanery [Iabeda]*, 1798), and as an example of a Ukrainian who became a Russian writer. He visited the Gogol home and, according to tradition (which is not very trustworthy in this case), put his stamp of approval on Gogol's juvenile literary efforts. He died when Gogol was fifteen, and Gogol wrote home to express his sorrow (letter to his parents of January 22 [o.s.] , 1824).

But there was a direct line running from Gogol's father. Vasily Gogol's esthetic inclinations found expression in a variety of ways: in sentimental serenades to his fiancée; in a no less sentimental passion for horticulture; in the arbors and grottoes he constructed in his garden and the "valleys of repose" he created in the woods; in the lyrical verses he wrote in Russian, usually as occasional pieces; and most strongly and fully in his Ukrainian comedies. He exemplified the bilingualism characteristic of all members of the Ukrainian intelligentsia at that time, with few exceptions. Ukrainian remained the language of the home (as was also the case with the Gogols, according to I. P. Zhitetsky's likely supposition) and of the folk-characters in comedies. Anything the least serious—a letter, a diary, a lyric poem—was written in Russian. A Ukrainian like Gnedich or Kapnist who found himself in Moscow or St. Petersburg easily shed his native language and, for the most part, his feeling of nationality as well. These were the social factors which determined the linguistic milieu in which Gogol grew up too. Throughout his life he wrote only one epigram and one letter in Ukrainain, although he never lost his knowledge and love of his native tongue, and would chide those who were ashamed of it.[11]

The comedies written by Gogol's father grew out of a tradition of character-types and migratory motifs as embodied in anecdotes. These were reflected in a variety of ways in the interludes, by then a dead form, in the still-vital Ukrainian nativity puppet play,[12] in the popular anecdotes, fairytales and songs that formed the basis of that type of play, and finally, in those same materials as embodied in written Ukrainian literature, which had undergone a revival in the first quarter of the nineteenth century. One of Vasily Gogol's comedies, *Dog or Sheep (Sobaka-vivtsia)*, which has been lost, was based on an anecdote about a fool who is talked into believing that his sheep is not a sheep but the mayor's runaway dog. (The simpleton-type goes back to the traditions of the nativity puppet play and the fairytale.) Roman is of the same ilk, in a comedy by Gogol's father which has survived: *The Simpleton, or, The Guile of a Woman Outguiled by a Soldier (Prostak, abo khitroshchi zhinky, perekhytreni Moskalem)*. It bears a close resemblance to Ivan Kotlyarevsky's well-known *Soldier-Sorcerer (Moskal'-charivnik)*. The coincidences of detail[13] show that each play is indebted to the other; but both also go back to the same tradition. The play by Gogol's father is closer to it, with the simpleton-type whom the crafty wife sends off hunting with a pig, and with the lector/ladies'-man type (instead of Kotlyarevsky's clerk). And we must remember something else about *The Simpleton:* Gogol made use of it for his own purposes, and through it, came into direct contact with the tradition out of which it had sprung. These comedies were presented in the private theater on Troshchinsky's estate. According to other information that is not entirely clear, Gogol was involved in putting on his father's plays at his school in Nezhin (more of which in a moment), and also tried his hand at writing some in the same vein.[14] Thus, we can assume the existence of a literary tie between father and son; and if it is too rash to assert that the father guided the boy's reading (he was scarcely capable of providing systematic guidance), it is indisputable that he shared the latest literary news with him and kept him supplied with books.[15]

In 1821, after a brief sojourn at the Poltava District School, Gogol left his family to enter the School of Higher Studies at Nezhin. Academically the school did not give him very much, although relatively speaking it was not bad. Here too there were literary people—some teachers who were actually writing, some pupils who were keenly interested. The tradition-bound teacher of literature, P. I. Nikolsky, was the author of triumphal odes and of a long poem entitled "Mind and Fate" ("Um i rok"). The young Latin specialist I. G. Kulzhinsky had just begun to appear in print. In 1827 he published a book entitled *The Little Russian Village (Malorossiiskaia derevnia)*, in which material that had been more or less conscientiously selected from Ukrainian folklore underwent a reworking in the spirit and style of sentimental Ukrainophilism.[16] Gogol ridiculed this book in one of his letters, branding it a "literary freak," yet he could not help but take an interest in it.[17] Among Gogol's fellow-students were some future writers: the playwright and novelist Nestor Kukolnik; the poet and translator V. I. Lyubich-Romanovich (who was older than Gogol); and E. P. Grebenka (Gogol's junior), who wrote in both Ukrainian and Russian. They were all writing during their years at school. So were N. Ya. Prokopovich and K. M. Bazili, who were classmates of Gogol. The writers from the different classes would get together for literary evenings, reading from their own compositions and criticizing each other's efforts. They also put out journals.[18] There are discrepancies in the information we have about these journals; but apparently several did exist, and Gogol was in charge of one of them. However, his fellow-writers not only did not regard him as an authority, but actually wanted him to bow to their authority. Prokopovich even attempted to give him a literary education. Unfortunately, Gogol's trust in Prokopovich was to be of long standing: even after *Dead Souls* had been completed, he was still authorizing him to make corrections in (and thereby water down) his style. It is curious that Gogol's short-sighted classmates tolerated his efforts in verse but rejected his first attempt at prose fiction, a tale entitled "The Brothers Tverdislavich." Bazili's verdict was: "You'll never make a fiction writer, that's obvious right now." Gogol promptly tore up the story and burned it. This was the first instance of manuscript-burning on Gogol's part, but not the last.

In his final three years at school, Gogol wrote rather a lot and made frequent mention of his compositions in letters to his mother. (His father died at the beginning of 1825.) In a letter dated November 23 (o.s.), 1826, he even spoke of a radical change in his writing: "You won't recognize my compositions; they've undergone a radical new change. They are of a completely special kind now." What kind of compositions were these, and what kind of radical change had taken place? We know virtually nothing about them, except for the titles. We do not even know the chronological order of the titles. The only recourse is to hypothesis, more or less irresponsible. People have in fact done just that, and a variety of conclusions is the result.[19] Here are the titles, and the scanty information we have about them: (1) "Two Fish," a ballad in which the author gives a very moving account of his fate and his brother's; (2) "The Brigands," a tragedy in iambic pentameter; (3) "The Brothers Tverdislavich," a Slavonic tale, "an imitation of the tales which were appearing in the literary miscellanies of the time"; (4) "Russia Under the Yoke of the Tartars," either a short or a long poem, whose opening lines have been reconstructed as Gogol's mother remembered them; (5) "Something About Nezhin, or, Fools Rush In Where Angels Fear to Tread," a prose-satire on various estates of society. All these have been lost, except for two of the poems.[20]

Of course, these titles can lead one to indulge in flights of fantasy (as has happened), seeing "the Brigands," because of the title, as an imitation of Schiller (why not of Pushkin?), or regarding "The Brothers Tverdislavich" as an imitation of Marlinsky by virtue of a statement made by Danilevsky in his old age as to its "lush nature descriptions" (although such descriptions are more characteristic of late Marlinsky, and would therefore have presumably not influenced Gogol). By arranging these titles in any order we like, we can discover any "radical change" we like.[21]

Let us try to be more cautious even in our suppositions. We cannot simply suppose that Gogol or his classmates were literary rebels and innovators at that time. They must have followed the line of least resistance and absorbed a tradition which had not only become common currency but which also suffered from the time-lag that was inevitable in a remote province. In the mid-1820s this tradition might still have been classicism, lightly tinged with sentimentalism in content and style, as in the works of Ozerov and Dmitriev. Classical traditions still held sway in the school: Nikolsky was an orthodox classicist, for whom even Derzhavin was a "new man." Classical comedies (Fonvizin, Knyazhnin, Krylov) and a tragedy by Ozerov (Oedipus, in which Gogol played the part of Creon) were chosen for presentation by the school theater. This is the sense in which we are to understand the "high style" in which the pupils at Nezhin were said to write, and which can be found in two lines of Gogol's that have come down to us: "Parting the silver-fleeced clouds,/The moon appeared atremble."[22]

But the pupils went further than that. The effects of the literary tempests raging at the time could be felt even in the backwoods of Nezhin, more readily in fact than the political tempests, if only because the press and the post office were at their service. New writing did reach Nezhin: the chapters of Pushkin's *Eugene Onegin* as they came out, one by one; Delvig's miscellany *Northern Flowers (Severnye tsvety)*; journals of the Romantic movement, *The Moscow Telegraph (Moskovskii telegraf)* and *The Moscow Herald (Moskovskii vestnik)*. What is more, the German teacher, Singer, would occasionally assign a lesson not from Klopstock but from Goethe and even Jean Paul. Anything that represented an attempt to shatter the old canons posed a threat to this stronghold of classicism—whether fantasy, or free-singing Romantic and even Sentimentalist lyricism, or biting realistic satire. In Gogol's letters from 1826 on (the year of the "radical change"), a new humorous style began to alternate with the old rhetorical manner, usually (though not always) depending on the addressee. It is possible that "Something About Nezhin" was being written precisely at that time: Gogol's very first compositions, as he himself later recalled, had been "almost all in a lyrical and

19

serious vein" ("An Author's Confession," 1847). The old classicist Nikolsky was now an object of ridicule: the boys would turn in poems by Pushkin and Kozlov, passing them off as their own, and would make fun of his criticisms and corrections. Gogol chipped in for subscriptions to new Russian publications, and on his own subscribed to an edition of Schiller in the original, even though he apparently did not have the necessary command of the language and absorbed the influence of "Germanism" more through Russian journals. In any event, *Hanz Küchelgarten* was written after the "radical change" had occurred.

An awareness of the esthetic undoubtedly awakened in Gogol while he was still at Nezhin, but it found expression in ways other than his literary efforts. He was also attracted to the stage and to painting. Even after he had gone off to St. Petersburg, he did not abandon his efforts in those areas. In the eyes of his schoolmates he did not possess much literary authority; but all, without exception, acknowledged his gift for the stage. He threw himself enthusiastically into the production of school plays. His comic roles stuck in the minds of his audiences: the nursemaid Vasilisa in Krylov's *A Lesson for the Daughters (Urok dochkam)*, Prostakova in Fonvizin's *The Minor (Nedorosl')*, and particularly a comic peasant role, probably in one of the Ukrainian comedies. But he also played the tragic villain Creon, in Ozerov's *Oedipus*. And he painted scenery and made drawings in pastel. He wrote his mother about his drawings with the same care he took in describing his literary compositions, and told his uncle, P. P. Kosyarovsky, about his ability to decorate walls "with paintings al fresco" (letter of September 8 [o.s.] , 1828).

Gogol was aware of his potentialities for creative work in the arts even before he found himself specifically as a writer; and this awareness was only part of his general conviction that he was exceptional. He was not very highly esteemed by the other boys or by his school; but at an early age he began to esteem himself. He found it difficult to open up to his schoolmates, and did so reluctantly. Apparently the only exception was G. I. Vysotsky, who was a dreamy type. Although outwardly Gogol lived the same life as the others and participated in the same activities, from plays to pranks, inwardly he shut himself up within his hopes and dreams. In the eyes of the other boys he was the "mysterious dwarf," a secretive individual.

It was not just that he shut himself up. He also derived a certain secret pleasure from being "considered an enigma by all." As he wrote his mother: "At home I am considered wilful; here I am called meek...in some quarters I am so very quiet, modest, polite; in others—sullen, pensive, uncouth... for some I am intelligent, for others I am stupid" (March 1 [o.s.] , 1828). Gogol's last two years at Nezhin, which he spent separated from Vysotsky, his close friend and the confidant of his dreams, further alienated him from his surroundings and impelled him to set his personality and his dreams in even sharper contrast to the "existers," the "self-satisfied mob" (letter to Vysotsky, June 26 [o.s.] , 1827). He was convinced that he was exceptional, even more, that he was one of the elect. He "burned with an unquenchable desire to make [his] life necessary for the good of the state" (letter to P. P. Kosyarovsky, October 3 [o.s.], 1827). He dreamed of working in the civil service, and at one point, even more specifically, of serving in the judiciary in order to do a heroic deed: battling injustice. But these adolescent dreams should not tempt us to see (as does Kotlyarevsky) an innate moralism in Gogol's character, or (as does Vengerov) an innate sense of civic responsibility, which was exceptional for those times. That would be a mistake.[23] In the idea that had taken possession of Gogol—"my heroic deed"—the emphasis fell on the word *my*. This was first and foremost the proud dream of carrying out *his* own mission, expressing *his* own individuality. In a letter to Vysotsky (June 26 [o.s.], 1827), he expressed a feeling of being oppressed above all by the need to "grovel" among the "existers," among "lowly unknown creatures"; he feared above all that fate would assign him to "dingy lodgings of obscurity in this world." Earlier, in a letter to his mother dated March 24 (o.s.), 1827, he had spoken of toiling "for the happiness of the citizens," "for the good of those like me"; but in the same letter he stated: "I blaze up in a fire of proud self-awareness." In a letter to his uncle, P. P. Kosyarovsky, in which he outlined his plans for doing battle with injustice, we find the following oft-quoted statement: "A cold sweat broke out on my brow at the thought that perhaps it would be my lot to perish in the dust without having marked my name with even a single excellent deed" (October 3 [o.s.], 1827).

And finally, twenty years later, in "An Author's Confession," Gogol recalled these adolescent dreams as follows: "It always seemed to me that I would become a well-known person, that a wide range of activities lay open before me, and that I would even do something for the common good." The word "even," coming as it does after the first statement, is characteristic of Gogol. Of course this was not mere ambition; it was unmistakable idealism, but idealism that had sprung from an egocentric mind. There is no looking for logic in people's psyches. This young man was capable of dissociating himself from the mob yet at the same time capable of dreaming about serving this same mob, merely bestowing the nobler name of "citizens" upon them. In the October 3 letter to his uncle (1827), Gogol gives concrete substance to his dream: he wants to become a judge. A year later, he is already dropping hints to his uncle about other plans which he does not fully reveal (September 8 [o.s.], 1828). They are no longer tied in with his dream of going to St. Petersburg or serving in the judiciary; rather, they have to do with making a journey of several years' duration to foreign lands—to America, according to Danilevsky.[24] We shall see that on later occasions as well, Gogol gave the most varied content to his dream of accomplishing a lofty mission. But the content we would expect—an association of his sense of mission with his newly-awakened awareness of the esthetic—is not to be found in this early period. "In the years when I began to ponder my future, the thought of being a writer never entered my mind": that is how Gogol recalled it in "An Author's Confession."

And in fact, while enumerating his gifts in the letter to his uncle, Gogol reminisces on everything under the sun—on painting, even on his talent for tailoring and cooking—but he does not utter a word about writing.

On the other hand, during those same years he did create a literary image of a dreamer who, in many though not all respects, resembled himself. And although he did not make this character specifically a writer or a poet, he at least endowed him with an awareness of the esthetic. This was the hero of his first long poem—or, as he significantly called it, his idyll: *Hanz Küchelgarten.*[35]

Hanz has a quiet and happy life to look forward to in an idyllic family with his beloved Lisa, the daughter of a farmer and the granddaughter of a pastor. But he is tormented by "a vague thought," by dreams of classical Greece and romantic India, and he flees this idyll only to return to it after wandering in foreign climes. This is the simple plot of the poem. However, the poem is important not for its plot but for its hero's psychology, which Gogol did not probe, but merely sketched. It would be futile to look for a definite literary prototype for Hanz. In some specifics, such as the character of the old pastor, the scenes of cosy family life, and certain combinations of words, there are echoes of Johann Heinrich Voss's idyll "Luisa," which Gogol could have read in Teryaev's Russian verse translation.[26] There is nothing in Voss that resembles the dreamer Hanz; but this was a character-type that had become traditional by the first quarter of the nineteenth century. In his preface to the translation of Chateaubriand's *René,* published in *The Moscow Herald* (No. 5, 1827), M. P. Pogodin refers to the hero as having the personality of "an enthusiast who is dissatisfied with surface life, which fails to gratify his inner needs.... This character has been depicted by many great writers of today (each in his own way), and there is no point in trying to find in them imitations of one another, as certain people do."

In effect, the very first lines of *René,* in the *Moscow Herald* translation, outline the general plan of *Hanz Küchelgarten*: "In settling among the Natchez, René, according to Indian custom, was obligated to marry; but he did not live with his wife. A disposition to reverie enticed him into the depths of the forests." The elegiac Hanz does not correspond to the passionate René (a detail common to both is an attraction to Greece), but Gogol did hew to the theme of the "sentimental journey," which was reflected in different ways in Chateaubriand, Goethe, Byron, and the German Romantics. It was not mere chance that he chose Germany as his setting and ended the poem with an apotheosis of Germany and of "the great Goethe," with whom he was familiar not only from Singer's lessons at school, but also from the cult of Goethe in which *The Moscow Herald* was steeped. The similarities between *Hanz Küchelgarten* and the letters Gogol wrote while at school have been noted on more that one occasion by V. I. Shenrok and others. But less attention has been paid to the dissimilarities. In both cases, the existers, "as low as the most despised of creatures," the *mob* (a word that crops up both in the letters and in the poem), are opposed by an exalted dreamer in whom the "desire for welfare and good," the idea of a personal mission, is closely bound up with a proud sense of individualism, a proud hope for "blessings" from his "descendants," and with the fear of "not marking his existence" (a literal co-incidence between the poem and the letters). But Gogol limits the scope of his dreams by resort to a ready-made form: government service. This was a form for which he had no real sympathy and which was very probably suggested by convention; and he either forgets or says nothing about the demands of his own true nature. Hanz, in his *Sehnsucht,* his yearning, has no goal:

> ...but what
> In all the agitation of his heart
> He quested with a mind unclear and fogged,
> The object of his covetings, his cravings,
> The object whence he strove so ardently,
> With soul both thirsting and impassioned,
> As if desiring to embrace the world—
> E'en that he could not truly understand.[27]

Gogol has good reason to bring the curtain down after Hanz flees, raising it partially for just a moment in the ruins of Athens, and then showing him already back home. We simply do not learn where Hanz's wanderings have taken him and for how long, and whether he has tried to make any connection between his efforts to reach "the luxuriant ends of the earth" and his search for a "better goal," "renown," "the agitation of the world" (Scene 8). On the other hand, we do know something about him that Gogol did not reveal about himself—his enthusiasm for things esthetic:

> Creators of impressions wonderful!
> I'll see your chisel and your brush,
> And all my soul will be suffused and filled
> With fiery flame from your creations bold.

In creating this vague but esthetically inclined hero through the intuitive processes of art, Gogol was able—by virtue of this very vagueness and estheticism—to come closer to what he himself had personally experienced than he could in his letters, which were the product of his conscious mind. The denouement is very important in this idyll. Hanz, like Gogol himself, is an individualist. The "Ballad" ("Duma"), which comes in Scene 17, depicts an ideal hero who serves the "noisy world" without being bothered by the noise:

> In vain insanely shouts the mob:
> Amidst these living fragments he stands firm,
> And all that he can hear's the grateful sound
> Of blessings his descendants render him.

The antithesis is traditional, and it had become so even before Push-

23

kin's "Iamb" and "Sonnet." We do not have to hark back to Horace or even to Derzhavin.[28] It is enough to cite Zhukovsky and his epistle to Prince Vyazemsky and Vasily Pushkin ("Friends, that poet is unfortunate" ["Druz'ia, tot stikhotvorets—gore," 1815]), which also ends with the same expression of confidence in descendants, cast in a rhythmically similar line. Undoubtedly Gogol had experienced this traditional antithesis personally: both his life and his art were to show that the expressions of individualism in the letters he wrote as a youth were not mere phrase-making. Thus, *Hanz Küchelgarten* is built on the same conflict between the individual and the mob; but as it turns out, Hanz's sense of individualism is shaken. From the very beginning, we can see how the poet's sympathy is divided between Hanz, who is a strange young man, and the good Wilhelm Bauch and his good household servants. Bauch's comfortable philistine existence is even painted in attractive hues, although, to be sure, they are borrowed from Voss: gobbling turkeys, tasty yellow cheese, sweet hot spiced wine, brown waffles.[29] After he has left the farmstead, Hanz is called a "cruel tyrant"; but a few scenes later, he is shown as being already disillusioned both by people and by fame:

> Attracted was he, pulled and tugged
> By fame. But false were its thick fumes,
> And bitter was the poison glittering.

Of course, "Lord Byron was of the same opinion, Zhukovsky said the same."[30] In the end, however, Gogol's hero follows not Byron but Zhukovsky: the latter's Aeschines returns to the Penates and is convinced by the quietism of Theon, who has remained true to the Penates ("Theon and Aeschines" ["Teon i Eskhin," 1814]). Incidentally, Batyushkov, in "The Wanderer and the Stay-at-Home" ("Stranstvovatel' i domosed," 1815), resolves the same basic plot in just the opposite way. As it turns out, the "Ballad" in Scene 17 of *Hanz* is just a pretext for posing the following question (for the first but by no means the last time in Gogol's work):

> But when the excitation of insidious dreams
> Creates a thirst for a bright destiny,
> Yet there's no will of iron in the soul,
> Nor strength to stand steadfast amidst the bustle—
> Is it not better, in secluded quiet,
> To move with ease across the field of life,
> Remain content with modest family ways,
> And disregard the hubbub of the world?

The answer is given in the denouement: "Yes, it is better." Hanz returns to an "unbright destiny," to Luisa. He calls himself "insane, muddle-headed," and gives up his "insidious dreams," though not without a twinge of regret. The poem actually becomes an idyll, an idealization of "existers."[31] Artistic images are not, of course, solid evidence of the results of conscious thought. But neither can they be mere accident; and we are justified in saying

that the idealization of the farmstead near Wiesmar or of the farm near Dikanka (which is the same thing) was one of the possibilities that presented
themselves to Gogol's conscious mind. Gogol had close, organic ties with tradition, with his environment, with the soil; it was inevitable that the harder
he tried to cut himself loose from them, the more he kept being drawn back,
again and again. In large measure, this rhythm of repulsion and attraction
shaped the drama of his personal life. The happy ending of his first idyll,
Hanz Küchelgarten, provides the earliest evidence of this drama.

Gogol's biographers connect *Hanz* with the first, rather puzzling trip he
made abroad, to Lübeck in 1829. It is of course impossible to suppose that
Gogol simply repeated in life what he had depicted in a poem. This is even
more so inasmuch as he was able to maintain a distance from his hero and give
some definite, even practical substance to his own dreams, which Hanz was
incapable of doing (although it is not entirely clear just what was involved in
the trip to Lübeck). We have seen that he conceived the idea of a trip abroad,
apparently to America, while he was still at school in Nezhin. His confederate
was Vysotsky, who, after arriving in St. Petersburg, tried to make the arrange-
ments, in company with another person whose identity we do not know (see
Gogol's letter to Vysotsky dated June 26 [o.s.], 1827). As is evident from
letters, Gogol's plans fluctuated. We do not know the details; we only know
that a few months after arriving in Petersburg he was informing his mother
that the death of some "magnanimous friend" had frustrated the "splendid
opportunity of traveling to foreign climes."[32] At this time, he was also attempting to give substance to his dreams in Petersburg itself. But he was aiming not so much at government service, of which he now spoke even disdainfully, as he was at finding some application of his esthetic potentialities (see
the letter to his mother dated May 22 [o.s.], 1829). The surest way would
have been to exploit his talent for acting, which everyone at Nezhin had recognized, without exception. In fact, at one point he did try to go on the
stage; but he failed to impress those who auditioned him, and was let go
either after the first reading or the first rehearsal.[33] But he still had *Hanz
Küchelgarten* in reserve, and he published it several months after arriving in
St. Petersburg, under the pseudonym of V. Alov. Evidently he pinned all his
hopes on this book; with it he intended to break out of the "dingy lodgings
of obscurity."[34]

But Gogol's schoolmates had done him a bad turn in convincing him to
write poetry instead of prose. *Hanz Küchelgarten* contains a number of bold
and striking images (e.g., "the sportive dragon-fly circled, chirring," and
"fiery roses"). On more than one occasion it shows that an artist is at work.
But he is an artist who has absolutely no command of verse technique. He has
trouble sustaining the two basic meters—blank iambic pentameter and a
rhymed tetrameter; slipshod rhythms unwittingly creep into the tetrameter;
and the blank verse sometimes rhymes unexpectedly. Inappropriate parenthetical words ("here," "already," "you know") crop up here and there for

the obvious purpose of filling out the line; Church Slavonicisms also appear unexpectedly, and in obvious service of the meter. In one place, where a particular verb does not fit the meter, Gogol boldy inserts an incorrect form. Nor does he hesitate to misplace word-stresses. There are strange neologisms, as well as neologisms which can be explained only by a poor knowledge of Russian. Sometimes we find a mixture of Russian and Ukrainian, and sometimes an out-and-out Ukrainian word. Generally speaking, for someone who had absorbed the style of the poets of Pushkin's school, Gogol was sometimes capable of displaying stupendous ineptitude and bad taste.[35]

It is not surprising that the critics (in *The Moscow Telegraph* and *The Northern Bee*), gave the idyll an unfriendly reception. A rather more favorable review by Orest Somov[36] appeared later; but at the time, the summer of 1829, Gogol saw his literary ambitions crash in ruins. He destroyed the book which had betrayed him: this was the *second* instance of book-burning by Gogol.

A few days after the review in *The Northern Bee (Severnaia pchela)*, he wrote his mother that he had made up his mind to go abroad with money he had received from her (in exchange for which he gave her power of attorney for his share of the family estate). This letter offers several simultaneous explanations for the trip; still others would be provided later. There is the desire to "cultivate my passions in quietude," in order to "broadcast good and work for the benefit of the world"—in other words, the same motives he had conceived while at Nezhin. Here too he expresses his unwillingness to "grovel" in government service. He hints darkly at "misfortunes," but makes no direct reference to the misfortune of *Hanz Küchelgarten*. Finally, he voices the need to "escape from myself," to escape an unhappy and tormenting love for a woman he considers "too lofty for me."

It has become customary to disbelieve Gogol and to regard everything he says about himself as mystification (unless either Danilevsky or Prokopovich knew of it). But the question arises: first of all, if someone had wanted to indulge in mystification, could he not have done so in a more calculating way, instead of simply piling professed motive on professed motive? In the second place, why should there necessarily be only one motive for human behavior? And in the third place, why is it so implausible that Gogol should have been hopelessly in love with someone, particularly in view of the oft-cited letter he wrote Danilevsky on December 20 (o.s.), 1832? Here he tells how he had *twice* been close to the "flame," the "abyss" of love, and how both times a firm will had overcome his desire. But the biographers had need of a legend about a Gogol who had never fallen in love. The more cautious of them attribute Gogol's confused statements of motive to his own confused feelings, and regard them not as mystification but as literary hyperbole.[37]

After failure as a writer, after personal experiences which unexpectedly proved painful rather than idyllic (as they had only recently been depicted by his creative imagination), after gloomy impressions of the surface life of

St. Petersburg, Gogol found it all the easier to return to his old plan, which no longer stood out so sharply in his mind but which he had not rejected: going abroad to accomplish his mission. We simply do not known the specifics of this mission. But he did not abandon the idea of writing. He was collecting "information about the Little Russians," adding that his work would be in a foreign language (very questionable indeed).[38] Looking back on it later, he observed that "the plan and goal of my journey were very unclear" ("An Author's Confession," 1847). It would probably be more accurate to say that the plans nurtured in Nezhin and revived in St. Petersburg were impractical and at times simply fantastic. However, Gogol did not lose his grip on reality, and he returned from Lübeck in less than two months.

The sense of individual mission which developed in Gogol's adolescence found expression in his personal life earlier and more strongly than in his writing. "Only the proud intentions of youth," he stated after his return, "which, however, flowed from a pure source, merely from the burning desire to be useful—only these lured me too far, not being subject to restraint by prudence" (letter to his mother, September 24 [o.s.], 1829). The proud intentions of youth strove to cut through and tear loose from the web in which tradition had entangled him, whatever the form in which this web presented itself to him, whether as the gray web of office work, or the pink web of the Lünensdorf idyll in *Hanz Küchelgarten*. But Gogol fell to earth in his first attempt at flying. Instead of reaching a fabled America, he ended up working in the Third Section, under Bulgarin's patronage.[39] He was well aware that such service compromised him; he carefully tried to conceal it, and at the first opportunity, he transferred to the innocuous Department of Crown Properties.

CHAPTER II

THE DEMONIC AND THE FARCICAL

The failure of *Hanz Küchelgarten* marked the failure of Gogol as a poet. Influenced by his schoolmates, he underrated himself as a writer of prose. Some of his early efforts in that form he destroyed ("The Brothers Tverdislavich"); some he lost through sheer indifference ("Something About Nezhin"); some he left unfinished ("The Dread Wild Boar"). But very soon after arriving in St. Petersburg, he realized his mistake. He quickly saw the direction things were taking in literature, and understood what kind of literature would enable him to put his powers successfully to the test. Since the mid-1820s, the question of nationality had been an urgent one in Russia. The assimilation of Romantic theories and traditions inevitably brought about a shift from the mere imitation of foreign models to the creation of something new out of native materials. In fact, some people had begun to take stock of these materials and subject them to study—namely, Snegiryov and Maximovich.[1] Romantic theory saw in the "chronicles, songs and folk legends" the "best, purest and most reliable sources for our literature" (Wilhelm Küchelbecker, writing in the Romantic miscellany *Mnemosyne [Mnemozina]*). In literary practice, the genius of Pushkin was still dealing with folk legends very cautiously, but was bringing the chronicles to life and paving the way for true originality. His art was stirring the theorists too, and compelling them to reflect on the essence of nationality.

It is not surprising that the Ukraine excited special interest. In one sense it belonged to Russia, but in another it did not: it was a neighbor, a blood relation, yet it could easily be seen, in the half-real light of Romanticism, as a "Slavic Ausonia."[2] Ukrainian folk songs, and verses by Ukrainian poets were published now and then in Russian journals, and in 1827, Maximovich's anthology of Ukrainian songs appeared. There were also publications bearing such titles as: *The Ukrainian Herald (Ukrainskii vestnik), The Ukrainian Journal (Ukrainskii zhurnal), The Ukrainian Miscellany (Ukrainskii al'manakh)*. More and more frequently, Russian writers—among them Ryleev, Narezhny, Pushkin and Aladin—were choosing Ukrainian subjects, for the most part historical. But the fantastic tale based on Ukrainian (and Russian) folklore was also making its appearance. Here Gogol's immediate predecessor was Orest Somov, the author of a tale about a drowned maiden who has turned into a water-nymph, is called back by her mother with the help of a sorcerer and his magic, and once again runs away to the water-nymphs ("The Water-

Nymph" ["Rusalka"], published in *The Snowdrop [Podsnezhnik]*, 1829).
He also wrote *Tales of Hidden Treasures (Skazki o kladakh)*, where stories of
popular superstitions, as told by an old corporal, are woven into the tale of a
simple-hearted major who is searching for hidden treasure (published in *The
Neva Miscellany [Nevskii al'manakh]*, 1830). He was also the author of *The
Haidamak (Gaidamak)*, which contains elements from folklore. He also wrote
tales of everyday Russian life based on folk legends ("The Werewolf" ["Obo-
roten'," 1829]; "The Hobgoblin" ["Kikimora," 1830]; and others). Here he
was joined by Olin ("An Old Pal's Bed ["Kumova postelia," 1829]), and in
part by Pogorelsky ("The Poppyseed-Cake Woman from Lefortovo" ["Lafertovskaia makovnitsa," 1825]).

For Somov, the introduction of Ukrainian folklore into literature was
no accident, but a very deliberate literary device. In one of the notes to *Tales
of Hidden Treasures*, he says flatly that his aim is to "bring together as many
as possible of the folk legends and superstitions that are scattered amongst
the simple folk in Little Russia and the Ukraine, so that they will not be entirely lost for future Archeologists and Poets." Therefore, "not wishing to
compile a special dictionary from them, I have ventured to disperse them
throughout various tales." N. A. Polevoy had a similar project: he concluded
his *Christmas Stories (Sviatochnye rasskazy)* with a promise to "relate everything I have heard from Shumilov [the narrator of the 'true' story] and from
my old friends: stories true and imaginary, Russian fairy tales, and narrative
preludes *(priskazki)" (Moskovskii telegraf*, No. 3, 1826). Thus, in the literature of the second half of the 1820s, the idea of taking poetic, mainly fairy-
tale motifs from folklore and bringing them together in a single work had already come to fruition. Neither Somov nor Polevoy actually realized their
projects. Gogol did, in *Evenings on a Farm Near Dikanka*, as did Nikolay Markevich, at the same time but in another literary form: a collection of ballads
entitled *Ukrainian Melodies (Ukrainskie melodii*, 1831), which, like Somov's
The Haidamak, was furnished with ethnographic commentaries.[3]

Evidently Gogol got to know Somov's work early, perhaps through his
friend Lyubich-Romanovich, who was also coming out with Ukrainian themes
at that time ("The Legend of Khmelnitsky" ["Skazanie o Khmel'nitskom"],
in *Son of the Fatherland [Syn otechestva]*, No. 7, 1829). It was Gogol's impression that "everyone here [in St. Petersburg] is interested in everything
Little Russian" (letter to his mother, April 30 [o.s.], 1829). By April of
1829, he was planning a series of tales on Ukrainian themes with historical and
contemporary settings, and with fantastic plots. He needed material. He had
to move in the same direction as Somov, but without copying him. Gogol's
own dim and superficial memories did not suffice; literature offered nothing
except Yakov Markovich's *Notes on Little Russia (Zapiski o Malorossii*,
1798), and Kulzhinsky's *The Little Russian Village*, which owed a great deal
to Markovich and presented Ukrainians all too obviously, as Somov put it,
"in the same guise as Florian's Spanish and French shepherds" *(Northern*

Flowers, 1828). And yet Gogol did avail himself of Markovich's book (which had been dedicated to D. P. Troshchinsky), and even of Kulzhinsky's; he also had recourse to Maximovich's collection of folk songs, along with the commentaries (at that time no collection of Ukrainian fairy tales as such had yet been made). In addition, however, he made several urgent requests of his mother to collect materials and send them on to him: superstitions, legends, descriptions of rituals, games, even dresses. His questions show that his own notions of such matters were very vague. Not only was he unaware of any other kinds of "spirits" than water-nymphs, he was also ignorant of the name of the dress worn by peasant girls, and thought that he had seen a girl in church wearing a dress whose style actually dated from before the time of the hetmans, that is, from roughly the sixteenth century. (Letter to his mother, April 30 [o.s.], 1829.) His mother, indeed the entire family, responded to his request; he copied all the information into a "miscellaneous notebook." And out of the suggestions he picked up from his mother, out of Somov's stories and other books, out of his own dim recollections, Gogol—guided by a power of creative intuition which he himself later called "clairvoyance"—recreated an entire world, a world so alive and so well-structured that his contemporaries were mesmerized, even those as relatively knowledgeable about such matters as Somov, and they believed in its real existence.

But Gogol did not reflect "real" reality in *Evenings on a Farm Near Dikanka.* For one thing, he had a poor knowledge of that world, having observed it mainly from the vantage-point of a country squire. For another, he had been brought up on the traditions of Romantic literature, on the ballads of Zhukovsky, on the tales of Tieck, of Washington Irving and to some extent of E.T.A. Hoffmann (all of whom were being regularly translated in the Russian journals of the 1820s), and on Romantic theories that were being championed by these same journals, *The Moscow Herald* in particular. His mind must have taken in such ideas as: "truth in art and truth in nature are different"; "the artist absolutely must not copy his works from the works of nature" (S. P. Shevyryov, in *The Moscow Herald,* No. 2, 1827); the imitation of nature leads to the creation of a brightly-painted puppet as the ideal (*The Moscow Herald,* No. 4, 1827); "a comic writer ought to seek to strengthen characters and never paint portraits" (M. P. Pogodin, "Paradoxes" ["Paradoksy"], *The Moscow Herald,* No. 2, 1827). He must have read with interest the translation of Sir Walter Scott's article "Novels of Ernest Theodore Hoffmann" (1827), which was published in 1829 (in *Son of the Fatherland* under the title "O chudesnom v romane"). There he could find Scott advising that "the imagination of the reader is to be excited if possible without being gratified," and giving advice on how to use and "embroider" folk legends.

In Tieck's tales he found models for a narrative genre of the fantastic. The Russian Romantics themselves had made a few experiments along this line. One was Pogorelsky's "The Poppyseed-Cake Woman from Lefortovo," which so delighted Pushkin. It is the story of how the innocent niece of an old witch is approached, after the witch's death, by a black cat (the devil) disguised as a titular councilor, who asks her hand in marriage, and how she luckily escapes union with the infernal powers. There were also: Titov's "The Solitary Little House on Vasilevsky Island" ("Uedinennyi domik na Vasil'evskom"), whose plot we know was suggested by Pushkin, and which features the same theme of the devil in human form; Olin's "An Old Pal's Bed," which deals with a peasant lad who is sold to the devil by his mother while she is experiencing a difficult childbirth, but who subsequently is saved by a magnanimous work-man (an old pal of Beelzebub), who takes the "contract" down to hell and destroys it; Somov's "The Water Nymph," which has already been men-tioned, belongs here as well. Gogol's stories look toward this genre. They even contain reminiscences of their predecessors: the crimson candle and the blood-red light in the witch's room in Pogorelsky are echoed in "Basavryuk," with its blood-red light effects; the journey into hell made by the hero of "The Lost Letter" harks back to a similar journey made by Olin's hero; Somov depicted the search for hidden treasure on St. John's Eve as being ac-companied by the same frightening effect—a mysterious laugh—as did Gogol in his "St. John's Eve"; in Somov's "The Hobgoblin," there is a cat with claws of iron, just as there is in Gogol's "A May Night." Even the opening sentence of *Evenings on a Farm Near Dikanka* is close to the opening of Somov's "The Werewolf."[4]

But in the process of assimilating a genre that was beginning to develop in Russian literature, Gogol introduced a great deal that was completely new. It was not a question of new materials, of which there were few, but of two other factors: on the one hand, his close ties to another literary tradition that was alien to his predecessors, even Somov—the Ukrainian comedy; on the other hand, his deeply personal attitude toward his themes. Later he spoke of the "tag-ends of my state of mind at that time," that is, the time when *Even-ings* was written (letter to A. O. Smirnova, December 24, 1844); and he found both a style and a syntax all his own to fit that state of mind.[5]

In the same letter in which he first asked his mother for material, Go-gol also requested that his father's comedies be sent to him: he intended to put them on "in the theater here." No such production took place. But it was not completely pointless for his mother to have sent him the comedies, for they revived in his mind the tradition of the nativity puppet play and the anecdote. The epigraphs to "The Fair at Sorochintsy" reveal a knowledge of P. P. Gulak-Artemovsky's work[6] and of Kotlyarevsky's translation of *The Aeneid*. This same tradition determined the tone that was used for all the characters and scenes from ordinary, "real" life, and, to some extent, for the "unreal" ones as well—for anything that could be perceived and depicted as being comic. The ludicrous devil, the shrew, the boastful Pole and the brave Zaporozhian Cossack, the rascally gypsy, the peasant simpleton, the lector with the high-falutin way of speaking—all these are characters out of the Ukrainian nativity play. In "The Lost Letter," Gogol even garbs the

Zaporozhian Cossacks in "the traditional costume of the nativity puppet play."[8] In that type of play, the depiction of Christ's birth was followed by scenes based on ordinary life, where the characters were usually presented in pairs.[9] Gogol makes use, especially in "The Fair at Sorochintsy," of the same compositional device, in his skilful alternation of comic couples and couples in love.[10] In the fourth chapter of "The Fair at Sorochintsy," we see a married couple—the shrewish Khivrya and her simpleton-husband; in the fifth chapter—Gritsko and the gypsy (who does not, however, represent the nativity-play type in all respects); in the sixth—Khivrya and the priest's son, who is close to the lector-type of the nativity play and folk tale, and even closer to the lector/ladies'-man type in *The Simpleton,* the play written by Gogol's father. The whole scene showing a rendezvous that does not come off is a variant of the same scene in *The Simpleton* and in *The Soldier-Sorcerer.*

In "Christmas Eve," we see a new series of couples: the devil and the witch, the devil and the blacksmith, Chub and his kinsman, the couples who come and go in Solokha's room, where again the lector/ladies'-man type appears. The comic effects in *Evenings* are shaped by the same tradition, which, broadly speaking, is that of the farce, with its beatings, concealments and pratfalls. A clump of mud flies at Khivrya; a stone sails through the mayor's window; market-women fling "curses and crayfish" at one another; Levko swings his fist at his father; Khivrya is on the point of seizing Solopy Cherevik by the hair; Vakula uses his fists to settle accounts with Chub; the kinsman's wife sets to with a poker; the "drunken Jew" (also a character out of the nativity puppet play) "knees a woman in the rear end" ("The Fair at Sorochintsy");[11] the sexton's wife spits at the weaver's wife; the weaver's wife spits at the sexton's wife but instead hits the mayor in the face. Kissing also misses its intended target: the lads, thinking they are kissing the fair maid Ganna, are actually kissing Makogonenko. Levko does not recognize his father, the mayor does not recognize his sister-in-law, Kalenik and Chub do not recognize the hut; the sister-in-law is caught instead of the rowdies, and Solopy, who has been robbed, is caught instead of the robbers themselves. Solopy flees after placing a basin on his head instead of a hat (just as later, in *The Inspector General,* the mayor places a box on his head). Khivrya hides her lover on the stove-bench; Solokha hides hers in sacks; the priest's son falls down (just as Bobchinsky does in *The Inspector General*); the sacks containing Solokha's lovers are mistaken for provisions that have been laid in for Christmas. The old men break into a dance (Solopy, Kalenik, the grandfather in "An Enchanted Spot"), as often happens in the nativity puppet play. The blacksmith catches the devil by the tail, and this again is a scene out of the nativity play. Migratory anecdotes are introduced: the peasant whose mare is unhitched by thieves ("The Fair at Sorochintsy"), the learned student who steps on the wrong end of the rake. Finally, the surnames (which proved so upsetting to the patriotic Kulish) are calculated for the same effects: Golopupenko, Sverbyguz, Goloputsek, Patsyuk.[12]

That is why statements to the effect that Gogol is realistic (at least in his depictions of the older generation) must be qualified.[13] As early as *Evenings on a Farm Near Dikanka,* gross caricatures of the kind that would be typical of his later works are in evidence, even though they lean heavily on the Ukrainian comic tradition.

But Gogol creates images that are meant to be terrifying as well as amusing. Here he almost always differs radically from his Russian predecessors, Olin in particular, who depicted terrifying things in the condescending manner of gentlemen making fun of the ignorance of the simple folk. I say "almost always" because in this first effort Gogol himself sometimes destroys the effect by poking fun, as when he shows Basavryuk's face on the head of a roasted ram, or a kneading-trough that dances. But generally speaking, in treating demonic themes, Gogol does not mix the comic and the serious.[14] In his approach to the former, he makes contact with the tradition of the nativity puppet play, and in his approach to the latter, contact with the psychology and general outlook of a story-teller from the folk, through the Romantic tradition to which he was personally close.

Among the Romantic writers of the Jena circle, it was primarily Tieck who possessed the elements of a tragic sense of life. Hence his penchant for demonic images and themes, which blossomed forth in late Romanticism, especially in E.T.A. Hoffmann. For that dualistically-inclined literary generation, the devil of the fairy tales became the incarnation of universal evil, and the structure of a Romantic tale of fantasy was usually determined by two themes: the exposure of the devil concealed in human form, and the tragic lot of a man who delivers himself over to the devil. Therefore, the tragic plots of the stories in *Evenings on a Farm Near Dikanka* bear a similarity to the tales of Tieck, not only as far as these themes are concerned, but in specific details as well. "St. John's Eve" resembles "Love's Spell" ("Liebeszauber")[15] in the scene where the child is murdered at the instigation of the witch, and in the motif of the hero's forgetting the horrors he has seen. "A Terrible Vengeance" resembles "Pietro Apone" (which appeared in translation in *The Moscow Herald* in 1828), particularly in the scene where the sorcerer conjures up Katerina's soul.

The closer Romantic traditions brought Gogol into contact with the folk tale, the more thoroughly he absorbed the traditions themselves. And the folk tale touched a chord in him, not only by virtue of the comic and anecdotal elements which were embedded in it (and which had become an integral part of the nativity play and of Ukrainian written literature), but also by virtue of the basically demonic element that it contained. Here the traditions of the folk tale mingled with the view of the world that Gogol had absorbed from his family. If we can speak of reflexes of that demonic element in the young Gogol, then it is only in terms of myth and ritual, and not in terms of personal religious experiences: God and the devil are the powers that rule the world; the historical church is the representative of heaven on earth and the

33

only possibility for man's emerging victorious in his struggle with the devil. Even more cautiously, we can say that there are no factual data which enable us to determine just what Gogol's personal view of the world was in those years; and yet, the images in *Evenings* derive from something resembling precisely that.

The eight stories in *Evenings* can readily be divided into four pairs, which group two to each of the two parts of the book. "The Fair at Sorochintsy" and "Ivan Fyodorovich Shponka and His Aunt" do not fit this scheme. "Shponka," an instance of a unique genre, owes absolutely nothing to the demonic element. "The Fair at Sorochintsy" owes *almost* nothing to it: the story of the red jacket is only a clever invention, although we should note the peasant who chops the jacket up after making the sign of the cross over his axe. The remaining three pairs are a variation on one theme: *the invasion of people's lives by the demonic and their battle against it.* Two stories which belong together by virtue of common narrative devices (both are related by a sexton) and the same hero (the narrator's grandfather) tell of this in anecdotal fashion. They are "The Lost Letter" and "A Bewitched Spot." Here the demonic power takes the form of minor devilry. The weapon employed against it is the sign of the cross; but the difference is that in the first story, the hero makes the sign over the demonic cards just in time to avert catastrophe, while in the second, only bitter experience teaches him to sign all suspicious spots in this fashion. These stories reflect only the comic side of the folk tale and the nativity play; and the literary anecdote that underlies them might have been perceived as mere comedy, with nothing "terrifying" about it. Immediately after the first part of *Evenings* appeared, Gogol related another brief anecdote of this same kind in a letter to Zhukovsky.[16]

The other pair consists of two love stories, two "nights": "A May Night" and "Christmas Eve." These have happy endings, and the elements of comedy and lyricism are much weaker. Both speak in graver tones of the contest between the powers of light and darkness. In "A May Night," the witch is overcome by the good heroes, the pure souls (the innocent young martyred maiden and the ideal "knight" Levko), though without direct assistance from heaven. The literary parallels (Somov's "Water Nymph" and others) are of little importance here, inasmuch as the greatest stimulus in the 1820s for all water-nymph themes was provided by the opera *The Dnieper Water Nymph (Dneprovskaia rusalka)*, arias from which were sung by all "provincial beauties," according to N. A. Markevich. "Christmas Eve" features a devil straight out of the nativity play and the folk tale, endowed with exaggeratedly comic traits; but he is vanquished by a pious blacksmith, quite in keeping with the way demonism is treated in folk tales. In popular tradition too, the blacksmith appears as the defender of Christ and as the victor over the devil (although we also find the other image of the demonic blacksmith-sorcerer.)[17] In the version which served as the immediate source for Gogol's tale (even though it has a different ending), the blacksmith is an icon-painter, as he is in Gogol.

Finally, the last pair—"St. John's Eve" and "A Terrible Vengeance"—consists of two tragedies, except that a comic element is introduced at the end of the first one. They come closest of all to Romanticism of the Tieck variety. Now it is not just petty demons who are contending with human beings, but the powerful Basavryuk and the sorcerer: they goad people into committing unnatural crimes, and annihilate anyone who tries to oppose them. In "St. John's Eve" Petro turns into ashes and persishes. In "A Terrible Vengeance," Danilo perishes, his young son perishes, and so does his wife Katerina, who has spurned the amorous advances of her father, the sorcerer.[18] In both stories, the cloister is set in opposition to the demonic world that invades the life of man. There Pidorka hopes to save herself by taking the vow of silence ("St. John's Eve").[19] Even the sorcerer, in "A Terrible Vengeance," imagines the monastery to be his last hope; at first he is hypocritical about it (when he tries to persuade Katerina to release him from the underground cellar), but then genuine (when he is in the hermit's cell). But Pidorka and the sorcerer resort to the cloister too late. Both these gloomy stories end with the demonic powers triumphant (in "A Terrible Vengeance," retribution comes only in the epilogue, after the sorcerer has done his work). In the sixth chapter of "A Terrible Vengeance," the sorcerer lies chained in the cellar, whose miraculous walls have been built by a hermit; they are *almost* responsible for bringing him to his doom, but Katerina releases him. Here cloisters do not save people from demons, but they do serve to emphasize the existence of demons, while remaining inaccessible to them.

We see that the essential theme of these stories is the same, whether they are constructed as anecdotes, novellas or tragedies. There are two sides to life. On one side stands the unclean power—devils both small and mighty, witches and sorcerers. They come into people's lives, sometimes in the form of harmless befuddlement or petty swindling, but sometimes in a really serious form, as an attempt on someone's life, as persecution, as some mortal threat. On the other side stands the church in all its historical completeness, up to and including the rules prescribing the foods that are pleasing to God (see "A Terrible Vengeance," chapter four). The very least of its rituals is sufficient to ensure miraculous victory over the unclean power. A person who places himself under the church's protection is saved, whether by shutting himself up in a cloister, decorating the wall of a church, or perhaps resorting to a religious talisman in good time.

Gogol's closeness to the essential spirit and substance of the folk tale is more important than closeness in specifics. Many coincidences of detail—in motif and even in plot—can be found between his stories and the folk tale. Scholars have already done some work along these lines,[20] although it is not always possible to say just which specifics derive from a folk source (perhaps from tales that escaped the attention of later collectors), and which from a literary source. Actually, later transcriptions of folk tales might well contain echoes of Gogol's own stories. The devil expelled from hell, the devil's search for his property ("The Fair at Sorochintsy"), the transformation of the witch into various animals, the lopped-off hand of the witch ("A May Night"), the devil as a thief and the search for something stolen, the card game played with devils ("The Lost Letter"), the theft of the stars (by a witch in the folk tales), the ride on the devil's back ("Christmas Eve"), the great sinner who kills a holy man ("A Terrible Vengeance")—all these motifs, in any event, are present in later transcriptions of folk tales. The scattered treasure, the fern-blossom, the drowned maidens who have become water nymphs, the journey into hell, and certain other details all existed in literature before Gogol. The motif of selling one's soul to the devil ("The Lost Letter") can be traced back not only to Goethe and Zhukovsky but also to Gulak-Artemovsky's ballad "Tverdovsky." The conflict between the church and the demons, as found in folk tales, is not only taken over by Gogol but played up: his Cossack wins after making the sign of the cross over the cards ("The Lost Letter"), whereas the soldier in the folk tale wins by virtue of *his own* adroitness and cunning; and Gogol's sorcerer ("A Terrible Vengeance") does not gain fogiveness, as does the sinner in the folk tale. This motif alone—and the fact that Gogol returns to it again and again in his art—compels us to conclude that the system of imagery in his early works is not the result of mere chance, but, at the very least, of the "tag-ends of [his] state of mind."

What Gogol called the "tag-ends of [his] state of mind" in his early works ties in directly with another well-known statement: "I would be overcome by attacks of melancholy, which I myself could not explain...in order to divert myself, I would think up everything funny that I was capable of devising. I would invent a whole cast of funny faces and characters, and mentally put them into the funniest situations, without the slightest concern as to why I was doing this or what benefit anyone would derive from it" ("An Author's Confession"). Thus, the element of farce in *Evenings* is explained as being entirely the result "of a certain mental need," as in fact is the element of lyricism, or everything that resisted transformation into farce.

Tales of four types can be distinguished in *Evenings*. The first—exemplified by the popular anecdote type and by "St. John's Eve"—is the *epic monologue,* which is determined by the very fact that the story is told by a narrator. Here the manner of narration more or less resembles that of the pre-Gogol tale, although sometimes, especially in "St. John's Eve," it makes too free a mixture of devices drawn from the language of literary Romanticism, folk songs, and the popular anecdote. The second type can be called the *lyric-dramatic,* examples being "The Fair at Sorochintsy" and "A May Night." Here the author appears in the role of a director, who lyricizes and comments on the scenes he makes the actors play out before the reader-audience. He shifts the settings at will, and sometimes yields completely to the actors, as in "A May Night," where certain of his statements serve as nothing more than stage directions ("the proposal was approved...the door was opened...the

36

sister-in-law crossed herself''), or especially as in "The Fair at Sorochintsy," where some chapters (the sixth, and in particular the fourth) are nothing more than scenes from a drama, or dialogues from a nativity play. This was also noticed by P. A. Pletnyov, who wrote to Zhukovsky in 1832: "I have always been struck by the drama-like passages in his tales." Both stories are framed by lyrical introductions and endings. Sometimes too a chapter within a story begins with such an introduction (chapter five of "The Fair at Sorochintsy," and chapter two of "A May Night"). And in these lyrical monologues, the author feels himself free, in a good Romantic way: he is not bound either by the plot or the tone of the story, but sometimes achieves effects by contrast, as in the marvelous elegiac finale of "The Fair at Sorochintsy," which is yet another place where the "tag-ends of [his] state of mind" poke through. In "Christmas Eve" and "Ivan Fyodorovich Shponka and His Aunt," dramatic representation is almost completely subordinated to epic narration, as is the lyrical element that is interspersed throughout the story. This is the *dramatic-epic* type, in which the drama is not simply accompanied by authorial monologues and comments, but rather, is declaimed by the author himself. And finally, "A Terrible Vengeance" should be singled out as a special type, despite the abundance of dialogue in it: the *lyrical monologue*. There is a complete unity of prose-diction here, a unity that is conferred mainly by the rhythm.[21] In the earlier stories of this collection, rhythm could be heard in this or that monologue; in "A Terrible Vengeance," it is present from beginning to end; and lyrical exordia, such as the famous Dnieper scene at the beginning of chapter ten, are rhythmically no different from the depiction of the most ordinary kinds of scenes.[22]

The unique charm of Gogol's monologues—what we oversimplify by calling the "poetic quality" of his stories—depends primarily on their rhythm and syntax.[23] Through stylistic analysis, we can see that his epithets and comparisons are only approximate, unexpressive, and monotonous: the sky embraces the earth, the pond embraces the sky, the evening embraces the earth, the wind kisses the leaves. To describe a moonlight night Gogol hit on one epithet which he repeats over and over: "silvery"—silvery mist, silvery moon, silvery gleam. One harsh critic, I. E. Mandelshtam, even dubbed this early period of Gogol's the period of "the absence of all style," which is, of course, inaccurate and unjust. The task of the realistic and ethnographic critic is even easier, because to look for the actualities of Ukrainian life in Gogol's stories is the same as looking for the actualities of German life in *Hanz Küchelgarten*. Pushkin had the clearest understanding of this aspect of Gogol: he *forgave* Gogol for the "disconnected quality and lack of verisimilitude of certain stories." And Polevoy was only factually, not psychologically wrong when he suspected Gogol's Rudy Panko of being a city-dweller. The other critics, with the exception of Andry Tsarynny, did not notice the inaccuracies of realistic detail, because they were mesmerized by Gogol, whose dramatic scenes and lyrical rhythms gave life not only to traditional comic characters, but also to those couples in love who spoke in the language of Ukrainian and even Russian songs, or for that matter in Gogol's own words. Nadezhdin thought that Ukrainians had "a kinship with the irrepressible but harmless mountain-dwellers," and it is therefore not surprising that he found *Evenings* to be "painted in bright Ukrainian colors." More curious is Kulish's observation: "One has to be an inhabitant of Little Russia...in order to comprehend the extent to which the overall tone of these scenes is 'faithful to reality.'" Several years passed, the hypnotic spell wore off, and this same Kulish, writing in 1861, hurled thunderbolts at *Evenings* for its *lack* of faithfulness to reality.[24]

When he was not taking a Sentimentalist tiller of the soil from the stories of Kvitka (the Ukrainian Grigorovich)[25] and substituting him for a real Ukrainian, Kulish was of course right in defining the overall tone of *Evenings* as "phantasmagorical exaggeration" and as "a masterpiece of caricature," and, to some extent, in saying that "if one were to invest [*Evenings*] in different garb and remove all the Ukrainian words from its language, then we would all wonder just what kind of people these were: Spaniards, Greeks, Moldavians, Serbs, or Poles." This, however, is only partially true: the comic tradition with which Gogol worked was Ukrainian, not Spanish or Moldavian. Kulish is right in particular about the inaccurate details, most of which, however, were noted as early as 1832 by Tsarynny: matchmaking while the fair was still in progress, as well as at harvest-time; a wedding without the marriage rituals; young people pursuing nocturnal diversions on weekdays; a wedding in May—all these things were impossible in real Ukrainian peasant life. But Kulish was applying a measure to Gogol which Gogol never applied to himself: it is just as easy to fault "The Fair at Sorochintsy" and "A May Night" for their rapid denouements as it is to find a lack of verisimilitude in the classical comedy, with its obligatory unity of time. These stories, by their very structure, are dramatic.

However, even the harshest of the realist critics always made an exception for "Ivan Fyodorovich Shponka and His Aunt." This is actually a story with different purposes, and it should be studied in a different context.

The external history of the writing of *Evenings* is the history of Gogol's first literary success and his discovery of himself. Conceived before his trip abroad, the stories were written after his return—beginning in late 1829, continuing throughout 1830, and ending in 1831. "Basavryuk" was the first to be completed, and it was published separately in *Notes of the Fatherland (Otechestvennye zapiski,* No. 2, 1830). This was the journal of P. P. Svinin, who was a devotee of olden times and of ethnography. The first part of *Evenings* was set in print in the summer of 1831, and it made the typesetters laugh. It was published in the fall, and sold out within a few months. In March of 1832, the second part appeared. Even Polevoy, who had earlier been hostile, now spoke of it with praise. Throughout 1830 and 1831, Gogol also published a few articles and fragments in Delvig's *Northern Flowers* and *The*

Literary Gazette (Literaturnaia gazeta). He was brought into these publications probably by Somov, who himself was very actively involved in them. From this time on, Gogol's literary position was defined by his close relationship with Pushkin's circle; from this time on, the development of his intellect and his art proceeded under the aegis of his close relationship with Pushkin.

CHAPTER III

ESTHETICS

Gogol's esthetic self-awareness could be more acute at certain times than at others, but it remained a decisive force throughout all his years of young manhood.[1] It could evince itself indirectly, as a spur to creativity, or directly, as a theme in his writings. It was a theme in *Hanz Küchelgarten;* the theme of the first work to be published under his own name, the article entitled "Woman," in *The Literary Gazette* in 1831; and also the theme of a lyrical dialogue in prose, "Boris Godunov," which was written that same year but not published. Finally, it was the theme of a rather considerable number of articles and stories on which Gogol was working during the first half of the 1830s and which went into *Arabesques* (1835), the first book to appear after *Evenings on a Farm Near Dikanka.* His personal relations with Zhukovsky and Pushkin during the four-year period between these two books, and the unequivocal success of *Evenings,* which set him on the path of professional writing—all this developed and strengthened his esthetic self-awareness, and made estheticism the dominant element in his psyche at that time.

Earlier scholars tended to idealize the relationship between Gogol and Pushkin. More recently, doubt has been cast on how close this relationship really was.[2] That, however, does not alter the essentials. Gogol served his literary apprenticeship under the influence of Zhukovsky and Pushkin. We know how such influences are intensified by personal encounters: through the sounds that could only have been guessed at by the reader, a living voice begins to be heard, and the mind can associate the impressions it has formed with a face that can actually be seen. All this is even more true if regular *literary* contact is involved as well. Certainly such contact existed in this case, although it was perhaps not so close as people once thought. For Gogol, Pushkin was the supreme exemplar of an esthetic personality through and through, the incarnation of what he himself was striving to be. Later, Gogol said that "not a single line was written without my imagining him standing before me" (letter to P.A. Pletnyov, March 16, 1837). Certainly this cannot be psychologically false. Both Nadezhdin and Bulgarin praised Gogol for *Evenings on a Farm Near Dikanka;* Somov even praised him for *Hanz Küchelgarten;* but Pushkin was the first to see Gogol as a *phenomenon* ("this is all so unusual in our present-day literature that I have not yet come to my senses").[3] Significantly, the five years during which Gogol knew Pushkin (May, 1831 to May, 1836) marked the period when everything that made Gogol a great artist—from the final stories of *Evenings* to *Dead Souls*—was either written, begun, or conceived.

Even before meeting Pushkin, Gogol sketched out a few ecstatic pages inspired by *Boris Godunov*, which he had just read, and dedicated them to Pletnyov, who was in fact to be responsible for bringing Gogol and Pushkin together. Here, in the same rhythmic periods that shape the lyrical monologues of *Evenings*, and with even stronger rhetorical effects, Gogol characterizes the stupendous effect of art: "the lightning of fiery sounds...flaming planets have turned into words and letters... a spiritual sea...a flood of grateful works...the ringing of the silver sky."[4] This luxuriance of style reflected a psychological intensity which was even greater than in *Hanz Küchelgarten*, and which showed itself in particularly concentrated form in the closing vow that was taken by Gogol (or rather, by his mouthpiece) over "this eternal creation": a vow to be pure and not defile the sounds that had been extracted from his soul. The article entitled "Woman" appeared in print at the same time. This was a hymn to beauty, and was psychologically and stylistically similar to the unpublished article on *Boris Godunov*. Only this time it was not artistic beauty that Gogol had in mind, but living, female beauty. The artist endeavors to "express divinity in its very materiality." (Even in "Boris Godunov," the soul, on reading the "marvellous creation...trembles, horrified at having summoned God up out of its own limitless bosom.") Woman herself is just such a material divinity; the soul tries to find "its father, eternal God, in the ethereal bosom of the soul of woman." That is, "das ewig Weibliche zieht uns hinan": "The eternal feminine draws us on." Willy-nilly, a Romantic parallel suggests itself: it is evident that "Woman," which is a dialogue between Plato and his pupil Telekles, is a product of Platonism as it was understood by the German Romantics. But the Romantic idea of the feminine was perceived by Gogol as an esthetic idea: the feminine as female *beauty;* and it was in beauty that Gogol wished to infer and comprehend the divine principle, as did certain of his contemporaries.[5] We shall see that Gogol would again evince this same desire, but that it would be overcast by the idea of pure estheticism.[6] Still, the image of the ideally beautiful woman, Alcinoë, before whom man prostrates himself in the dust (in this case Telekles, who grumbles at Zeus for having created women), would be found in Gogol's later works on more than one occasion.

After this early esthetic manifesto came articles on art, which were written between 1831 and 1834. They were included in *Arabesques*, which was published almost simultaneously with *Mirgorod*, at the beginning of 1835. Gogol himself characterized *Arabesques* as "a mishmash, a potpourri of everything, a porridge," promptly adding "in which you have to judge for yourself whether there is any butter" (letter to M. A. Maximovich, January 22 [o.s.], 1835). There is no doubt that Gogol himself valued the "butter" in his books, and that this "butter" consisted of two basic ideas which also shaped his view of the world at that time: the esthetic and the individualistic.

At this point we are concerned with the first.

Russian esthetics of the 1820s and the beginning of the 1830s had assimilated the various nuances of Romantic esthetics, and certain of its representatives were already attempting to express disagreement with their predecessors. For the esthetics of German Romanticism, art was a supra-sensual revelation of pure infinity, a language in which man spoke with the divinity. The most perfect of the arts was music, which carried man away from this earth into other worlds. This notion pervades Wackenroder's book *Effusions of the Heart of a Monk Who Loves Art*.[7] Schelling defined art as a synthesis of the finite and the infinite, and this idea was taken up by Friedrich Schlegel and by Novalis. One of Schelling's Russian followers was A. I. Galich, the author of *An Attempt at a Study of the Beautiful (Opyt nauki iziashchnogo,* 1825). "Man," he wrote, "is a citizen of two worlds, the visible and the invisible"; but in art, there is no gap between these worlds, they are one. "Man, who is like a microcosm by virtue of the unity of his being, would like to possess the perfection of his nature in the aggregate. This need on the part of a spiritual and sensual being...is called esthetic." The Romanticism of Wackenroder and Zhukovsky (Galich cites his "Mysterious Visitor" ["Tainstvennyi posetitel' "]), which brings the "absolute" down into the "world of the senses," is not the ultimate achievement, as far as Galich is concerned: an *agreement* should be found between "the ideal and the natural," between plasticism (i.e., classical antiquity) and Romanticism: a *romantic plasticism.*

Likewise, for Nadezhdin, "material delight" was the "consequence of a mysterious sympathy that links our entire being with nature," and he thought that this delight had only to be heightened. "Esthetic pleasure as such begins when our spirit, *beneath the rude crust of matter,*[8] begins...to sense the presence of a higher life that is akin to it."

The Russian Romantics of the 1820s who were grouped around *The Moscow Herald*—D. V. Venevitinov, Prince V. F. Odoevsky, S. P. Shevyryov, V. P. Titov, and others—were closer to Wackenroder's version of Romanticism than to Schelling's: it is significant that Wackenroder's book appeared in their translation in 1826. Characteristic of this group is the paean to *architecture* in Titov's article entitled "A Few Thoughts About Architecture" ("Neskol'ko myslei o zodchestve," *Moskovskii vestnik,* No. 1, 1827). In architecture, as in music, they saw pure idea, unconditioned by any proximity to nature. In Titov's view, man "is not content with the depiction of the infinite in finite objects." At the same time, even Galich considered architecture merely a "relatively fine art," and P. A. Katenin, in his hostility toward Romanticism, flatly refused to number not only architecture but also music among the fine arts.[9]

There is no doubt that ideologically, Gogol belonged with the Moscow Romantics: his "Boris Godunov" and "Woman" express their ideas, but with greater emotional intensity. The articles in *Arabesques* are also evidence of the link: "Sculpture, Painting and Music" not only repeats the title of an

42

article by Venevitinov, and his central image of three goddesses (in Gogol they are three sisters, queens of the world), but also echoes his style, and develops his basic idea. The articles on architecture are a development (albeit more original) of Titov's articles, with which Gogol was evidently familiar.[10] And yet Gogol did not merely repeat his predecessors; on the contrary, he often contradicted them, and on occasion himself as well. The differences here are more important than the similarities.

For Venevitinov, sculpture already contains "the presence of a secret divinity"; painting makes the idea of the infinite comprehensible; music complements nature and carries the soul far away from this earth into a new world. Gogol sharpens these distinctions, which were blurred by Venevitinov. In effect, he picks up, points up, and partially renews Galich's scheme, according to which painting is Romantic: sculpture is sensuous, painting represents a fusion of the sensuous and the spiritual, and music is pure spirituality. Gogol's ideas about music are close to those expressed in "Woman": in antiquity, "all of religion consisted...of the god-like beauty of woman," but this is now a stage that has been passed; and it is music, which transports man out of his own body, that must become "the essential property of the new world," and not sensuous sculpture, or sensuous and spiritual painting. This is how Gogol endeavors to fit his esthetics into Galich's scheme. And, as it happens, he finds a truly inspired style and rhythm to describe sensuous sculpture: "White and milky, exuding, in marble translucent, beauty, languour, voluptuousness, it preserved one idea, one thought—beauty, the proud beauty of man." In speaking about painting, he betrays some hesitation: the manuscript version tells of the viewer who took delight in the other world while standing before the face of the Madonna, but this is omitted in the printed text; and about music and its pure spirituality he speaks in vague and general phrases. Highest of all are his hopes for the moral influence of music. The is the first, as yet shy and hesitant sign of moralism in Gogol ("may...the troubled soul of the robber feel, if only for an instant, the pangs of conscience, may the speculator lose what he has counted on gaining"). Least of all for Gogol is what was most important for the Romantics: the religious influence of music. To be sure, he does introduce an example of the mighty power of music "under the endless dark vaults of the cathedral"; however, this refers not to music in general, but to a special kind of music in special surroundings.

In another article, "The Last Day of Pompeii,"[11] Gogol speaks of painting apart from his preconceived scheme; indeed, he contradicts the scheme. What he has formerly ascribed to sculpture alone—the idealization of the "beautiful human being"—now proves to be possible for painting as well. As if thinking better of it, Gogol makes the following qualification: the merit of Bryullov's canvas lies in the fact that "sculpture has finally [!] given way to painting, and moreover has become infused with a certain secret music." No matter how much Gogol may have overrated Bryullov, even he would hardly have been capable of believing that Bryullov was the first and only plastic painter in the world. Still, he goes on to ascribe to Bryullov's canvas everything that he has formerly deemed characteristic of sculpture, only now all those "pagan" features redound to Bryullov's credit: "precious to us is our beloved sensuousness, precious to us is this beautiful earth of ours. He has captured this idea in all its power...his woman exudes everything that is best in the world. Her eyes, luminous as stars, her bosom, exuding languor and strength, give promise of a luxuriance of bliss...." Bryullov's woman is a new Alcinoë, but she is no longer set back in the dead world of paganism.

Of course, these contradictions are not evidence of Gogol's "paganism," but only of the rigidity of the schemes into which he tried to fit his ideas. The article "On the Architecture of the Present Day" begins with a sigh of nostalgia for the Middle Ages. At the very outset we find a sentence that could easily have been translated from Novalis: "They have passed, those ages when faith, fiery burning faith impelled all thoughts, all minds, all actions toward one thing, when the artist strove to elevate his creation higher and higher toward heaven." This is a sigh of nostalgia for the Gothic. As Christian architecture, it is set in opposition to all other architectural styles. Also noted are its esthetic perfections and the mystical feeling it arouses (in an appropriate esthetic setting, to be sure: an *unreal* gloom, the light through stained-glass windows, lancet arches). This is the tradition of the return to the Gothic which derived from Wackenroder and in Russia was upheld by Titov, who perceived a profound significance in the triumph of the Gothic *straight line* over the ancient *circle*: the violation of a harmonious relationship with the "material world" and the almost forcible elevation of the soul.

Titov ends his article with a paean to the Gothic; Gogol begins with it. He is also concerned with the idea of the relationship of the circle and the straight line, but he goes further. Judging by the beginning of the article, we would expect him to call for the restoration of the Gothic. But that is not the case. In the article on Bryullov, we did not find the expected idealization of painting or of music, but rather, an idealization of the "sculptive" Bryullov and of sculpture itself, "as enchanting as life, as the world, as sensuous beauty." Likewise, we now find an idealization not only of the Gothic, but even more explicitly, of sensuous architectural styles. The cupola is idealized: "voluptuous, airily protruding, [it] was to embrace the entire structure and luxuriantly repose its white cloudy surface on the entire mass.... The dazzling whiteness conveys an inexpressible fascination and fullness to its gently protruding form." (The manuscript has "fascination and voluptuousness," which sets the image that Gogol is hinting at in even higher relief, and which is significant to anyone who knows his work.)[12] *Eastern architecture* is idealized: it is as fascinating "as an eastern beauty...with black eyes bright as lightning, in her particolored attire and her necklaces of precious stones." Finally, the article ends with a call not for the revival of the Gothic, but for an act of daring, for the creation of new forms. To Gogol, an important feature of both

44

the old forms and the new was *the colossal,* above all. Here he could find support in certain paragraphs of Galich's esthetics; and sometimes he virtually repeated E.T.A. Hoffmann ("The Devil's Elixirs") in his gibes at "pretty little toys" and petite churches and bridges. But his own artistic requirements were a factor here as well.

It has been asserted that Gogol's inner life moved in a straight line, that he absorbed religious mysticism with his mother's milk, and that it remained within him unchanged to the end of his days. If that were so it would be natural to expect that he would have been engulfed by Romantic esthetics and as a result would have become a religious esthete of the first water. In point of fact, something else happened. On three occasions, Gogol attempted to link esthetics and religion, and all three times the linkage proved flimsy. His scheme whereby the arts evolved from sensuous paganism to spiritual Christianity was demolished by the fact that painting, which defined the transition-point in the scheme, struck him as being plastic, and therefore non-Christian, according to the scheme. From here it was only a step to the idealization of pure "pagan" plasticism. As soon as Gogol began to talk about architecture, his sympathies again swung between Christian and pagan styles; and the hint he dropped about a revival of the Gothic remained only a hint.

Gogol's esthetics did not correspond with Schellingianism either. He arrived at no "harmony" between spirit and matter; and after hinting at such a harmony in "Woman," he again vacillated between the two worlds. There are echoes of "Woman"—that paean to sensuous, god-like beauty—in the three articles on art. There are echoes of his article on *Boris Godunov*—that esthetic lyric inspired by his impressions of poetic creativity—in the article "A Few Words About Pushkin" (1834). Moments like the one recorded in "Boris Godunov" are not forgotten; and the man responsible for them—Pushkin—was long destined to dominate Gogol's mind and cast a spell over his deepest emotions, which were basically esthetic, as could be seen even in the unfinished "Boris" article. This was especially true after Gogol actually came into personal contact with Pushkin, despite the fact that the contact was never close. In this unpublished fragment, Pushkin is called "great"; in the article "On the Poetry of Kozlov," written in the 1830s, he is proclaimed "boundless"; in "A Few Words About Pushkin" he is "an extraordinary phenomenon and perhaps a unique manifestation of the Russian spirit." With uncommon perspicacity and uncommon firmness, this last article insisted on Pushkin's significance at a time when he was under attack from the "judgment of fools," when doubt was being cast even on his talent.[13]

Gogol begins his line of thought with an expression of enthusiasm for the personality of Pushkin ("Here is a Russian man...his very life is Russian through and through"). This is consistent with the intense self-awareness of the young Gogol. (By contrast, in attempting an evaluation of Pushkin ten years later, Gogol would show no desire to define his personality.) The main thing he emphasizes in Pushkin's personality is its intensely esthetic nature.

In this article, Gogol for the first time begins to speak of the artist's freedom to choose any theme—from "the mountaineer in martial garb" to "the judge in a threadbare, tobacco-stained tailcoat." For the first time he makes a contrast between a "forced style" and false passion, on the one hand, and "inaccessible inner poetry, which has rejected all coarse trappings," on the other. In short, he was the first to suggest the terms of the parallel between himself and Pushkin that critics would make in the future. But for the time being, the demands that he was making for realistic breadth in art had none of their future sting, that is, no moralizing; for the time being, the whole point was that a "forced style" was incompatible with "the fine discrimination of the poet," and that the depiction of objects which were unappealing to "the crowd of admirers" could have strong esthetic merits "in the eyes of a few genuine connoisseurs." The entire article was a challenge to Gogol's contemporaries and their philistine esthetics.

The metaphor which Gogol uses to point up the distance between himself and his contemporaries is a curious one. In order to understand Pushkin, he says, one must "be to a certain extent a sybarite who has long since become satiated with coarse and heavy foods, and who now eats game no bigger than a thimble and savors a dish of the kind whose taste seems utterly indefinable and strange to a person accustomed to swallowing the concoctions of a peasant cook." We recall the caustic label that Apollon Grigoriev pasted on literary critics of the Druzhinin type—"literary gastronomy."[14] Whether Grigoriev had Gogol's article in mind, we do not know; but it is worth noting that Gogol was serious about the gastronomical metaphor and therefore, as later critics understood it, was taking estheticism just about as far as it could go. For those familiar with certain of the finer points of Gogol's biography—namely, his love of eating—this metaphor, which might otherwise appear ironic or overly naive, has a convincing ring to it.

The experience that Gogol had accumulated in the writing of *Evenings on a Farm Near Dikanka* took on greater complexity as his own awareness of the esthetic continued to develop. It is therefore not surprising that he went on from his articles to explore the theme of the esthetic in subsequent works of fiction. The two books that appeared at the beginning of 1835—*Arabesques* and *Mirgorod*—contain three stories featuring this theme: "Viy," "Nevsky Prospect," and the first version of "The Portrait." Scholars suppose that all were written at more or less the same time (1833-1834). They can be set apart from everything else Gogol wrote during that period. While they do have things in common with the articles on esthetics in *Arabesques*, the underlay of myth links them directly with *Evenings* as well. The invasion of men's lives by the demonic was the theme of *Evenings*. The invasion of the *beautiful* by the demonic is the modified version of this same theme which shapes the three new stories. The *beautiful* in "Viy" and in "Nevsky Prospect" is represented as female beauty, and in "The Portrait" as art.

The demonism in "Viy" comes out of the folk tale, as it does in *Evenings*

46

too. However, Gogol expands, combines and changes the folk-tale motifs of the witch riding on the man and the man riding on the witch, the reading of the Psalter over the witch's body and all the attendant horrors. The witch gradually turns into a beautiful woman—not "gradually" in the story-line itself, but rather, in the process of Gogol's own revisions. In the manuscript, Khoma Brut merely imagines that the witch is not an old woman; in the first published version (in *Mirgorod*), the old woman's face assumes youthful features; and only later, in the reworking, does the witch actually turn into a beautiful woman. Thus, two folk-motifs have merged into one.

Gogol's depiction of the demonic sometimes follows the folk tale (e.g., the witch), and sometimes departs from it completely, as he invents monsters out of his own head in great profusion: a pyramid with a tongue on top, "something black" with many hands, "something reddish-blue" with two probiscises, something "thin and long" consisting entirely of eyes, and so on. Gogol was reproached by Shevyryov and Belinsky for the superfluous detail of such supposedly scary images. Later on he eliminated much of it and achieved better effects by omission (Khoma Brut does not have the courage to take a close look at the monsters) and by suggestion (wings and tails). Gogol himself called his main figure, Viy, a "colossal creation of the popular imagination" and at the same time the chief of the gnomes—creatures which were and are unknown in the Ukraine or in transcriptions of folk tales. If in fact Gogol was working from some folk-figure we know nothing about, he had a very foggy notion of it: at first, Viy is a giant; later, a squat, ungainly creature (this of course goes better with the image of eyelids that reach to the ground). Gogol also made a change in the typical folk-hero, by using a seminary student, who is reminiscent of the lector/ladies'-man type that was well known to him from the nativity puppet play. He endowed him with a philistine imperturbability which set the fantastic and demonic element in even higher relief,[15] and surrounded him with the details of ordinary, everyday life that were repetitions and variations of Narezhny's *The Seminary Student (Bursak*, 1824) and *The Two Ivans, or, A Passion for Lawsuits (Dva Ivana ili strast' k tiazhbam*, 1825).

The basic problem posed in "Viy" becomes evident when we compare this story with the article "Woman." The Cossack's daughter is endowed with an esthetic quality that is as authoritative and efficacious as Alcinoë's: Khoma is fascinated by her "coruscating beauty," just as Telekles is by Alcinoë's "dazzling radiance." But in "Viy" the fascination is demonic, and the resolution of the problem can be understood only in the context of *Evenings*. Here, as there, the church is the one and only fortress in the war man wages with the demons; and the siege that is laid to this fortress constitutes the drama of the story. For a time, Khoma does resolute battle using a tried-and-true weapon—the ritual incantations of the church. (The reading of the Psalter over the dead was just that—an incantation—for the residually pagan mind, and Gogol does a splendid job of revealing the kernel of myth embedded in the folk tales that contain this motif.) But the denouement of "Viy" can be compared with "A Terrible Vengeance," the difference being that in "Viy" the demons' victory over the church remains unavenged: "and so the church was left for ever and ever, with monsters stuck in the doors and windows." The very thought that beauty could become the spoils of the powers of darkness led to the gloomy and pessimistic ending, which does not occur in Russian or Ukrainian folklore: there the hero always gets help and is saved.[16] Gogol's originality is very noteworthy: it is obvious that this was not just a literary problem for him, but one of which he had personal experience, quite apart from his art.

In "Nevsky Prospect," the same esthetic theme is transposed into a contemporary setting. When Gogol moves from attempts at creating genre-scenes in a Ukrainian setting (more about them later) to scenes with a St. Petersburg setting, he is inclined to show this setting in an unreal light. By the very fact that they are only sketchily outlined, his impressionistic images approach caricature, and from there it is no great distance to the fantastic. The style becomes nervously lyrical, and the "third person" of the narration is in constant conflict with the first, the persona of the author, who interrupts the narration with questions and exclamations. This is the case in the sketches for the novel "The Dread Hand," with its impressionistic touches: the white dress in the gloom, the triangle-shaped face, the mass of flesh wrapped up in a cloak and cap. So it is too in "Nevsky Prospect," where there is no fantastic story as such, but where the lyrical and impressionistic narrative manner bathes all of the most commonplace characters in an unreal light and leads inevitably to the conclusion that "everything is deception, everything is a dream, everything is other than it appears to be."

By the first half of the 1830s, the Hoffmannesque tradition of the fantastic nature of the commonplace had already come into Russian literature. After initial efforts by Pogorelsky and Titov, it emerged fully in V. F. Odoevsky's *Motley Tales (Pestrye skazki,* 1833), and was reflected in a distinctive way in Pushkin's "Queen of Spades" ("Pikovaia dama," 1834). Odoevsky, during the period when he was writing *Motley Tales,* was primarily a satirist, who even made his devils mock the nineteenth century.[17] Gogol, in his *Arabesques* and *Mirgorod* period, was primarily an esthete, whose most cherished theme was the fate of beauty. But basically, Odoevsky and Gogol were similar not only in their sense of life, but also in the artistic devices they used; they also became friendly in those years; and Gogol even helped Odoevsky with the publication of *Motley Tales.*

To a certain extent, "Nevsky Prospect" is close to "Viy." In both stories the hard core of tragedy is softened by the scenes of ordinary life, where there are no inconsistencies. Khalyava and Tibery Gorobets ("Viy"), like Lieutenant Pirogov ("Nevsky Prospect"), are representatives of that lower, immobile level of society (see Chapter X of this study) which is impervious to inconsistencies. Khoma himself ("Viy") belongs body and soul to this level of society, and it is only because of the requirements of the story that he is called out of it to do battle with the unclean power. The artist Piskaryov ("Nevsky Prospect"), on the other hand, consciously fights for an esthetic idea and is martyred to it. In both stories, beauty, incarnate in a beautiful woman (a descendant of that near-divinity Alcinoë), is profaned and perishes. In "Viy," beauty is handed over to the unclean power without further ado; but in "Nevsky Prospect," there are only suggestions that demons are involved in the defeat of beauty, whereby a divinity is transformed into a prostitute. About the unknown woman who captivates Piskaryov, Gogol writes: "She would have been a divinity in a crowded ballroom...in the presence of the silent adoration of a crowd of her admirers prostrate at her feet." (Compare Alcinoë, toward whose feet "the young man turned in amazement, in adoration.") But "by some horrible will on the part of the fiendish spirit, eager to destroy the harmony of life, she had been flung down, with laughter, into this dreadful abyss."

The statement about the fiendish spirit and his battle against the beautiful ("the harmony of life") could have been simply fortuitous, were it not for the closing lines of the story: "It deceives at all hours, this Nevsky Prospect, but most of all when...the demon himself lights the lamps with the sole purpose of showing everything in a false aspect." This image throws light on the basic problem of the story.

Everything that happens on the Nevsky Prospect is painted in the colors of the puppet theater. Here Gogol's indebtedness is seen in basic technique, rather than in specific details. Old men and old women waving their arms and talking to themselves; *pale* misses and *pink* mademoiselles; employees of the foreign office with *black* side-whiskers, and those of other departments with *red* ones; the ladies like a sea of butterflies, with waists "not a bit thicker than the neck of a bottle"; ladies with sleeves resembling two balloons; a foreman "in whom everything is in motion—his back and his hands and his head"—all these are marionettes moved by someone's hand.[18] At night, that "mysterious time when the streetlamps cast an alluring, mysterious light on everything," this puppet-theater quality becomes even more pronounced: "Everything is deception, eveything is a dream, everything is other than it appears to be." In the concluding sentence, the power responsible for the deception is actually named, the power which has played the two big tricks in the story: having a women of the streets mistaken for Perugino's Bianca, and having a German artisan's wife taken for a high priestess of pleasure. In the human perspective, one of these tricks is a tragedy, the other, a farce. The first is the tragic answer to the question of the fate of beauty as the highest value in this world, which is posed by man's esthetic sense. Beauty perishes morally, and man's esthetic sense cannot accept this fact. ("It would be one thing if ugliness went along with it [vice], but beauty, tender beauty....") As the character who is endowed with this sense, Piskaryov also perishes. However, his esthetic faith does not perish; on the contrary, it becomes more powerful and vivid, and turns into illusionism, a cult of incorporeal phantoms, ideals and dreams. ("Oh, how disgusting was reality. What was it compared to dreams?... Oh Lord, what sort of life is ours—eternal discord between dream and reality!...") Piskaryov denies reality in the name of imagination, and feeds his imagination on narcotics. Hereby he points ahead to highways and byways that would be taken by esthetic illusionism in Europe; he is the first decadent in Russian literature. This represents the highpoint of Gogol's estheticism: he no longer feels the need to hang the talismans of church ritual on the character who represents this estheticism.

For Pirogov, with his complete lack of any philosophy of life, the revelation of the truth merely hastens the farcical ending of the whole episode in which he is in involved. (The artistic perfection of this character was much admired by Belinsky, who called it "a type of types," and by Dostoevsky, in *The Idiot* and in *Diary of a Writer*.) [19] There are also signs of a true farce-tradition in the scene where Schiller nearly has his nose cut off, in Pirogov's unsuccesful attempts to kiss the German woman, and particularly in the scene where Pirogov is beaten (which Pushkin liked so much, and which was toned down in deference to the censor). All this would also have been possible in the *intermedii* of the Middle Ages and in the popular farce, where, incidentally, the thrashing would probably have constituted the denouement. But Gogol adds a subtle psychological touch: Pirogov, the roundly beaten Lovelace, forgets his indignation once he is confronted with layer cakes, *The Northern Bee,* and the mazurka. Pushkin had good reason to call "Nevsky Prospect" the fullest of Gogol's works.[20] Its "fullness" depends not only on the variety of character-types, but also on the combination of the two elements of Gogol's art: tragedy, which underlies the ideology and psychology of the story, and farce, which is the most finished and symmetrical element as far as the structure is concerned. The ironic remarks of the author, which give higher relief to the caricature-like kaleidoscope of the street and the farce in Schiller's house, cease when Piskaryov's tragedy is being depicted: here the exclamations and questions on the part of the narrator take on an unmistakably pathetic quality and do not sound like authorial interventions, but rather, like a commentary on Piskaryov's experiences.

"The Portrait" is written in the same tone as this section of "Nevsky Prospect" (that is, the first version of "The Portrait": for the moment, this is the one we are talking about). But the rhythm is less marked; it also shifts from lyrical monologue into dramatic-epic monologue, and then into purely epic monologue in Part 2, where the narrator is introduced as a character. Stylistically, "The Portrait" is even further removed from "A Terrible Vengeance." But the two are close in other respects: "The Portrait" is the first work after "A Terrible Vengeance" in which Gogol ruthlessly excludes everything comic. It lacks not only the kind of comic fantasy we find in the anecdotal stories of *Evenings,* or in Senkovsky's works as a rule and Odoevsky's oftentimes, but also any comic treatment of ordinary life, such as we find in

"A May Night," "Viy," and "Nevsky Prospect." Here everything is tragic and serious, as is appropriate to the seriousness of the basic problem that is being treated. If "Nevsky Prospect" is stylistically the "fullest" of Gogol's works, then "The Portrait" is the "fullest" ideologically. The theme remains the same—the invasion of the beautiful by the demonic—but now both demonism and estheticism stand forth in very high relief. In retrospect, the earlier versions of the theme now look like mere sketches for "The Portrait." The opposition of icon-painter and unclean power is reminiscent primarily of "Christmas Eve"; but now the unclean power is no petty demon, but rather, a power of the same magnitude as the sorcerer in "A Terrible Vengeance," and possessed of the same capabilities as the demonic powers in "Viy." The inner life of the icon-painter is also developed, as is the very meaning of his art: here the esthetic is not merely an attribute of church observance, but an independent force; and the demon launches his attack not against isolated manifestations of the beautiful, but against beauty itself, which is embodied in the work of art ("he strives to penetrate into everything: our affairs, our thoughts, and even the very inspiration of the artist").

The portrait, which Chertkov fatefully cannot resist buying (even though he knows he is spending his last kopeck) and which miraculously appears by itself in his rooms, is the portrait of the Antichrist. Rather, it is the Antichrist himself, inasmuch as it comes to life and steps out of the frame. Chertkov has been struck by the lifelike quality of the eyes. The motif of a portrait that is irresistibly lifelike or that actually comes to life is a favorite of the Romantics, perhaps because it affords a ready way of emphasizing the irrational "magic" of art, which creates new realities. It goes back to the hagiographic theme of icons coming to life; it even has a pre-Christian past in legends about statues coming to life; and ultimately it has its roots in myth, in the belief that part of a person's life passes over into any representation of him. Therefore, the task of picking out Western parallels to "The Portrait" is very rewarding but of little value in the case of a motif which already had such a long tradition behind it. The immediate stimulus could have come from Maturin[21] and Washington Irving, from a story by Spinello, which had been translated by Somov,[22] or from Pushkin's "Queen of Spades," where the old Countess's face appears on a playing card. Pushkin's story has direct connections with E.T.A. Hoffmann's "The Devil's Elixirs."[23] In the history of this theme in Russian literature after Gogol (Mikhail Lermontov, V. F. Odoevsky, Konstantin Aksakov, Alexey Tolstoy), one cannot distinguish individual influences, but the general Romantic tradition is obvious.

Gogol turns the portrait motif into a demonic motif. As he reflects on the supernaturally lifelike eyes, Chertkov says: "Why, then, is it so terrible to cross the line that has been drawn as a boundary for the imagination? Or can it be that beyond imagination, beyond the surge [over the line] there is reality, that terrible reality into which the imagination leaps off its axis, impelled by some outside hand?..." From what follows we see that art, once it leaps

51

off its axis and crosses the line, falls victim to demonic powers, which enjoy absolute autonomy within the realm of "terrible reality," that reality which stands opposed to beautiful reality.

The demon, or the Antichrist, does battle with beautiful reality on two fronts. Internally, he corrupts the artist's soul; externally, he compels him to destroy works of art. In the first version of "The Portrait," the radical change in Chertkov is psychologically unmotivated. His Salieri-like doubts about the feebleness of his own talent do not really foreshadow the artist-spectator who eventually emerges. On the contrary, Chertkov exemplifies an artist who is capable of selflessness, not only in his attitude toward paintings done by others, but in his own as well. This faith remains unshaken in Piskaryov, despite all the trials it undergoes. In Chertkov it dies —not, however, because of his own instability, as is largely the case in the second version of the story, but rather because a demonic force intrudes from outside.

Here Gogol comes close to the interpretation of the Salieri character-type as demonic, which we find in Odoevsky's story "The Improvisator" ("Improvizator").[24] The Antichrist appears to Chertkov in a dream and tempts him with the alluring "truth of nihilism";[25] it is very important that this nihilism is a denial precisely of *esthetic* faith. The consequences are first seen in Chertkov's initial efforts as a professional artist, when he substitutes the sketch of Psyche for the portrait of the girl. The lady who commissions the work fatefully appears in an unexpected manner, as though she has been sent by the Antichrist: the phrase "a fiendish thought flashed through the artist's head" is hardly fortuitous. The ensuing consequences are seen in paintings cast in "monotonous forms that were long ago outlived," and finally, in the conclusion that "there is no revelation from on high in this world." At last comes Chertkov's destruction of the paintings he buys up: from a psychological point of view, this would hardly have happened unless the old man in the portrait itself had originally planted the idea in his mind. Here too the epithet "fiendish" is repeated three times in the account of Chertkov's frenzied destructiveness (fiendish intention, the dreadful laughter of fiendish enjoyment, fiendish desire).

Ideologically, Part 2 of "The Portrait" is a commentary on Part 1: the basic images of the demonic and the beautiful are explicitly set forth here. Structurally, it is the second act of a drama, or, more precisely, a story about the past (*Vorgeschichte*) and a frame-epilogue, which show the demon vanquished. Here the evil spirit is shown to have taken on human form (as the pawnbroker), in keeping with the Romantic tradition, which had already been reflected in two of Gogol's earlier works, "Basavryuk" and "A Terrible Vengeance." The evil deed of the sorcerer and the pawnbroker are similar: in "A Terrible Vengeance," Danilo, the child and Katerina are destroyed, one after the other; in "The Portrait," the same thing happens to the artist's wife and child. What is new is the evil spirit's attitude toward the beautiful: he attacks it in the hope of turning art in a "fiendish direction." The epithet "fiendish" now has a literal meaning, and this leads us to suspect that the same meaning applies to earlier usages of the word as well.

The battle with the evil spirit is won by the painter, who is living out his days in a monastery under the name of Father Grigory. One would like to call him "the monk who loves art," as Wackenroder called the imaginary author of his book, and from there trace the threads back to the icon-painters of the medieval legends, such as the eleventh-century Alimpy (also called Alipy) mentioned in the Kiev Caves Paterikon.[26] That is, the demon is once again taken on by the church and her representative—a man who is a combination of the simple-hearted icon-painter Vakula (in "Christmas Eve"), and the hermit in "A Terrible Vengeance." But now the church ritual by itself is inadequate to the contest; and Gogol, for the first and only time in his art, offers us a religious type, a man who has "turned completely into a religious flame." Judging by the overly generalized phrases in which he speaks of the experiences of Father Grigory, and by all the evidence of his own life during those years, we must conclude that he treats these matters superficially, as mere possibilites which had flashed through his mind in artistic form, but which he had not yet experienced in his own life. But it is important to note that religious experience, even in this artistic guise, is shown as the result of esthetic experience, of which Gogol himself undoubtedly had first-hand knowledge: Father Grigory is not merely a hermit, but also a painter. Everything that Gogol had experienced, whether in actuality or in potentiality, is concentrated in this, his last "demonic" story. The victory that is won over the devil here is not meant to be merely a personal victory: the devil is universal evil, which must be defeated throughout the world. Even Father Grigory does not accomplish this immediately. As far as he personally is concerned, he escapes the evil that is spread by the portrait of the Antichrist he has painted. But the portrait is still in existence, together with the evil spirit that has come to life in it. The story of Chertkov that is told in Part 1 takes place, as a *Vorgeschichte,* after the events the painter relates to his son in Part 2. The final victory—which comes as a result of the painter's "labors and prayers"—is put off for another twenty years and occurs in the story's epilogue, when the mysterious portrait turns into an insignificant landscape.

"The Portrait," then, is a synthesis of myth and the Romantic literary tradition. The awareness of the esthetic, which largely shaped Gogol's inner life in the 1830s, predominates here too; but it was already beginning to touch upon contiguous areas of his mind.

"I never felt any attraction to the past," Gogol wrote in "An Author's Confession" in 1847. This paradoxical statement applies, of course, only to the Gogol of that particular year, not to the Gogol of the 1830s. In that earlier period, he had indeed felt a very strong attraction to the past. Moreover, this attraction lay at the very heart of his attempts to define himself and the mission he had been dreaming of since he was an extremely young man.

In 1830 he worked as a civil servant and studied painting. He published only "Bisavryuk" and a chapter of *The Hetman* (on Lapchinsky and Glechik).[1] In 1831 he left the civil service and became a teacher at the Patriotic Institute in St. Petersburg; he made the acquaintance of Pushkin and Zhukovsky, and published two chapters from "The Dread Wild Boar," as well as "A Few Thoughts on the Teaching of Geography to Children," "Woman," and the first part of *Evenings on a Farm Near Dikanka.* In 1832 he continued teaching; that summer he made a trip back home; in Moscow he met M. P. Pogodin, M. A. Maximovich, S. T. Aksakov, and M. S. Shchepkin; he published the second part of *Evenings.* In 1833 he went on with his teaching; toward the end of the year he entertained hopes of being appointed to a chair at Kiev University; he became good friends with Odoevsky; he published nothing. In 1834 he was still continuing to teach; in July he secured a chair in history at St. Petersburg University; he was planning to write a history of Little Russia; he published historical articles and "The Tale of How Ivan Ivanovich Quarrelled with Ivan Nikiforovich." In 1835 he worked at his professorship right up to the end of the year; at the beginning of that year he published *Arabesques* and *Mirgorod;* and he was planning a history of the Middle Ages.

This is a quick survey of the most notable events in a five-year span of Gogol's external life. Of course, much was determined by chance. But hopes of finding a vocation had not been abandoned. Only now the vocation was no longer government service, and it was not yet writing. Were these hopes bound up with teaching? There are only indirect answers to this question: Gogol's passion for pedagogy, as reported to Pushkin by Pletnyov; a note to his article on geography, which says—even before his appointment as a teacher at the Patriotic Institute—that the author has "completely devoted himself to his young charges"; the unrealized plan to publish his lectures at the Institute in the form of a book entitled *The Earth and Its Peoples.* In any event, Gogol's article on teaching geography contains much that is still fresh and valuable even today: ideas on the use of visual aids, on teaching not by the book but by maps, drawings and outlines, on organizing the course in concentric circles, and on heeding questions asked by the pupils themselves.

But if the mission of pedagogue did not occupy the center of Gogol's attention for long, there is certainly no doubt that the mission of historian filled him with enthusiasm. His only hesitation was just how to accomplish it. Would his mission be: historian as writer or historian as professor? Events pushed him in the second direction, which least suited his talents. Fatefully, his plans for scholarly works kept falling through; and works of historical fiction, toward which all his historical studies invariably veered, were not connected in his own mind with the sense of mission. His sense of mission as a *writer* developed at the same time, quite apart from his endeavors in the field of history.

Gogol's biographers have long regarded the episode of his professorship as a riddle. Shenrok assumed that it represented self-deception on the part of an over-confident man. That was mild by comparison with many of Gogol's own contemporaries, who bluntly called him a charlatan. From here it was only a step to seeing charlatanism as a psychopathic state; and that step was taken too. However, F. A. Vitberg, A. I. Kirpichnikov, and later, S. A. Vengerov were able to view Gogol's work as a professor more seriously and to place it in more of a historical context.[2] Given the conditions of his time, Gogol's lack of preparation was nothing out of the ordinary. In fact, material published later showed that he was trying to make up for this lack by hard work, sometimes even in original sources. Once this became clear, scholars were compelled to re-examine the role of this entire episode in his development. Some began to talk about civic enthusiasm (Vengerov), others about the more generalized enthusiasm of the altruist (Kotlyarevsky).[3] But these are all anachronisms, which make use of a knowledge of Gogol's mature mind to interpret his mind as it supposedly was at a much earlier period.

The only kind of "enthusiasm" we can see in Gogol at the beginning of the 1830s is the same as was evident during his years at Nezhin: the enthusiasm of the individualist. In July of 1833, he was hoping to join Maximovich and move to "ancient, beautiful Kiev," where "one can renew all one's powers" and "do much good."[4] By "good" he means—as is evident from other letters written at the time—collecting folk songs and other materials, and working on his own projects. In a letter to Pushkin (December 23 [o.s.], 1833), he expresses the hope that he will be set apart from "the crowd of sluggish professors that are packing the universities." In Kiev, he says, his projects will begin bubbling along, he will "take out and dust off" his history of the Ukraine and will write "a world history, which so far, unfortunately, does not exist in an up-to-date form, not only in our Russia, but even in Europe." One moment he places himself a head higher than all other Russian scholars, the next moment he hopes to tower above all European scholars as well.

A week after writing this letter, Gogol greeted the new year of 1834 in a rapturous, lyrical outburst. "What, then, will you be, oh my future? Glittering? Broad? Will you teem with great deeds for me? Or?... Oh, may you be glittering! May you be active.... Mysterious, inexpressible 1834! Where will I mark you with great labors?..." ("1834"). The entire page is written in this highly personal tone, and ends with a thrice-repeated oath (or is it an incantation?): "I shall accomplish!" Gogol sees before him not his close friends, but only himself and his Genius, whose face is still shrouded in mist. Evidently he was giving more thought to the process of accomplishing the great deed than to the results. Apparently he had grown cold to the idea of making his mark as a university professor, although he had barely been given the opportunity; and he began to see that this great deed consisted of the *writing* of history. But here too he really could not picture the results clearly, even though he had an announcement of a forthcoming history printed up. It is simply arbitrary to suppose that the history—at least, the one of Little Russia—was written and then burned. It is no less arbitrary to consider everything Gogol said about his work on the history as an attempt at mystification. But it is indisputable that he simply could not bring off the writing of a history. This is borne out by the fact that even his plans changed quickly—one gave way to a second, a second to a third. At first it was the history of "our poor, unequalled Ukraine"; then, Little Russian and world history; then came a radical recasting of the whole plan; and finally there emerged the idea for a history of the Middle Ages, in some eight if not nine volumes. All this happened in the course of little more than a year.[5]

It is obvious that Gogol's dream of personally doing some great deed was all but divorced from any actual substance. Along with his high opinion of himself went its companion—contempt for the "rabble." Gogol's biographers have been troubled by the fact that he advised Maximovich to take it easy, to work straight off the top of his head (letter of June 27 [o.s.], 1834). But we would like to compare this with the opening of Pushkin's poem "The Poet and the Crowd" ("Poet i tolpa," 1828): "the poet was strumming his inspired lyre with a distracted hand." It is clear that Gogol detected in himself the power to "accomplish something out of the ordinary," not through pursuits requiring perseverance, but in a single surge of inspiration. In the actual implementation, this grand idea unavoidably ended in compromise. Gogol soon understood that inspiration alone was not enough; but he did not master all the techniques of the scholar either. The synopses, the outlines and the other remnants of his historical studies give the impression that he was feverishly collecting material for the purpose of laying a firm foundation under his ambitions. He seemed to be performing this drudge-work stealthily and with a feeling of shame, while uttering only glittering generalizations for public consumption—for example, the two lectures, polished to a high gloss, that were printed in *Arabesques*.[6] This unavoidable compromise was perverting his original conception and paving the way to disillusionment, although he was not immediately aware of that.

At first, even the awareness of his own mistakes merely heightened his self-importance; it merely alienated him anew from the "sleepy listeners" who were not struck by the "bright truth." Once again, his self-awareness coincided with Pushkin's, once again it was defined by the formulation in Pushkin's poem "The Poet and the Crowd": "You will hear the judgment of the fool and the laughter of the indifferent crowd." This was precisely how Gogol felt as he contemplated the "sluggish professors" and the "sleepy listeners" who disapproved of him: "Nobody listens to me! If only a single being among the students understood me....They are a colorless lot, like Petersburg itself" (letter to Pogodin, December 14 [o.s.], 1834). Gogol could not find a single understanding "being" in the student body because he was looking over their heads, straight on, into a distance that only he could see.

Even after he had "kissed the University goodbye"—and not of his own volition, as we know—Gogol maintained his old self-importance intact. "Unrecognized, I assumed the chair [of history], and unrecognized, I am relinquishing it. But in this year and a half—a period of ignominy for me, because it is the general opinion that I took up something unsuited to me—in this year and a half I have derived a great deal from all that and have added to the treasure-house of my soul. I have no longer been stirred by childish but by lofty thoughts, filled with truth and of awesome magnitude." He let such thoughts "sink to the bottom of his soul," although not forever, but only until they "awake once more," and "the shameless impudence of the learned ignoramus, the learned and unlearned rabble, the ever-consenting public, et al., et al., will not dare to resist them." (Letter to Pogodin, December 6 [o.s.], 1835.)

Gogol's attitude toward his historical studies was too lyrical (because he did not cease to be an artist) not to reflect his personal ideology. If nothing else, his choice of period shows this. He was attracted only to the Middle Ages and the history of the Ukrainian Cossacks, and was steered in those directions by the two traditions so powerfully at work in him: Western Romanticism and Ukrainian nationalism. In addition, his strong sense of himself as an individual, which was expressed in his attitude toward his new vocation, came out in the way he evaluated historical data. When he approached historical events not as an artist but as a maker of theories, he looked for individuals. Events for him were shaped primarily by heroes—primarily if not entirely, although even departures from this basic tendency still fitted into his overall view of life.

At first glance, no hero at all is present in the article "On the Middle Ages," which was Gogol's introductory lecture at St. Petersburg University. We do not even find any names, except that of Hildebrand, who is mentioned in passing. However, that is not because the idea of the individual is being opposed by some other, but only because Gogol's first lecture is not a work of history at all. It is a brilliant work of art, which speaks of the Middle Ages in the unmistakable tones of a fairy tale. A "strange brightness" and a "gigantic

57

sense of the colossal" are for Gogol the signs of the Middle Ages; its events are more than once called *miraculous*. Concerning the phenomenon of the Arabs, he poses a question which is appropriate to the ending of a tale of fantasy, and is in fact repeated in the closing lines of "The Portrait": "did [this unusual people] really live and exist, or is it a most beautiful creation of our imagination?" In chivalry he sees "a miraculous, almost fairy-tale-like quality." Finally, the description of the alchemist's dwelling place is a page straight out of a fairy tale: "In the deep of night a bluish smoke rising from the chimney attests to the indefatigable vigilance of the old man, who has already gone gray in service of his questings." The conclusion he draws about the Middle Ages—"everything then was poetry and instinctiveness"—is implicit in the article (or the "fairy tale") as a whole. But the fairy tale must have a hero. And there is one here too: the Pope, although he has no name, like the nameless tsars of the fairy tales. "He is the mighty possessor of these young ages, he brings all his powers into play, and, like Zeus, directs their destinies with a mere beck of his hand. In short, the entire history of the Middle Ages is the history of the Pope."

In the article "On the Teaching of World History," the importance of the individual in history is followed through consistently. To be sure, the history of mankind is represented primarily as the history of *peoples*. Does this mean that Gogol took a stand on the side of N. A. Polevoy, the author of *History of the Russian People (Istoriia russkogo naroda)*? In those years, this book, by its very title and purpose, boldly challenged the authority of Karamzin, the author of a history of the Russian *state*, and met with rebuff from many, Pushkin among them. No, that was not the case with Gogol, because in his article the people are reduced to playing the role of an inert, faceless mass, which either follows its leaders wherever they may take it, or is crushed by the iron will of individual personalities. Cyrus, Alexander the Great, Columbus, Luther, Louis XIV, Napoleon—these are the landmarks in Gogol's view of world history. Cyrus *united* diverse peoples by force. Alexander *subjugated* the Greeks. The commerce of Venice was *killed off* by Columbus, the impoverished Genoan. Luther *smashed* the power of the Pope. The Dutch were seizing control of world commerce until they were *undermined* by one exceptional ruler. Napoleon, the titan of the nineteenth century, *blocked* the way of the English, and *stunned* Europe with his rapid movements.

United, subjugated, killed, smashed, undermined, stunned—this is how highly complex historical developments appeared to Gogol.[7] The leap from Louis XIV directly to Napoleon—bypassing the French Revolution—is remarkable; such utter silence about such a long stretch of history cannot be attributed to any consideration on Gogol's part for readers from official government circles, or to any fear of the censor.

Looking closely at "A View of the Formation of Little Russia," where not a single name from Ukrainian history seems to be present, we also find an individual of "gigantic dimensions"—Gedymin, whose appearance on the

scene violated all the norms of history. When Gogol is depicting "the movement of peoples at the end of the fifth century," in the article of the same
name, he introduces the even more wondrous, fairy-tale-like figure of Attila.[8]
"He was a small man, almost a dwarf, with a huge head and small Kalmyk
eyes; but they were so quick that none of his subjects could bear to look at
them without involuntarily trembling. With a glance from them alone, he
commanded all his tribes...." From whatever source Gogol borrowed the legend of the power of Attila's eyes, there is no doubt about its connection
with "The Portrait," which was written at the same time: this is evidence of
the fuzziness of the line dividing the history he was then studying and the creations of his own imagination. Sometimes he obviously wove his own conjectures into history in "gigantic" images of a similar kind: "By his head-
quarters, Attila was able to display such a large pyramid of decapitated heads
that the very sight of them served to discourage most people who were desir-
ous [of rebelling] ."Attila's march on Rome, and his retreat the moment the
Pope came out to meet him with crucifix and banners, is narrated in the manner of someone telling a simple anecdote. The same anecdotal quality can be
found in many of the excerpts and synopses that were first published by
Tikhonravov. The decline of Rome is explained by "a lack of spiritual firmness on the part of the successive Caesars." The fall of the Eastern Roman
Empire is explained by Justinian's traits of character. The wars during the
reign of Clothard II are even attributed to the personal enmity between the
wives of two of the earlier French kings.[9] A glorification of the individual,
which tended to turn into anecdote and which bordered on fairy tale—this lay
at the heart of Gogol's understanding of history. But he was not consistent in
his dedication to individualism, even in the years when his individualistic view
of life was honed to its keenest edge. He sensed the possibility of yet another
approach to history.

This was not to be from the standpoint of the life of the masses: Gogol
the scholar took scant interest in them, far less than did Gogol the artist, and
he always perceived them as a homogeneous whole. Rather, this other approach was from the standpoint of "visible nature," "material nature." Gogol was very much interested in M. P. Pogodin's historical aphorisms, and the
following might well have stuck in his mind: "Man at first is a slave to the
land; it is here that one must seek the source of religions, forms of government, and the relationship of geography and natural history to history itself.
The more man develops, the more his spiritual side evolves toward perfection,
then the more he frees himself from the power of material nature until he becomes its master instead of its slave" (*Moskovskii vestnik*, No. 6, 1827). In
fact, when speaking of the earliest periods of history—in his articles "On the
Movement of Peoples at the End of the Fifth Century" and "A View of the
Formation of Little Russia"—Gogol devotes a great deal of attention to the
geography and nature of Central Asia and the Ukraine. He even says:
"much in history is determined by geography." Despite his great interest in

geography, he of course understood that it could not explain *everything;* and whenever he recognized this fact, he would go back to the role of the individual in history.[10]

Finally, a third concept of history—the providential—creeps into Gogol's articles in an ill-defined and timid way.[11] Suggestions of it are to be found in two articles: "On the Teaching of World History" (in a vague statement to the effect that the mysterious ways of Providence should be noted), and in his introductory lecture at St. Petersburg University, "On the Middle Ages," where he supposes that Providence intervened in the development of the Papacy and in the destinies of chivalry. That is all. As close as he came to the view of the world expressed in the Old Russian Chronicles, he did not grasp their religious didacticism, and the possibility of seeing life in those terms remained only a glimmer to him in those years.

Individualism, realism, religion: in varying degrees and at various times these ideas took possession of Gogol's mind. In this particular phase of his development, they were interrelated, as was evident in the articles on history. Realism was the foundation, the solid ground: hence his habit of taking empirical explanations of history as points of departure. Religion was still a potentiality as yet unrealized. Individualism was a crucial, albeit temporary stage.

As far as Gogol was concerned, the dividing line between a scholarly and an artistic approach toward history was virtually imperceptible, and he crossed it time and again in his writings. He ended his article on three historians—Schloezer, Miller, and Herder—by indicating three other men who were to serve as models for the future historian.[12] They were not scholars but poets: Schiller, Sir Walter Scott, and Shakespeare. What he valued in Shakespeare was the "art of developing important traits of character within narrow limits." Schiller's sense of the dramatic, and Scott's ability to hold the reader's interest should influence the external form of the historian's narrative. Even here, Gogol's own estheticism played the decisive role; but some influence was also exerted by the then-current view that history was part of esthetics. In Section 174 of his treatise on esthetics, Galich regards world history as the ideal epic work. Even Pogodin writes: "Events take their shape in the eyes of the clairvoyant historian and appear to him like a work of fine art that exists in space rather than in time" *(Moskovskii vestnik,* No. 6, 1827). And Gogol presents the broadest of his historical generalizations—a picture of the ancient world—in the article entitled "Life" *(Arabesques),* which is a specimen of out-and-out lyricism, being cast in rhythmic sentences and saturated with imagery.

Gogol looked on history as material for art before he began to devise theories about it. "A Chapter from a Historical Novel" was one of his earliest appearances in print (at the end of 1830). Historical settings or historical episodes are presented in three of the stories in *Evenings on a Farm Near Dikanka.*[13] And while working on *Evenings,* he was also writing purely historical tales: the unfinished *Hetman* and the first version of "Taras Bulba." Some of the traditions that had been incorporated into *Evenings* continued to operate in these new contexts as well—notably, the Ukrainian comic tradition and the highly emotional rhetoric of the Ukrainian folksong. But here the historical narrator also had to deal with the tradition of the Russian historical novel. S. P. Shevyryov once said that "Karamzin sharpened the quill for Russian prose; everyone is writing accordingly" *(Alcyone [Al'tsiona]*, 1832). This could also be seen in the historical tale, not so much in lexicon and syntax (which were easy to depart from) as in the epic-monologue manner and the schematic depiction of character. The action of the historical tale was not well developed in Karamzin: usually it was created by stringing incident upon incident, as in the adventure story. This was done with relative artistry by Narezhny, in "The Seminary Student," and with no artistry whatever by Bulgarin in *Dmitry the Pretender (Dmitrii Samozvanets,* 1830) and *Mazeppa* (1833). As it emerged from Bulgarin's ineptly sharpened pen, the Karamzin style became indistinguishable from the characteristic style of official government correspondence ("I request that you inform me," etc.); dialogue merely served to convey "facts" and sententious homilies; and plot effects amounted to nothing more than the sudden appearance of maidens who had been saved from drowning, and similar excursions into naiveté. At the same time, the free narrative style of Sir Walter Scott, which was at once dramatic and epic, was coming into Russian literature. Here the author allowed himself to indulge in commentary but not in lyricism, in idealization but not in the grotesque. Practices that derived straight from Scott were revitalized in Pushkin's historical prose: while sticking to a traditional kind of action (the adventures of a separated couple), he gave his style a brilliantly terse quality, and made his characters psychologically convincing.

Still earlier, Zagoskin, with *Yury Miloslavsky* (1829), was moving out into the mainstream represented by the dramatic and epic story whose plotline broke off at appropriate intervals to allow for a change of scene. However, he retained the conventionally pallid figures of classical heroes and villains, and oversimplified or virtually eliminated the "struggle of passions" that was obligatory for heroes of classical tragedy. Zagoskin inspired several other novelists who more or less successfully carried on what he had done.[14] At the same time, the exaggerated characters and powerful effects of the French Romantics (headed by Victor Hugo) began to reverberate in the Russian tale, particularly of the historical variety. The loudest reverberations could be heard in the historical stories of Marlinsky: marauders refuse to touch the clothes of a traitor; a girl is killed not by a bullet but by her wedding ring, which has been put into a pistol. The middling man of letters borrowed from all traditions everything that was pleasing to the tastes and instincts of the middling reader—a sentimental lyrical sigh, over-simplified psychology, romantic effects, cheap moralizing. An example of this kind of amalgam can be seen in Yegor Aladin's *Kochubey* (1828). From here it was but a step down to chapbook literature, which appropriated "high" literature,

Gogol's works included, and refashioned it to its own purposes. By the end of the 1830s, Russian Romantic literary critics had begun talking ironically of the traditional devices of structure and style in the historical tale. An excerpt from *The Moscow Herald*'s review of *The Nevsky Miscellany* for 1828 will help make clear the extent to which Gogol still remained faithful to moribund forms, and the extent to which he was moving away from them:

> Little by little we are beginning to discover the secret of composing popular tales. Let us set forth certain basic fundamentals of this new theory. Take several historical personages, garb them in national dress, and create some sort of intrigue among them. For Russian authors, the preferred subjects for such stories are *the fall and the destruction of castles and towns,* and Mr. Bulgarin, following the example of his predecessors, has smashed Wenden. The choice is very convenient: in the first place, the description of a siege can be accompanied by much martial din and thunder; in the second place, one is allowed to introduce *two lovers, one of whom should come from the camp of the besiegers, the other from the camp of the besieged,* for greater interest. Among the historical characters the author should not fail also to place some fictional characters with magical powers—either a *sorcerer,* as in Mr. Bulgarin, or a *gypsy,* as in Somov's *The Haidamak,* or, best of all, a Jew, as Mr. Aladin has done. These Jews are *very fashionable;* they derive their ancestry from Shakespeare's Shylock and Sir Walter Scott's Isaac. This Jew must be omnipresent, he must appear everywhere, like a deus ex machina, ravel and unravel all the threads of the action.... As for the form of the story, it is best to divide it up arbitrarily into chapters, and begin each chapter *with a description,* either of morning or of night or of a storm, on the model of Mr. Aladin. As for style, the greater the number of *flowery* expressions, the better.[15]

We should keep in mind this ironic characterization by a contemporary of Gogol's.

Gogol also had predecessors who depicted the Ukrainian past in epic prose; but there was not one in whose steps he could follow directly. The adventure-tale structure favored by Narezhny did not tempt him; furthermore, in "The Seminary Student," the historical element is completely overshadowed by adventures of various kinds; and the Ukrainian setting of "The Zaporozhian Cossack" ("Zaporozhets," 1824) is utterly colorless and merely serves as a framework for the hero's adventures, which take place in Spain and Italy. The fragments of Somov's *The Haidamak* suggested that the finished version would have been an adventure story of the same type; and if they did find any echoes in Gogol's writings, then it was only in *Evenings,* in certain details of ethnography. Several of the chapters of Bulgarin's *Dmitry the Pretender,* whose action is set in the Cossack Host, could perhaps have served as a negative lesson for Gogol: rehashing historical sources in the speeches of the characters does not make a novel historical. The same thing is true, in general, of Bulgarin's *Mazeppa:* only one scene was reflected in Gogol (the Jew thrown into the water), and perhaps one character (Bulgarin's crudely drawn Paley, an intercessor on behalf of the common people). Nor did Gogol go the way of Aladin, that belated follower of Karamzin, and merely draw on generally accepted traditional techniques. All these descriptions of the manners and mores of times past had no specifically Ukrainian coloration. That was supplied by Gogol, and he found it in the same sources he had used for *Evenings*: the folk song and the popular anecdote.

In addition to "Taras Bulba," two fragments published during Gogol's lifetime—"A Chapter from a Historical Novel" and "The Captive"—have survived, as well as several unpublished chapters and fragments. The longest of these consists of five chapters that are complete, and one that is not; it tells of the return of the hero Ostranitsa to his native region, and of his love for the Cossack girl Galya. On more than one occasion, attempts have been made to regard these fragments as components of the novel *The Hetman,* the first part of which Gogol said he had burned. The major obstacle here has been internal chronology: the action of "The Captive" is set specifically in 1543, that of the Ostranitsa-fragments in 1645, and that of the Glechik-chapter after the rebellion of Bogdan Khmelnitsky, i.e., roughly after 1650. These doubts can be laid to rest now that a continuation of "The Captive" has been discovered. Here Ostranitsa appears as a "bloody bandore-player" (whence the title of the fragment), who is skinned alive, and the mysterious captive proves to be his own beloved Galya.[16] Gogol has no trouble in wandering off his chronology by as much as an entire century. The same thing happens in "Taras Bulba," where he is sometimes in the fifteenth century, sometimes in the sixteenth, sometimes in the seventeenth. It was even easier for him, then, to err by ten or twelve years in *The Hetman* and attribute to the 1640s something that should have happened in the 1650s. Therefore, all the surviving fragments can be attributed to *The Hetman,* and we are entitled to speak only of two projects for historical fiction on Gogol's part: *The Hetman* and "Taras Bulba."

In *The Hetman,* Gogol is trying out a style, or, more accurately, several different styles. The monologue is basically of the dramatic-epic variety. Only occasionally does it become rhythmic, in the places where Ostranitsa and Galya speak in the manner of a folksong (on the model of Petro and Pidorka, or Levko and Hanna, in *Evenings*). Sometimes Gogol has his hero "pour out his thoughts" in a long monologue, following the example of the classical tragedies, and with the openly avowed goal of having the reader "find out something about the hero's life." No lexical unity has yet been achieved; barbarisms do crop up.[17] The basic love intrigue is made more complex by the introduction of sundry horrors, in certain images (e.g., "a frog of almost gigantic size," and other "fiendish gnomes" in a cave) and in the plot itself (skinning Ostranitsa alive). The censors had banned "The Bloody Bandore Player" (in which these two examples occur) for just this sort of thing. The disguise-motif, which Gogol never once employed in his comic scenes, is now brought in to create a dramatic effect: the captive proves to be a woman. The arrogant Pole and the caricatured Jew ("he sprawled on the ground like a frog"), both of which derived from the nativity puppet play, had appeared perfunctorily and sketchily in *Evenings*. Now they are more sharply delineated, but there were literary models for them too: the Pole in Zagoskin, the Jew in Bulgarin and Somov. Ostranitsa's exterior is even more sketchily drawn than that of the Cossack lads in *Evenings*; but in Galya we can see an attempt, albeit still tentative, to offer something more individualized than the clear eyes and pink lips of the Dikanka maidens. New features have been added: "a bared shoulder, blushing slightly, peeped out tenderly, like a ripening apple, while under the shift on her bosom the young breasts quivered resiliently." Gogol painstakingly polishes this image and repeats it many times; for him it becomes synonymous with the impression created by womanly charms.

"Taras Bulba" was the only historical tale that Gogol brought to completion. However, the "Taras Bulba" of *Mirgorod* is not the same story that all of us have known since childhood: it was completely reworked between 1839 and 1840, and only in this final version did Gogol achieve a complete unity of rhythm and style. They resemble the rhythm and style of "A Terrible Vengeance," but to an even greater extent, they incorporate devices from the epic tales and the folk songs, which served to confer a unity on the lexicon and style. The final version no longer has the "ebony brows" of the Polish girl, nor eyelashes as long as "reveries," nor an electrically fiery cheek, nor "oh! what an osculation!" The structure underwent considerable reworking as well. In the first version, all the traditional elements on which Gogol built his story are much more in evidence. Subsequently these were concealed in the devices of an epic prose-narrative told in a lyrical manner, which was an entirely new departure for longer prose fiction in Russia.[18] Belinsky called even the first version a supreme model, ideal and prototype of a Homeric epic; and he could have said the same of the second with greater justification.

On reading what the critics in *The Moscow Herald* had to say about historical novels, in the long passage quoted above, we cannot help thinking of Gogol's "Taras Bulba": there is a town under siege, a pair of lovers, one of whom is on the side of the besiegers and the other on the side of the besieged. The love between two enemies, the conflict between love and duty, represents of course a very old tradition; and it must be traced back beyond Zagoskin's historical novels to the classical tragedy, to Corneille and the reverberations his plays made in Russia.[19] In the reworked version, Gogol succeeded in showing Andry's act of betrayal as a gesture of despairing renunciation. But in the first version, Andry seems to bring it off with astonishing rapidity: this is part of the general impression of "sketchiness" which Shevyryov pointed to as a fault.[20] The story rushes ahead without the slightest concern for the "law of retardation" prescribed for the epic by Galich's esthetics; instead, it reflects the dynamics of the classical tragedy, with its unity of time. The action in the first version develops almost as rapidly as in the journeyman reworkings of "Taras Bulba" that were made for the stage—except that in the latter, Taras himself is captured immediately after Ostap. The fourth chapter features the siege of Dubno, the appearance of the Tartar-girl, and Andry's act of betrayal, all of which were later developed in two long chapters, the fifth and the sixth. In the fifth chapter of the first version, Taras kills Andry during the first battle (later this does not happen until chapter nine), and in the sixth, Ostap is captured.

The figure of the Zaporozhian Cossack was derived from the nativity puppet play and first appeared in "The Lost Letter" (*Evenings on a Farm Near Dikanka*). In "A Terrible Vengeance" he became a Romantic knight. In "Taras Bulba" this Romantic knight is endowed with characteristics that are plausible historically. If they are not exactly accurate historically, from the viewpoint of modern scholarship, that is because Gogol had to depend on the historical literature available to him, and also because he was not trying to create a real Zaporozhian Cossack, but an ideal figure in the spirit of the Ukrainian ballads. It was precisely during this period that Gogol, like Maximovich, was reading and studying folk songs (including ballads), collecting songs himself, and waxing enthusiastic over them. "What are all the stale chronicles through which I am now rummaging by comparison with these ringing, living chronicles!"[21] The article "On Little Russian Songs," which appeared in *Arabesques,* is suffused with the same kind of enthusiasm. It also contains what seem in effect to be preliminary sketches for "Taras Bulba": the bitter lot of the Cossack's wife, the sorrow of the mother, the campaign, the battle, the execution, the dead Cossack, the picture of the measureless steppe as a "wonderful ocean of flowers," and all the "expansive will of Cossack life." Here the Cossack himself is "stubborn, unbending," and is endowed with "strength, joyfulness and might, with which he abandons the quiet and security of home life." This article makes it clear where Gogol found the colors for his historical palette. He is not an archeologist but a poet. He is capable of confusing chronology by entire centuries, simply not realizing in which historical period the action is taking place, any more than the oral epic does.

If the historians of today have formed the impression that "Taras Bulba," for all its anachronisms, is set during the time of Bogdan Khmelnitsky, then that is all to the credit of Gogol's intuitive sense of rightness, and not any conscious intent on his part. A statement made by Kulish, which proved so offensive at one time to the blind admirers of Gogol, is still convincing: "When we re-read 'Taras Bulba' now, we very often find the author groping in the dark; but the moment a song, a chronicle, or a legend give off a spark of light, his extraordinary sharp-sightedness makes use of their faint glimmer to identify objects nearby. Nonetheless, what strikes the expert about 'Taras Bulba' is precisely the purely accidental exactitude of its colors and the glitter of the fantasy-world that is being created; but it is far from satisfactory where historical and artistic truth are concerned."[22]

Such were the sources of the rhetorical strain in Gogol. Out of them he created something all his own, something without any immediate predecessors. But a comic tradition is reflected in "Taras Bulba," that same tradition which derived from the nativity puppet play and the popular anecdote. The very first scene—the fistfight between father and son—could certainly have occurred in the popular farce, if not in the nativity play. Significantly, it begins with a dialogue which would not have been out of place in Kotlyarev-sky's *Aeneid*. The boastful Poles appear even more fleetingly here than in *The Hetman*. On the other hand, the nativity-play Jew, who appeared only in vague outline in "The Fair at Sorochintsy" and in *The Hetman*, now for the first time is developed as a character who is also important to the action of the novel. (Once again we must remember that article in *The Russian Herald*.) All the scenes involving the Jew Yankel are calculated for comic effect (N. V. Stankevich could not think of them without laughing); even the cruel scene where he is thrown into the water is narrated in a manner appropriate to the farce. But this scene reflects literary models as well. Both Aladin and Bulgarin readily resort to drowning to kill off their characters: the Jesuit in *Kochubey* drowns Maria's nurse; the pretender in *Dmitry the Pretender* drowns the mistress of whom he has grown tired. And in Bulgarin, the Zaporozhian ataman on several occasions throws into the water Cossacks who have committed some offense, or Turkish prisoners; also, a Jew is hanged for virtually no reason at all, and the execution is accompanied by loud laughter from the robbers. Finally, Paley, in Bulgarin's *Mazeppa*, throws a Jew into the water (" 'Eternal Sabbath!' cried the Cossacks. Their laughter was repeated in a rumble"). What is new in Gogol is the comic effect of the legs dangling in the air; it is interesting that the original sentence—"the hardened souls of the Cossacks accompanied this with laughter"—was struck out.

Gogol's habit of looking at history in terms of individuals required a hero. But his sense of what was artistically appropriate, and his own traits of personality, made it impossible for him to follow standard literary practice and take a hero from his own times. And so he found a hero in the past. The folk tradition of song and epic also provided him with the palette that would make this figure artistically convincing. But this same tradition also involved the life of the masses, the Cossacks as a whole; and Gogol—who was incapable of being tendentious as an artist—therefore shifted attention away from Taras himself onto the masses, far more emphatically than in his articles about history. It is just as easy to try to demonstrate Gogol's concern with society on the basis of the mass scenes in *The Hetman* and "Taras Bulba" (as Vengerov endeavors to do in the book we have mentioned), as it is to demonstrate his concern with the individual on the basis of the role Taras plays in the story. Neither emphasis constitutes a demonstration. In the first version of "Taras Bulba," artistic and esthetic considerations carry the day. There is not a single instance of aphorizing or preaching (attitudes that neither Zagoskin nor Bulgarin had hesitated to strike, any more than did Gogol himself in re-working the story). Nor is there any moralizing: the father's murder of his son and the cruel reprisals taken against the Jews and the Poles are depicted in a completely dispassionate manner. Gogol remains an esthete first and fore-most, in his substitution of an esthetics of history for a theory of history, in his attitude toward his subject, and in his lyrical outbursts. In the manuscript version, a panegyric to music comes after the Cossack dance: "Only in music does man have freedom. Everywhere he is in fetters. He forges for himself even heavier fetters than those imposed on him by society and authority.... He is a slave, but he is free only when he loses himself in a frenzied dance; here his soul does not fear his body." Artistic consistency required the omission of these lines too from the published version. But they are further evidence of the basic element that governed the author of *Arabesques*.

CHAPTER V

THE CONTEMPORARY WORLD AND THE SECOND IDYLL

Toward the end of his life, in "An Author's Confession" (1847), Gogol tried to show that his early works owed their comic quality to a need for "self-diversion" on his part. This explanation is only partially justified by those comic elements we have considered so far. In the fairy-tales that make up *Evenings on a Farm Near Dikanka*, and in "Viy," the comic is intertwined with the demonic, which is capable of revealing its uncomic aspect at any moment. In the longer fairy-tales, the historical tales, and "Nevsky Prospect," the comic is also interwoven with an elegiac lyricism, with the idealized figures of couples in love and epic heroes, and with situations that are unmistakably tragic. In looking back on the creative process as it operated in him, Gogol seemingly might have been thinking of those works in which plot and characters are comic through and through. In fact, he did create works of this kind whenever he returned from the remote regions of history and fantasy to the Ukraine of his own days. The Dikanka stories are not contemporary; they exist entirely in an unreal space and time (as is appropriate to fairy-tales); historical datings and settings (sometimes specified, sometimes not) are irrelevant. The Petersburg tales[1] are contemporary in setting, but it was very easy for Gogol to combine this contemporaneousness with Romantic fantasy. However, he was able to show the Ukraine of his time in a purely comic light, without any element of fantasy.

While at Nezhin, Gogol wrote a satire, which has been lost: "Something about Nezhin, or, Fools Rush in Where Angels Fear to Tread." In *The Literary Gazette* for 1831, two chapters of the tale entitled "The Dread Wild Boar" were published (it has not survived: either is has been lost or it was never completed). Included in *Evenings* is a story which is deliberately left unfinished, "Ivan Fyodorovich Shponka and His Aunt." But "The Tale of How Ivan Ivanovich Quarrelled with Ivan Nikiforovich," included in *Mirgorod*, is indisputably complete. These are all comic descriptions of the ordinary Ukrainian life of Gogol's own times set in towns or among small landowners, with an appropriate cast of characters. Here the comic element in Gogol is seen in its purest form (though it is not entirely pure); and Gogol's statement about the comic serving as a diversion is relevant to these particular stories above all.

The first chapter of "The Dread Wild Boar," entitled "The Teacher," outlines a theme that was to reverberate in Gogol's major works: the comic commotion stirred up in a stagnant little philistine world by the appearance of a new character. Here it runs the gamut from remarks that are comic by virtue of their pseudo-profundity to a scene of pure farce, where two women flail away at each other (the future "two ladies" of *Dead Souls*, except that those do not actually come to blows). The central figure is a philistine school-teacher who pompously attends to the "process of satiation." He is a former seminary student and therefore a modification of the clerk-figure in the nativity puppet play. In outward appearance he is also a caricature, with a face like a bottle, a mouth that stretches from ear to ear, and bright green eyes. The second chapter (entitled "The Success of a Mission") shows the clumsy attempts made by Onisko, the keeper of an eating-house, to declare his love for the "blond beauty" Katerina. [2] This falls somewhere between Somov's crude scenes of pastoral love and the operetta-like duets of the Dikanka stories. It comes closest to the scene between Vakula and Oxana in "Christmas Eve"; there is nothing comic in that scene; only at the end of the chapter in question does the comic suddenly erupt, in the farce-like touch of placing a cap instead of a chicken on the spit.

The major comic effect in "Ivan Fyodorovich Shponka" is one of incompleteness: the story is suddenly broken off just as the aunt is concocting a new scheme, which is to be carried over into the following chapter that was never written. Gogol set great store by this device of the same story repeated over and over. (Let us recall that Sir Walter Scott advised the writer to arouse curiosity but not satisfy it.) Of course is does not matter whether the story was originally conceived with this effect in mind, or whether the explanation in the preface—that the paper had been used for baking meat pies—was added later.[3] Another comic device is the gravity with which the most trivial matters are narrated, the serious tone in which we are told, for instance, about the "occupations" of Shponka, who is one of Gogol's earliest loafer-types. A variant of the typical farce-device of absent-mindedness occurs here as well: the aunt, Vasilisa Kashporovna, holds out a morsel to the dog, which she mistakes for an imaginary great-nephew. There is a servant who gets down on his knees to attend to a guest. Then comes the earliest suggestion of a scene that would later appear in the play *Marriage*: the "conversation" between the suitor (Shponka) and the young lady, after a silence which in this case lasts about a quarter of an hour. Finally, there is Shponka's dream, which has all the elements of caricature.[4] Touches of caricature also creep into descriptions of the personages: the aunt is "of an almost gigantic height," the old woman is "a perfect coffee-pot in a cap." This story is dramatic and epic simultaneously: the author remains in the shadows; only now and then does he introduce a sentence in the first person, and only once (in the haying scene) some unalloyed lyricism, although here too he tries to pass off his lyrical effusions as commentaries on the feelings engendered by his hero's "meek soul." This story is intended as an epic. And in fact, it presents not only strongly marked individuals but also a detailed backdrop, a whole little world whose existence is based on turkeys baked with plums and the pickling of cucumbers.

In the story of the quarrel between the two Ivans, the comic aspect is not only played up but is constantly being intensified by authorial intervention. The author exchanges winks with the reader and jokes about what is going on, for example, about the way Agafia Fedoseevna seizes Ivan Nikiforovich by the nose. Sometimes he himself tries to make the reader laugh, as, for example, when he waxes enthusiastic over the "beautiful puddle" in the main street of Mirgorod. The plot is only remotely connected with Narezhny's novel of love and adventure entitled *Two Ivans, or a Passion for Lawsuits,* and with one episode in the same author's *A Russian Gil Blas, or the Adventures of Prince Gavrila Simonovich Chistyakov (Rossiiskii Zhilblas, ili pokhozhdeniia kniazia Gavrily Simonovicha Chistiakova,* 1814). Narezhny's didacticism makes a happy ending obligatory, and his methods of character-depiction do not resemble Gogol's at all. In Gogol's story, the principals are even more sharply caricatured than in "Shponka," and the same device of unexpectedly concrete comparisons that we find in "The Dread Wild Boar" is used: Ivan Ivanovich's head resembles a radish with the tail pointed down, Ivan Nikiforovich's head resembles a radish with the tail pointed up, Ivan Ivanovich's mouth looks like the letter V, Ivan Nikiforovich's nose is like a ripe plum, Agafia Fedoseevna has "a cap on her head, three warts on her nose, and a coffee-colored housecoat with little yellow flowers on it," her figure is like a tub, and her legs are shaped on the pattern of two pillows. The scribe is a particularly vivid caricature: a "typical scribbling inkslinger," swarthy, with spots all over his face, three pens stuck behind his ear, and a glass bottle tied to a button; he eats nine pies at one sitting (a glutton straight out of the farce!) and sticks the tenth in his pocket.[5] This "small semblance of a man" is referred to in an impersonal manner.

The various scenes are all calculated to create an impression that seems comic. In the conversation between Ivan Ivanovich and the old beggar woman, Gogol simply repeats the kind of dialogue that can be heard between the Cossack and the gypsy woman in the nativity puppet play. The only difference is that Ivan Ivanovich says to her, "Well, what are you standing there for? I'm not beating you, after all," whereas the Cossack, on learning that the gypsy woman wants to be given some coins, actually gives her a beating. In the second chapter, the actors are comically arranged in a group that resembles the mute scene which would later end *The Inspector General:* a naked Ivan Nikiforovich, Ivan Ivanovich striking the pose of a Roman tribune, the gaping woman, and the boy picking his nose. Sheer farce enters into the scene where Ivan Nikiforovich gets stuck in the doorway and has to be shoved through, and in the scene of the attempted reconciliation, where people try to push the two Ivans together and this is likened to a game of ball. That is, we have the confrontation of two enemies where, traditionally, one is tragically defeated. Finally, there is the scene that does not jibe with the best-intentioned efforts to interpret this as a "realistic" story: the brown pig carries off Ivan Nikiforovich's petition and itself becomes a character, whose criminal act is discussed in all seriousness by the mayor. The comic aspect of the story does not depend just on the characters and scenes as such, but also on the manner in which the action develops. Here Gogol applies what he had noted as "an old principle" in 1832, one that he invariably used in his comic plots: "He is just about to get something and grasp it with his hand when suddenly there is some obstacle and the desired object is removed to an enormous distance."[6] This is the case here: the two Ivans are just on the point of being reconciled when suddenly everything is removed to an enormous distance after Ivan Nikiforovich utters the fateful word "gander."

But this particular effect is not always comic. S. P. Shevyryov, in reflecting on the essential quality of humor (with reference to *Mirgorod*), defined it as the absurdity of life.[7] The "removal of the desired object" can either make the absurdity less perceptible (in the most naive kind of plot where "virtue is triumphant"), or else can intensify it (as is the case here, where the absurd quarrel is dragged out endlessly). Here it is no longer a question of pure "laughter," but, as Belinsky put it in another context, "laughter diluted with bitterness."[8] This is made clear and unambiguous by the epilogue as a whole, and not just by the concluding sentence—"It's a dreary world, my dear sirs"—as people usually insist. Throughout the story, Gogol limits his authorial role to that of a comic commentator, who stands by the footlights, points out what is funny, and laughs on behalf of the audience. He immediately suppresses any outbursts of lyricism (for example, in the description of the night in chapter three) with some qualifying comment: "Oh, if only I were a painter, I would depict..."; and further on he repeats "I would depict" three times. Only once does lyricism seem to break through and follow along a chain of associations: the play of bright sunlight has evoked the colorful spectacle of a travelling puppet theater, which in the setting sun reminds the narrator of "the fresh chill of the southern night," and this is turn calls to mind the "fresh shoulders and breasts of plump farm girls." But in the epilogue, lyricism is given full vent. At the beginning of the story, Mirgorod is merry and sunny, and there is good reason why the play of sunlight on Ivan Nikiforovich's uniforms and on the point of his sword reminds the narrator of a puppet theater "which vagrant entertainers cart around from farm to farm." The epilogue offers nothing like the merry puppet theater—just autumn, mud, mist, "an unnatural greenness," all of it described with an appropriate choice of epithets (sad, dreary, gloomy, sickly, mournful, unpleasant), and in a lyrical outburst which is now unrestrained and ends with a final apostrophe to the reader. The heroes, who were comic so very recently, have now grown old and pitiable.

Of course, this contrast is an artistic device as well, and Gogol was very much aware of its effect. As he wrote during the same years, in his article "On the Architecture of the Present Day": "A true effect comes from sharp opposition, beauty is never so vivid and evident as it is when set in contrast....Its

71

various parts are in harmony according to the same laws by which pale yellow harmonizes with dark blue, white with light blue, pink with green, and so on. Everything depends on taste and on the ability to arrange," or, in other words, on the art of composition.[9]

This contrast-effect explains Gogol's purposes as an artist. But it is also deeply rooted in his own psychology, notably in his individualistic outlook. Only at first glance does this individualism appear to be incompatible with the depiction of ordinary life. At the end of "The Two Ivans" the narrator exclaims: "It's a dreary world, my dear sirs!" He might well have gone on to add what had burst forth from Gogol himself in a letter written to Vysotsky seven years earlier: "And I must grovel amidst these existers!" In drawing such caricatures (whether of the crudely traditional variety or of greater refinement and artistry), Gogol was doing something in his writing that he considered necessary in his personal life as early as 1827: rejecting the "existers," the "loafers" (a favorite term of Pereverzev's), the "lampoons of humankind" (Belinsky's expression). Of each of his heroes, of each of the four Ivans in his works (Ivan Osipovch, Ivan Fyodorovich Shponka, and Ivan Ivanovich/Ivan Nikiforovich), he could have said exactly what he had said of the people at Nezhin: "With the crust of their earthliness they have crushed the lofty allotted task of man."[10]

Gogol's own psychology is involved here, but so is the literary tradition: the dualism of late Romanticism, with its non-acceptance of the world and its creation of other worlds. This tradition chimed with Gogol's psychology and was therefore assimilated by him. The uglier the faces of the "existers," which are fashioned out of dark clay, the more tender and incorporeal are the denizens of that ideal universe which is created by the artist in his visions or by his heroes at his behest. This is what we see in Gogol, with his ideal lads and lasses, who are recreated by two or three allusions to folk songs (Evenings), with his demi-goddess Alcinoë ("Woman"), with the divine stranger created by Piskaryov's will, first on the Nevsky Prospect and then in his opium-induced delirium ("Nevsky Prospect"). One more step and the heroes would begin falling in love with specters that had no ties whatever with the real world, as is the case with E.T.A. Hoffmann (especially in "The Golden Pot"), and V. F. Odoevsky (especially in "The Sylphid" ["Sil'fida"]). But this was a step that Gogol did not take, because he had a truly dualistic view of the world, one which critics have long noted but have never correctly interpreted.

The duality in Gogol did not consist of a conflict between paganism and Christianity, as Merezhkovsky thought (in those years Gogol's esthetic individualism was not Christian), or between Romanticism and realism, as Kotlyarevsky put it (Gogol's realistic satire was an expression of the same "Romantic" sense of life). Rather, this duality amounted to a *rejection* of the traditional social and cultural roots, together with an *attraction* to these very same roots.[11] It was this duality which compelled him, during his years at

Nezhin, to "burn with an unquenchable desire to make [his] life necessary," and, at the same time, to take a keen interest in such mundane things as distilling, farm-buildings, and the cut of frock-coats. This duality was also reflected in his creative work. The earliest example was *Hanz Küchelgarten*, where it turned a Romantic poem into a Sentimentalist idyll. The second instance can be seen in "Old-Fashioned Landowners," which was written several years later.

The contrast-effect can be seen in this story as well. With the words "but my narrative is drawing near to a very sad event which forever changed the life of this little corner," there begins a second chapter, as it were. Although this chapter is different from the first, the contrast-effect is underplayed. It was Belinsky who pointed it up: he found "the banality...vileness... of an animalistic, misshapen, caricatured life" in the story, and, in the heroes, "two parodies of humankind" (which is only slightly gentler than the "lampoons of mankind" that he had used for the preceding story), "actors in a stupid comedy." Yet he did sense a certain "charm" in the story. This he explained by the fact that even in this banal and absurd life, the author had discovered a human feeling: habit. Still, he thought that Gogol had drawn the following conclusion: "Oh, poor mankind! A pitiable life!"[12] Of course, Gogol does not conceal his compassion for the old couple, who do nothing but "drink and eat, eat and drink." The lyric-epic monologue form and the first-person narrator enable him to weave in pure lyricism and to break the narrative with ejaculations: "good old woman!" "good old people!" However, this is a compassion he feels not just for the old couple, but for the entire old-fashioned way of life, the "bucolic life" in which "not a single desire wings its way across the fence," a compassion for the very "air of the old-fashioned farmstead."

Here the life of "existers" is depicted in the tones appropriate to an idyll instead of a satire; and it would seem that Gogol's trip back home in the summer of 1832 provided the stimulus for such an idealized approach. The following lines in a letter to I. I. Dmitriev are very significant: "I am now living in a village which is of exactly the same kind as described by the unforgettable Karamzin. It seems to me that he was copying a Little Russian village, so bright are his colors and so similar are they to nature as it is here" (about July 20 [o.s.], 1832). Of course it was not by mere chance that Gogol made mention of Karamzin's idyll in a letter to Dmitriev, who was a follower of Karamzin. It is not clear whether he had in mind Karamzin's story "The Village" ("Derevnia," 1792), or the later and more openly aristocratic "Letter of an Inhabitant of the Country" ("Pis'mo sel'skogo zhitelia," 1803). In any event, both these pieces by Karamzin express a definite renunciation of youthful dreams of a golden age of universal brotherhood, and a sense of tranquility in the Horatian ideal of contentment with what exists. The reference to Karamzin reveals the historical basis of the psychology that underlay Gogol's vacillations between the individualistic rebelliousness of Romanticism and the idyll of reconciliation preached by Sentimentalism. This second idyll of Gogol's, like the first, is a dream, an idealization, and not simply a reflection of impressions drawn from real life. This is shown by the fact that the tone used to characterize the prosperity of the landowners is that of a fairytale (no matter how many "dreadful robberies" are perpetrated by the servants, "the blessed earth produced everything in such abundance" that they go unnoticed), by the comparison of the heroes to Philemon and Baucis, and finally, by those "rainbow colors" which are anything but true to reality and which Gogol uses to depict the life of the small landowners with which he was familiar: in his idyllic dream ("from here I see," etc.), the bird-cherry tree is in blossom, the cherries and plums are ripening, and the apples are being dried—all at one and the same time.[14]

Through careful attention to the text of "Old-Fashioned Landowners," we can see that Gogol himself was aware of the contradiction between his individualistic impulses and his attraction to the nirvana of the old-fashioned farmstead. This is indicated by the italicized words (my stresses) in the following sentences: "I *sometimes* like to descend *for a moment* into the world of this unusually isolated life...all this holds an inexpressible charm for me, *perhaps because* I see them no longer and because *everything from which we are separated is dear to us*...you cannot help but renounce, *at least for a brief spell*, all ambitious dreams, and you imperceptibly pass with all your heart into this humble *bucolic* life." This is a temporary flight from the individual's struggle for life and beauty, which Gogol had already depicted more than once in a tragic vein as a struggle against universal evil, against demonic powers, and not against "existers." There is an indication of this in the story too. "The life of their modest owners is so quiet, so very quiet that *for a moment* you are lost in forgetfulness and imagine that the passions, the desires, and the restless handiwork of *the evil spirit,* which trouble the world, do not really exist and that you have only seen them in some glittering, dazzling dream." Gogol flees into the humble bucolic life (even when idealized, it remains humble), into the "chemical laboratory" of Pulkheria Ivanovna, just as Pushkin's Aleko flees into the humble simplicity of the gypsy camp ("The Gypsies" ["Tsygany"], 1829). Were Gogol's hopes justified?

Pushkin's answer to Aleko's hopes is as follows: "And everywhere are fateful passions, and against the fates there is no defense." Gogol replies in the same way, except that he replaces passions with habit, which he could also have called love (for after all, the habitual nature of the relationship between the two Ivans did not prevent their comically absurd quarrel). As for the second part of Pushkin's reply—"and against the fates there is no defense" —this is repeated specifically in the fatalistic ending of Gogol's story. First the mysterious reappearance of the cat disturbs the idyll by forecasting Pulkheria Ivanovna's death; then comes death itself; and after her death comes the inconsolable grief of Afanasy Ivanovich, who is now alone. The depiction of incomprehensible forces in terms of an amorphous fate, rather than in the overly concrete images of demonism from the folk tradition, was more appropriate to Gogol's own amorphous mysticism in those years. But something else may have been at work here as well: a reaction, in Russian Romantic circles at the end of the 1820s, against the kind of unsophisticated excursions into the fantastic that were characteristic of fairy tales. This was expressed as follows by S. P. Shevyryov, in his review of Pogorelsky's *The Double (Dvoinik)*: "If we still have any reserves left for fantasy, they exist...more in those miracles, those imaginary incongruities, those unresolved phenomena which are part of the visible world" (*Moskovskii vestnik,* No. 14, Part X, 1828).

Thus, the idyll of "Old-Fashioned Landowners" is merely an *episode* in the history of Gogol's personal and artistic development, although it is an extremely significant episode. We cannot make a *direct* link between this episode and the kinds of idealization in which he later indulged. He himself was to link his third idyll (see Chapter XI) with the ideology he had worked out for himself by that time. This second idyll, like the denouement of the first, represents an escape from all ideology. Gogol was not tempted by the example of Karamzin (even though he did mention it), that is, he did not try to use moralism and social conservatism as sustenance for his idyll. Nor was he tempted by the example of V. I. Karlgof, who had published an idyll entitled "The Stationmaster" ("Stantsionnyi smotritel'") in *The Slav* in 1827.[15] Here the family happiness of an *educated* schoolmaster is depicted in the Karamzin style (among the components of this happiness are also a substantial home-cooked meal of rich cabbage soup, aspic, and home-grown veal). Karlgof's edifying idea—"every occupation is more or less useful to society; consequently, every one is more or less honorable"—would later become one of Gogol's favorites ("it is necessary to take up an occupation," in *Selected Passages from Correspondence with Friends,* 1847). But at this point we can find no direct link, as far as ideas are concerned, between the Gogol of *Mirgorod* (1835) and the Gogol of *Selected Passages.* The only link lay in the power exerted by historical and cultural roots, to which he sometimes gave assent, yet which again and again he denied.

CHAPTER VI

THE MISSION OF A COMIC WRITER

In "An Author's Confession," written in 1847, and in a letter to Zhu-kovsky that dates from about the same period (January 10, 1848), Gogol sketched out the course of his development as a writer. It fell into two radically different phases, with *The Inspector General* as the dividing point. The first phase, as he put it, was one of "youth, during which no questions came to mind," a time of carefree and spontaneous laughter, which answered to his need to divert himself during attacks of melancholy. *The Inspector General* was the first work conceived with the aim of exerting a good influence on society: here the "laughter" was different from what it had been before; now undertones of sadness could be heard. "The need to divert myself with innocent, carefree scenes ended along with the years of my youth."

Gogol's statement that in his youth "no questions came to mind" cannot be taken literally. Many questions arise and are resolved throughout his early works, beginning with *Hanz Küchelgarten*. But they are all questions stemming from an awareness of the esthetic. The humor in Gogol's early works is of the same origin as well. His statement can be interpreted as follows: it was only with *The Inspector General* that he began to connect the idea of a personal mission with the act of writing, to see that the mission was not to consist of serving "the good of the state," or performing any other kind of service, but rather, of fulfilling the role of a *comic writer* who could "exert a good influence on society." Thus, a moral individualism entered the picture, to give greater complexity to the already existing esthetic individualism.

Gogol had first advanced the possibility of art's *moral* influence in the article "Sculpture, Painting and Music." This did not of course rule out "innocent, carefree scenes": there are a great many of them even in *The Inspector General,* especially in the first version. That fact alone would make the sharp distinction between innocent and calculated laughter impossible. Moreover, the first signs of Gogol's awareness of his mission as a comic writer must be dated from an earlier period, even before he received his teaching position at the University (1834). After "kissing the University goodbye" at the end of 1835, he merely saw this mission in sharper perspective. The first signs can be detected in a conversation he had with S. T. Aksakov in the summer of 1832 in Moscow, from which Aksakov understood that "the Russian comedy preoccupied him more and that he had his own original view of it." We have this statement of Aksakov's; we know that Gogol praised Zagoskin for his "merriment" and disapproved of him for "not writing what he should." We even have his remark that "the comic lies hidden everywhere, and even though we live amidst it, we do not see it." Yet nothing definite can be said about his "original view" of the Russian comedy.[1]

But Gogol was indeed preoccupied with *comedy*; and evidently he was prepared to connect the idea of his mission as a writer with precisely this form of art. In Moscow he made friends with Zagoskin, who at that time was director of theaters, and with the celebrated comic actor Mikhail Shchepkin, who, according to tradition, gave him the plot of "Old-Fashioned Landowners." At the end of that same year, Pletnyov wrote Zhukovsky that a comedy was whirling around in Gogol's head; and at the beginning of the following year (February 20 [o.s.], 1833), Gogol himself wrote Pogodin that he had *lost his head* over a comedy, that the title was *The Order of St. Vladimir, Third Class,* and that it was to contain much *malice, laughter* and *piquancy.* But he went on to say that there was no hope of its being passed by the censor, and that he had stopped working on it (this was the only reason he gave). It was not until the middle of 1834 that reports of comedies by Gogol again began circulating. It was said that he had already written one, which he was reading to friends and was planning to produce, and that he was writing another "on the sly." But inasmuch as the comedy entitled *The Suitors* (which later developed into *Marriage*) was also being written at that time, we cannot definitely say which was which.[2]

Marriage was completed in 1835. Gogol gave it to Pushkin for comment, and at the same time his "hand was quivering" to write another comedy, in five acts and "funnier than the devil." He asked Pushkin for a plot, a "purely Russian story." That was in a letter dated October 7 (o.s.); and two months later, having become a "carefree Cossack," having given up his university post but not the "lofty ideas full of truth and awesome grandeur," Gogol wrote to Pogodin: "Let us now laugh and laugh as much as possible. Long live comedy" (December 6 [o.s.], 1835). In those two months *The Inspector General* had already been written, and four months later it would be produced. Thus, in the course of three years (1833-1835), Gogol made preliminary sketches for three comedies, and in the course of another seven years, he devoted more painstaking and protracted labor to them than to any of his works of prose fiction. Two comedies—*The Inspector General* and *Marriage*— took final form only in 1842. Everything that remained of a third comedy *(The Order of St. Vladimir)* was polished up, and a fourth was added to the list: *The Gamblers.* This, in brief, is the external history of these works.

It is an immediately striking fact that in his comedies, Gogol looks for heroes and plots in a world he completely avoided in *Evenings on a Farm Near Dikanka,* in *Mirgorod,* and in all the stories of *Arabesques* save one. This is the world of officialdom—at first, of St. Petersburg, then of the Russian provinces. Of course, heroes and plots from this world could also (and did) provide occasion for "innocent, carefree scenes" as well as for laughter with an end to self-diversion during attacks of melancholy. Such scenes had been associated with Gogol's own "states of mind" and with his contempt for "existers." Now, however, when he discovered that these "existers" were also to be found in society at large and in government service, his attitude toward them changed. So did the quality of the "laughter" he directed at them: it was now suffused with "malice and piquancy." In his adolescent dreams, service to the state had been one possible way of accomplishing "man's lofty mission." Now he felt obliged to subject those who had crushed such possibilities with "the crust of their earthliness" to particularly savage laughter. His choice of heroes and plots endowed the "amusing situations" he had created even before *The Inspector General* with significance as social satire.

We can form some judgment about Gogol's first project for a comedy, *The Order of St. Vladimir, Third Class*, on the basis of the four scenes he worked up into final form, when they are considered together with what has been preserved in rough drafts and in the memories of his contemporaries. These scenes are: "An Official's Morning," "A Lawsuit," "The Servants' Quarters," and "A Fragment." The central figure is an ambitious official named Barsukov, who dreams of receiving a decoration. However, he is a swindler who has forged a will. Other people who are just as unscrupulous and ambitious weave a web of intrigue around him—Prolyotov, the head secretary, and Zakatishchev, an official, together with Barsukov's brother, a landowner from the steppes who has been the victim of the forged will. Barsukov is a loafer, a gambler, and a stickler for form; he behaves arrogantly toward his subordinates and lives for only one thing: the decoration. Reports have it that there was one scene which was particularly good but which has been lost: Barsukov stands in front of a mirror trying on the decoration he imagines he has received. But the intrigue does its work: he does not get the decoration. This is a blow that robs him of his reason; and he goes insane imagining that he himself is the Order of St. Vladimir, Third Class.

This is the basic line of the play. There are also secondary motifs and characters—among them the virtuous Misha Povalishchev, who is in love with Odosimova, the equally virtuous daughter of a poor civil servant. The match is ruined by Misha's mother (with the aid of the intriguer Sobachkin, who is the same as Zakatishchev):[3] she accuses Misha of liberalism, freemasonry and a passion for the poetry of Ryleev, and she wants to marry him off to Princess Shlepokhvostova. A number of characters are also introduced in the servants' quarters of the Barsukov house. It was probably the complexity of the whole project, no less than apprehensions about the censorship, that induced Gogol, who was as yet inexperienced in matters of dramatic composition, to leave the comedy unfinished. Both these factors were cited by Pletnyov in a letter to Zhukovsky (March 11 [o.s.], 1833).

The Order of St. Vladimir, Third Class, cannot be regarded as a dramatic whole, but that does not diminish the importance of the central character-type and the central theme: the insanity of an ambitious man. The story "Diary of a Madman" has a direct connection with this play. It would seem that after experiencing failure with the comedy, Gogol returned to his usual genre, prose fiction, in order to depict the same theme, although the specific form—a diary—was new for him. The figure of Barsukov is now compressed into the episodic character of the director of a government department who wonders whether he will be awarded a decoration and then, when he does get it, boasts about it even in front of his dog.[4] But the theme of insanity resulting from ambition is assigned to another character—Poprishchin—and as a consequence, the story gains in sharpness and depth.

The theme itself was not new in the literature of the time. The journals at the end of the 1820s were eager to publish factual data about the insane, and fictional treatments of them as well. Several factual accounts appeared in No. 34 of the journal *The Butterfly (Babochka)* for 1829, among them the story of a French officer who imagined himself to be King of Spain and was mulling over a plan for a new Spanish constitution. Still earlier, in 1826, an article appeared in *The Moscow Telegraph* entitled "An Insane Man of Ambition" ("Sumasshedshii chestoliubets"), where mention was made of several similar cases: one madman insisted he was the Emperor of China, others claimed to be dictators and military leaders. In the 1830s this same journal printed an article by the publisher, N. A. Polevoy, entitled "The Insane and the Sane" ("Sumasshedshie i nesumasshedshie"), which advanced the idea that in the society of the time, it was impossible to distinguish the two categories. In 1832, V. F. Odoevsky was planning to put out a collection entitled *The Madhouse (Dom sumasshedshikh)*, based on the same idea[5] and also of course owing something to the plot of Griboedov's *Woe from Wit* and to the madmen in E. T. A. Hoffmann's stories. Thus, Alexander Herzen, in "Dr. Krupov" (1847), had a solid tradition to rely on. In 1831, *The Telescope* published Hoffmann's "The Sandman" (in Part 6), Balzac's "Sarrasine" (also in Part 6), and a story by an anonymous English writer entitled "The Statesman" (in Part 5), and proposed that a comparison be made of three kinds of insanity among three different peoples. Faddey Bulgarin's "Three Pages from a Madhouse" ("Tri listka iz doma sumasshedshikh") dates from 1834, and again deals with the theme of insane men of ambition. As far back as 1822, Verstovsky's translated vaudeville, *The Madhouse, or, A Strange Wedding (Dom sumasshedshikh ili strannaia svad'ba)*, used the theme of insanity for comic purposes.[6]

No other story by Gogol is so permeated with the element of comedy as "Diary of a Madman"; yet it is a tragedy. Barsukov's madness, in *The Order of St. Vladimir,* is not tragic: it reflects the traditional theme of the punishment of vice, here the vice of obsessive ambition and swindling. Poprishchin's madness is tragic because his obsessive ambition is the secondary cause, whereas the primary one is his love for the director's daughter, who is unattainable. In the world of freaks, where every clerk was "exactly like the document he was copying," Gogol found not only clerks but a tragic emotion as well: love. In those stories where he did not defer to the tradition of folk song and fairy tale (as he had in *Evenings*), he depicted love only as a tragic emotion which leads to delirium, both induced and involuntary (Piskaryov, in "Nevsky Prospect"), to crime (Andry, in "Taras Bulba"), or to madness. This is how he himself spoke of love in his letters, when he was being serious.[7] But in "Diary of a Madman," psychology is given greater complexity, by sociological factors. The shattering of every hope, when Poprishchin's beloved becomes engaged to a court chamberlain, turns an inconspicuous titular councilor into a social rebel. ("Everything that's best in this world, everything goes to court chamberlains or generals. If you find some piddling treasure and think it's almost in your hands, a court chamberlain or a general will snatch it away from you.") Again, as in *The Order of St. Vladimir*, Gogol's pen "snagged on passages which the censor will never in the world let pass";[8] and in fact, Poprishchin's tirades were thrown out by the censor, as was his comparison of the court chamberlain to a dog. Only after this terrible blow does it occur to Poprishchin's deranged mind that "perhaps I...I only seem to be a titular councilor," and his reading of the newspaper suggests the conclusion: "in Spain there is a king...this king is I."

This insane idea takes possession of Poprishchin because he has been wrenched out of the social norm. And to his deranged mind, this norm itself looks like the work of demonic powers: "the woman is in love with the devil ....And she will marry him, she will...." It is here that the story connects with *Evenings on a Farm Near Dikanka*, "Viy," "Nevsky Prospect," and "The Portrait," and with Odoevsky's *Motley Stories* and "Princess Mimi" ("Kniazhna Mimi," 1834). Immediately after *Arabesques* was published, Gogol made one more attempt to depict the world of clerks in the light of fantasy; but on this occasion he did not associate the fantasy-element with the insanity of the hero, who had finally become utterly insignificant. This was in "The Nose," which was written in 1835. Kovalyov, the hero of the story, is incapable not only of ideals or dreams (unlike Poprishchin) but also of great ambition (unlike Barsukov). He is reaching out after something small: he wants to be called a major, he wants to dress well and flirt irresponsibly. Suddenly this very normal "exister" finds himself wrenched out of every imaginable human norm, and he must bend all his efforts to one end: recovering his nose, so that he can become the same as everyone else. This is not the first time Gogol has his "normal" heroes land in highly abnormal situations which emphasize their insignificance. The plot of "The Nose," like that of "Diary of a Madman," is based on traditional stories about noses,[9] but is worked out by Gogol in a highly original way.

But even Gogol's third attempt at depicting St. Petersburg clerks "snagged on passages" that were unacceptable to the censor, however "innocent" the basic story was in itself. In the published version, all the details about the policeman disappeared (the bribes in the form of sugar, Kovalyov's

80

"gratitude," the "persuasion" of the peasant by means of a kick in the teeth, as well as the encounter with the Nose in the Kazan Cathedral). The only thing left for Gogol to do was to "devise the most innocent plot, at which even a policeman could not take offense" (letter to M. P. Pogodin, February 20 [o.s.], 1833). Gogol wrote this even before he had penned his offensive words about the policeman in "The Nose," and even then he had objected: "But what sort of comedy is there without truth and malice!" (Same letter.)

The Suitors and the first version of Marriage represented a comedy of just this kind. But The Inspector General, which had its premiere on April 19 (o.s.), 1836, offended more than just policemen. This play marked Gogol's first appearance in public as a writer of comedy. The final versions of Marriage and The Gamblers reflected all his experiences and thoughts in connection with the play's premiere and the various public reactions to it. Therefore, it is particularly important, apropos of The Inspector General, to raise the question of how far Gogol absorbed the traditions of comedy, and how far he went beyond them.

The Russian comedy grew out of the French classical tradition. But this tradition was not homogeneous. Its formal indicators—the three unities (to which Pushkin added a fourth: "unity of style"), positive heroes, a love intrigue—fail to account for all its variety. For his comic devices Molière is indebted on the one hand to the French farce, and on the other to the Italian comedy, which developed out of the commedia dell'arte, with its stock character-types (the simpleton and the boaster, the clever servant, etc.) and its "jokes appropriate to the theater," such as pratfalls, beatings, concealments, disguises, etc. But elements of another tradition figured in Molière's drama, and were less characteristic of it: the "decorous" comedy, in which dialogue predominates over action, and caricature is played down. In the eighteenth century this became the prevailing tradition, and it achieved its greatest refinement with the "capricious pen" of Marivaux.[10] With Destouches it absorbed elements of sentimentalism and didacticism; and finally, through many minor representatives, this tradition spread to Russia, where by the end of the century it overshadowed the Molière tradition, which was already being revived in France in the comedies of Beaumarchais. By the beginning of the 1830s, the genteel society-comedy reigned supreme on the Russian stage and was kept alive by such conscientious purveyors as A. A. Shakhovskoy and M. N. Zagoskin. Griboedov was also loyal to it, except that he was able to endow the conventional characters with a "portrait-like" liveliness. (Krylov, on the contrary, came closer to the plays of Molière.) But in the first quarter of the nineteenth century, the vaudeville became entrenched on the French stage, and Scribe was its king. From there it quickly spread to Russia, where at first it found translators and then imitators—N. I. Khmelnitsky, A. I. Pisarev, P. A. Karatygin, D. T. Lensky, F. A. Koni, and others.[11] It represented a compromise between the two traditions, and it lacked the bite of either one: its plots and situations made use of outwardly comic though not overly striking effects, but the characters were flattened and drained of color. In Gogol's time the vaudeville took over the Russian stage. In his writings on the drama, he subjected it to sharp criticism, but in his own practice he borrowed a great deal from it.

Gogol had the Ukrainian interlude and nativity play in his blood, and he must have felt drawn to the elements of farce in the Molière tradition, as well as to the vaudeville tradition, insofar as it contained the same elements. The actor Mikhail Shchepkin, who was a close personal friend of Gogol's and a Ukrainian too, was just as much devoted to Molière. Evidently the same tendencies were present within the Russian Romantic movement as a whole. Galich defined comedy as "a contest between wilfullness on the one hand, and chance, whim, and stupidity on the other," and the characters in comedy as "perverted or negative ideals, i.e., caricatures."[12] A reviewer for *The Moscow Herald*, by way of finding fault with the "classical" comedy of Vasily Golovin, wrote: "An event is more or less interesting in proportion as the dramatis personae are wilier....We are sick and tired of the mediocrity of the naive characters who flit before us every day on the stage of society; if we see them duplicated on the stage of the theater, they will seem twice as boring. Just look at Molière's plots, and even more so, at the plots of Spanish comedies! How lively they are, how expressive is the physiognomy of each character" (*Moskovskii vestnik*, No. 5, 1827). Gogol revered Molière: "Oh, Molière, great Molière—you who developed your characters in such breadth and such fullness!"[13] Pogodin also wrote, in "Paradoxes," of the need for the writer of comedies to "heighten characters and never draw portraits." (Griboedov, as we know, defended "portraiture" and regarded the best of Molière's "heightened" characters as portraits.)

The critics of Gogol's time immediately noticed that *The Inspector General* was based on "an old anecdote, familiar to all, printed, recounted and treated in various ways and in various languages a thousand times over."[14] It was a traditional motif of the plot of the "comedy of errors"—"one person is taken for another"—and in a general way it had been used by Plautus and Shakespeare, and more than once by Molière. Sometimes it involved a conscious deception on the part of an impostor, sometimes just a chance misunderstanding. In Gogol we find a combination of both: Khlestakov has been accidentally taken for someone else, and once he understands his position, he begins to take deliberate advantage of it. One cannot help but drawn a parallel with Molière's *Les Précieuses ridicules*, where the servants pass themselves off as grandees. Gogol was also acquainted with a Russian imitation, Krylov's *A Lesson for the Daughters (Urok dochkam*, 1806 or 1807)—he himself had played one of the parts in it while at Nezhin—in which Semyon passes himself off as the "Marquis Glagol." The specifics of the plot were not new either: a letter is received; it leads people to expect a particular individual; a different one appears and is taken for the one expected; the error is brought to light either by the appearance of the real person or by some other means. For example, in Khmelnitsky's *Castles in the Air (Vozdushnye zamki,* 1818), Aglaeva expects a count to arrive under a different name, and when Alnaskarov appears, she takes him for the count until a servant discovers that he is not. The same is true of Khmelnitsky's vaudeville *There's No Getting Around Your Intended Husband (Suzhenogo konem ne ob"edesh',* 1821), and particularly of Verstovsky's vaudeville *The Madhouse (Dom sumasshedshikh,* 1822), which in basic story-line very much resembles *The Inspector General:* a doctor who treats madmen in the asylum receives a letter saying that Edward, his daughter's fiancé, is arriving; a second letter announces the imminent arrival of a mad patient; when Edward arrives he is taken for the madman, and he, in turn, regards the doctor as one of his own patients; Edward's name is revealed only at the end, following which a servant announces the arrival of the *real* madman.

But there are also more specific points of coincidence between *The Inspector General* and earlier comedies. For example, the commotion set up in a provincial town by the anticipated arrival of an inspector general was depicted by Polevoy (without any "comedy of errors"); the judge Tsapkin (cf. Gogol's Lyapkin-Tyapkin) and his associates tremble over their earlier misdeeds while awaiting the inspector-general's arrival. They clean up some things, sweep others under the rug, and make certain substitutions; but their greatest fear is that of being denounced. Polevoy's scoundrels get off scot-free: they succeed in bribing the inspectors (*Inspectors General, or, The Grass Is Always Greener on the Other Side [Revizory, ili Slavny bubny za gorami,* 1832]). [15]

Polevoy, then, presented the theme of the anticipated arrival and the subsequent bribery of the inspectors-general. But it was A. F. Weltmann, in the short-story form, who depicted a "comedy of errors" in a provincial town *without* the theme of prior anticipation ("Provincial Actors" ["Provintsial'-nye aktery," 1835]). [16] Here an actor, wearing theatrical costume, including fake decorations, falls out of a carriage and injures himself. He is taken for the governor-general; the townspeople hasten to put things in order; the delirious actor declaims lines from the role he is playing, and these are interpreted as a dressing-down; the mayor's apologies to him are very similar to the ones made by Gogol's mayor. [17]

A more careful study of the plots of comedies and, to some extent, of comic narrative prose, will undoubtedly confirm what Senkovsky said: "We are acquainted with several plays and episodes in French, German and Italian novels that have been fashioned from this anecdote." [18] And then, in the context of this particular tradition, the partial coincidence of the plots of *The Inspector General* and Kvitka's *A Visitor from the Capital (Priezzhii iz stolitsy,* written in 1827 but published only in 1840) will not appear so surprising. Of particular interest here is not the letter-reading scene that opens both plays (that was a traditional device), but rather, the general setting that both share: the scene in the mayor's house, the presence of provincial officials, and certain details such as the mayor's instructions to the policeman about establishing order in the town. Different are the character-types and the plot-development: in Kvitka's play, the adventurer Pustolobov is not entirely skillful at duping the stupid but basically honest officials, and for this he suffers double retribution: he is exposed and arrested.[19] There are stories of similar actual happenings in the lives of Pushkin, Svinin, the composer Mikhail Glinka, and others. It is more accurate to say that the theme of a false inspector general was a story that was making the rounds in those days and was reworked in literature on several occasions, as a variation on the "comedy of errors." In "An Author's Confession" Gogol mentioned parenthetically that the idea of *The Inspector General* came from Pushkin. Recently, in fact, an outline of a work by Pushkin with a similar plot has come to light. But one is equally justified in saying that the idea of the play came from Kvitka, from Weltmann, and from the tradition in general.[20]

The boaster and liar as a major character-type is also very old. Its history begins with Plautus's boastful soldier and continues with Shakespeare's Falstaff, Corneille's Liar, and Molière's Masquarille. Among many familiar examples in the Russian comedy are Knyazhnin's *The Boaster (Khvastun)*, Khmelnitsky's *The Windbag (Govorun)*, and the figure of Zarnitsky in Shakhovskoy's *If You Don't Feel Like It, Then Don't Listen (Ne liubo ne slushai)*. Gogol endowed this character-type with a subtlety all his own. He does not have Khlestakov lie, but merely fantasize in all ingenuousness about the things his petty little heart is instinctively set on—comfort, success, a brilliant career as a government official and even as a man of letters. More than the other characters in the play, Khlestakov comes closer to Gogol's general system of characterization: he is a caricature created by taking the traits of a real-life collegiate registrar from St. Petersburg and heightening them; at the same time, he becomes "typical of a great deal that is parcelled out among various Russian characters." Gogol was distressed most of all that Dyur, the actor who played the role, presented Khlestakov as the conventional "naughty child of the vaudeville," like Khmelnitsky's Alnaskarov.[21]

Here we have an instance that is characteristic of Gogol's whole attitude toward the tradition. He does not avoid the traditional situations of the theater; he sometimes even makes use of hackneyed ones; he even maintains the classical unity of time and only slightly violates the unity of place. But instead of giving us the pale and unremarkable figures of eighteenth-century comedies and of the newer vaudeville, he returns to the Molière type of caricature and enriches it by giving it a psychological subtlety that is downright Shakespearean. For that reason, traditional plot-features suddenly become convincing.

Here are some examples. In comedies one can find numerous instances of misunderstanding between two characters, who take each other for someone different.[22] But in Gogol, the mayor and Khlestakov are afraid of each other, and each looks for a hidden meaning in the simplest words the other utters. Here Gogol surpasses all his models. Khlestakov's comments about the dinner create an impression of having been borrowed directly from Kara-tygin's vaudeville *Woe Without Wit (Gore bez uma,* 1831);[23] but the alter-nation between ambition and self-abasement that we see in Khlestakov repre-sent a happy discovery on Gogol's part. The rapid shift of the hero's attention from one woman to another is nothing new in comedies and vaudevilles;[24] but only in Khlestakov, with his "extraordinary lightness of thought," is this psychologically convincing. The same is true of the hackneyed stage effect where the hero is on his knees in front of the woman he is wooing when sud-denly the door opens and the one person we are not expecting—the other woman—comes in.[25]

Gogol did not try to avoid the obvious trappings of comedy, but some of them disappeared in the course of repeated revisions of *The Inspector Gen-eral.* The story of how the teacher of rhetoric spat; the recommendation that the history teacher be tied to the table (cf. Lensky's vaudeville *An Attorney Under the Table*); the account of the partridge that was eaten; the story of how Pushkin wrote with the help of a bottle of rum; the postmaster's thumb-ing his nose at the mayor—all these touches of sheer farce in the first version did not survive in the acting version or in the first published edition. But it was only in the final version that Gogol dropped the scene where Khlestakov tries to defend himself against the mayor with a bottle, as well as the jokes about Bobchinsky's red nose and the mayor's thick one. In every version the mayor puts a box on his head instead of a hat, Bobchinsky falls into Khles-takov's room at the inn when the door comes off its hinges, and the mayor writes a letter to his wife on a bill from the inn.[26] The final mute scene re-mained and was polished with ever greater care. Gogol also worked hard on the development of the action: one important detail—Osip's advising Khles-takov to leave—is present only in the final version.

The dramatic action of *The Inspector General* follows the same "old principle" that Gogol had noted as early as 1832: "He is just about to get something and grasp it with his hand when suddenly there is some obstacle and the desired object is removed to an enormous distance." Here this applies to the mayor, in his various ambitions and aspirations for rank, fine food, etc., as well as to Maria Antonovna in her hopes for love and marriage. In his notebook Gogol was of course only outlining the "principle." We might flesh it out as follows: a "desired object" is not only "removed to an enormous distance" but proves to be a phantom; that fact becomes apparent, after which everything returns to where it was in the beginning, as in the fairy tale of the fisherman and the fish. Belinsky, during his Hegelian period, inter-preted Gogol in these terms: the mayor's dream about the rats is the begin-ning of "a series of phantoms which comprise the reality of the comedy"; Khlestakov is "a creation of the mayor's frightened imagination, a phantom or shade of his conscience." This interpretation coincided with the one that Gogol himself made in 1842, and it perhaps helped him understand himself as a writer: Khlestakov, he says, is "a phantasmagoric figure who, mendacious deception incarnate, speeds off in the troika Lord knows where."[27] The effect of Act V depends on the return from the world of phantoms to the world of reality. The reading of a letter characterizing each of the people present is not a new device for a denouement,[28] but Gogol introduces an unexpected touch: the gendarme bearing news of the arrival of a real inspector general.

In "Leaving the Theater after the Performance of a New Comedy," Gogol himself said that this denouement had the same significance as "inescapable fate in the tragedies of the ancients." Here too he called laughter the only honest character in the play. But Vyazemsky came just as close to what Gogol had in mind when he called the government the only honest character.[29] The moral and social idea of the comedy is revealed in the appearance of a representative of the government at the end. If there is no triumph of virtue here, as there is in Kvitka's play, where the officials themselves are essentially virtuous and where there are "positive" types as such, then there is at least the punishment of vice, as in Molière's *Tartuffe,* Fonvizin's *The Minor*, and Kapnist's *Chicanery*. The following remark, in "Leaving the Theater," alludes to this tradition: "It is strange that our writers of comedies cannot get along at all without the government; there is not one of our comedies that develops without it." But Gogol made a bold break with tradition in another way: not only did he not introduce virtuous heroes, he even denied his heroes any attractive features whatever, deliberately eschewing verisimilitude in order to present "the contemptible and the insignificant" with "terrible, almost caricature-like intensity." As is evident from this statement, Gogol was not afraid of either a lack of verisimilitude or of caricatures. When The First Member of the Audience in "Leaving the Theater" demands "respectable" heroes, saying that "if the comedy is to be a picture and mirror of our social life, it ought to reflect that life in all faithfulness," the Author, speaking through the Second Member of the Audience, replies: "You see, the setting and the scene of action are imaginary. Otherwise the author would not have perpetrated such blatant inaccuracies and anachronisms, he would not even have let certain characters make speeches that are inappropriate, considering their nature and their place in society." The first drafts of "Leaving the Theater" were made when Gogol's impressions of the premiere of *The Inspector General* were still fresh in his mind. In 1842 he made it the concluding piece in his collected works, and his theories of drama are therefore of special importance.[30]

Gogol's statement about the imaginary nature of the setting of *The Inspector General* ought to eliminate the kind of guesswork that attempts to determine just which real-life impressions produced the text of this play. Also, they ought to explain why it is that scholars who are unfamiliar with the psychology of creativity fail to understand how Gogol could have written this play without ever having lived in a provincial town. Bulgarin thought that the character-types in the play were Ukrainian (surprisingly, this view was supported by Vengerov); but this does not stand up under critical scrutiny either (in order to defend it, Vengerov was forced to ascribe a "highstrung" nature to Ukrainians).[31]

Gogol resolutely rejected the one feature of plot that was fundamental to the comedy which in our day is called "classical" and in his day was called "romantic" (in contrast to the comedy of antiquity): the love-intrigue. In his treatise on esthetics, Galich defines the "romantic" comedy as one that takes place "not in a social but a domestic circle, revolving around its immovable point—marriage." The surviving fragments of *The Order of St. Vladimir* do not enable us to judge what role was played by the love between the *virtuous* heroes—the idealistic Misha and the "poor but honest" Odosimova—and whether their marriage would have occurred, threatened as it was by the mother's scheme of making a profitable match for her son. But Gogol detected the changes taking place in that stratum of society which provided the models for his comic lampoons; and in "Leaving the Theater" he suggested another scheme for a comic plot, which still included the idea of profitable marriage, but not love. "Everything in the world has long since changed. Now a stronger element in the plotting of drama is the desire to obtain a profitable position, to shine and eclipse someone else at all costs, to take revenge for the contempt and the ridicule one has suffered. Is there now not more electricity in rank, in money-capital, in a profitable marriage, than in love?" This is the scheme of *The Order of St. Vladimir,* and, in some particulars, of *Marriage* (the electricity of a profitable marriage), of *The Inspector General* (the electricity of rank), and of *The Gamblers* (the electricity of money-capital). It also looks ahead to the basic scheme of Nikolay Ostrovsky's plays, which did not, however, ignore the theme of the electricity of love. But for Gogol, these "theatrical lovers with their cardboard love" are not only insignificant, but cannot possibly be made into anything more than cardboard. In the words of the Second Lover of the Arts ("Leaving the Theater"), the introduction of a love-intrigue destroys "the significance of social comedy," which was just what Gogol set particular store by during those years when he was keenly aware of his mission as a writer. It is essential to recognize that there is a hidden psychological reason why Gogol departed so decisively from the tradition in just this respect, a reason which biography, psychology and psychopathology have so far been incapable of revealing in all its aspects.

In *The Inspector General,* Gogol presents a parody of the love-intrigue. The unity of time required a rapid tempo, yet afforded sufficient scope within the confines of the five acts and the twenty-four hours in which the action of the play unfolds. As if making fun of this rule, Gogol inserts two declarations of love, a misunderstanding due to a rivalry, and a proposal and engagement into the span of half an act and several minutes, only to laugh at this "phantom" too in the final act. Senkovsky advised Gogol to liven up the comedy with a love-intrigue—to have Khlestakov running after some young provincial lady and to picture her in turn as being jealous of Maria Antonovna, the mayor's daughter. But this lame piece of advice unwittingly underscored Gogol's bold originality.[32] In *Marriage* it is no longer the love-intrigue that is being parodied but the emotion of love itself. Certain critics feel the "breath of Eros" in the house of Agafia Tikhonovna, but it must be said that Gogol was making fun of this "breath" in having Podkolyosin unexpectedly experience an almost romantic ecstasy, and then five minutes later having him jump out the window in order to return to his comfortable, philistine couch. Again, we have "the removal of a desired object to an enormous distance." This time, however, the removal is not physical but psychological, and is the hero's own doing. Again we are right back where we started, and this gives a phantasmagoric quality to everything that has happened. If *Marriage* were a piece of prose fiction, we would not be surprised to find it ending somewhat like the first version of "The Nose": "However, all that has been described here was seen by the major in a dream."

Gogol worked especially hard on *Marriage,* making changes not only in particular situations and turns of language, as he did in The *Inspector General,* but in whole scenes and characters too. *The Suitors* takes place in the country, which until very recently was incorrectly regarded as being "Ukrainian." The heroine is a sprightly landowner hunting for suitors at the fair with the help of Fyokla Fomishna, who is evidently not a professional matchmaker. Yaichnitsa and Zhevakin almost get into a fistfight. The would-be bride answers each suitor with "I find that very pleasant," and the fragment that remains breaks off with their expressions of bewilderment. Neither Podkolyosin nor Kochkaryov as yet exists. They appear in the version of 1836. Now the action is set in a town, but as yet there is nothing of the merchant-class milieu. That was introduced apparently at the behest of the actor I. I. Sosnitsky, and came rather hard to Gogol: as he went on revising, he left blank spaces which he intended to fill in after consulting with Shchepkin, Sosnitsky, and especially Pogodin, "who knows this way of life."[33] *Marriage,* however, became a comedy not of manners and mores, but of exaggerated character-types and comic situations. Here the comic situations depend even more on the tradition of the farce than is the case in *The Inspector General*—quarrels and reconciliations, peeking through the keyhole and eavesdropping, the flight of the would-be bride from the room, the chasing away of the suitors and the angry attack by Yaichnitsa, "arms akimbo," the misunderstanding over Yaichnitsa's name, a number of other anecdotes and plays on words, and finally, Podkolyosin's leap out the window—a scene in which Gogol, without any doubt, showed himself to be more of a Molièrist than Molière himself. It was clear that the public, which had already grown accustomed to "decorous" comedy and which had even torn *The Inspector General* to shreds for being a "farce," felt all the more obliged to reject *Marriage,* which was a genuine farce. And that was what happened. Opinions on *The Inspector General* varied; *Marriage* was hissed by one and all.

The plot of *Marriage* gave Gogol an opportunity to introduce a whole gallery of characters. Among them were "positive" types too, although not the lovers or the uncles of young girls that were so dear to the hearts and expectations of audiences, but rather, custodians of society's very foundations, whose ideas were congenial to Gogol's own growing social conservatism: Arina Panteleimonovna and Starikov, the rejected suitor. Gogol's conservative tendencies had not yet extended to the gentry: this class is ridiculed in *Marriage,* and all the evidence indicates that Gogol did not idealize the higher aristocracy any more than he did the bureaucracy in those years. (See his letter to Pogodin dated February 1 [o.s.], 1833: "The more exalted, the higher a class—the more stupid. This is an eternal truth. And the proof is seen in our own time.") All the others are caricatures, drawn with great artistry but with far greater exaggeration than in *The Inspector General.* Zhevakin is a remote descendant of the "captain" of the Italian *commedia dell'arte,* and Yaichnitsa is virtually a mirror image of the Zaporozhian Cossack of the Ukrainian nativity play. The two main characters hew particularly closely to tradition: Podkolyosin and Kochkaryov are variants of the traditional "indecisive" and "busybody" types.

The indecisive Sganarelle in Molière's *Le Mariage forcé* is beaten with a stick. In Khmelnitsky's translation of a society-comedy by Collin d'Harleville (*L'Inconstant,* 1786; Russian title *Nereshitel'nyi [The Waverer,* 1820]), the hero, Armidin, cannot decide which of two sisters to marry, Natasha or Lyudmila, and is bailed out by Zborsky, his future father-in-law, who in effect decides for him. Podkolyosin resembles Armidin in the scene where he comes out with a hesitant declaration of love; Khmelnitsky's hero also "did everything but bare his heart," although this was because he was wavering between the two sisters. Gogol took the characteristics of the traditional "waverer" and divided them between the suitor and the would-be bride: Agafia Tikhonovna wavers in her choice of suitors and casts lots to decide, in exactly the same way that Armidin resorts to fortunetelling to determine which of the two sisters will be his bride. Podkolyosin himself closely resembles the "fastidious suitors" of various vaudevilles (including one whose title describes this particular character-type [*Razborchivye zhenikhi*]), as well as traditional "sluggards": Krylov's Lentula (i.e., "lazybones," in the play *The Sluggard [Lentiai,* 1800-1805]), and the hero of the anonymous comedy *The Lazy Man (Lenivyi,* 1828), who among other things fails to attend his own wedding out of sheer laziness.[34] Here too, as always, Gogol builds up the character *as a whole.* This is a far cry from the conventional practice of personifying just one character-trait. Gogol hereby goes beyond the tradition out of which his own lampoons developed. In Podkolyosin, laziness and indecisiveness are the result of philistine smugness, characteristic of the majority of Gogolian heroes and in this case the source of the arrogance he feels about his rank. In Gogol, the portrayal of a *forced* marriage, in the literal sense, is toned down. There is no physical beating, as in Molière, but only strong verbal abuse on the part of Kochkaryov. In the same vein, the hero is not actually compelled to make a choice, as he is in Khmelnitsky: Kochkaryov merely resorts to strenuous (and useless) attempts at persuasion. And the faint hint contained in Armidin's final line—"It seems a pity I didn't choose the younger one"—gave rise to Podkolyosin's concluding monologue and his leap out the window (which goes back to the farce tradition).

Molière depicted a clever "busybody" in Scapin. But even closer to the plot of *Marriage* are the efforts made by Sbrigan, in *Monsieur de Pourceaugnac*, to remove the rival from Erast's path: he tells the suitor slanderous things about the girl, and the girl's relatives slanderous things about the suitor. Kochkaryov plays the same double game. (Earlier, in *The Order of St. Vladimir,* Gogol had sketched an intriguer type in Sobachkin.) The professional intriguer type, or the intriguer by virtue of position (such as the servant) merged, in the figure of Kochkaryov, with another traditional type: the meddler, who pokes his nose in other people's business for the sheer fun of it. Busybody types are the heroes of many vaudevilles, such as *The Busybody, or, Work Obeys a Master (Khlopotun, ili delo mastera boitsia,* 1825), by Pisarev; Khmelnitskiy's *An Incident in Good Society (Svetskii sluchai,* 1826); Lensky's *A Matchmaker Out of Place (Svat nevpopad,* 1828); and others. They dispense advice on running the household, they reconcile adversaries and most often engage in matchmaking (which proves unsuccessful), either on behalf of others or themselves. Self-confident to the point of blindness, they unwittingly create good luck for their rivals. Gogol endowed this type with the insolence and adroitness of the professional intriguer: the web woven so quickly and skillfully by Kochkaryov is broken only by Podkolyosin's leap out the window.[35]

Let us also note that the amateur matchmaker type (who is not an intriguer but a "positive" character) sidetracks the professional matchmaker in Shakhovskoy's vaudeville *Gavrilych the Matchmaker (Svat Gavrilych),* which on one occasion was staged along with *The Inspector General.*

In *The Gamblers* Gogol made even greater use of traditional materials and departed even further from them. It has not been precisely determined just when this play was written. There are some grounds for dating it as 1840: after returning from abroad the previous year, Gogol could have gathered the material he needed for his setting in the same way he always did: by talking with "someone who knows this way of life," and then going on to create by "intellection."[36] But material was also furnished by the literary tradition: gambler-cheat types had been portrayed by A. E. Izmaylov in *Eugene (Evgenii)* and by Faddey Bulgarin in *Ivan Vyzhigin.* From the eighteenth century on, the comedy had begun depicting gamblers for avowedly didactic purposes, emoting over the "spendthrift reformed by love," or chastising someone who could not be reformed, as, for example, in Jean-François Regnard's *The Gambler,* which was also well known on the Russian stage (under the title *Igrok*). It was a felicitous theme for melodrama too, as was shown by the enduring success of Ducange's *Thirty Years, or The Life of a Gambler* (Russian title: *Tridtsat' let ili zhizn' igroka*). Gogol depicted the life of the card-sharp

90

in an original way that was consistent with his own moralistic aim. He did not admit a single positive hero into his cast of characters, and therefore did not admit even the possibility of the "triumph of virtue." He had the card-sharp suffer at the hands of his own accomplices, and he showed vice as both triumphant and punished in the very same ending. As Pogodin wrote, in "Paradoxes": "The moral purpose of a work does not lie in the triumph of virtue or the punishment of vice. Let the artist compel me to envy virtue oppressed and scorn vice triumphant" *(Moskovskii vestnik,* No. 2, 1827). This same idea was developed by Gogol in "Leaving the Theater." But the opposite extreme was no less inhibiting to the author's freedom; and, along with vice triumphant, Gogol shows vice punished—just as he does in *The Inspector General* when he lets Khlestakov make his getaway but does not allow the officials to escape the real inspector general.

The plot of *The Gamblers* is built on a very ancient device: substitute characters are introduced for the purpose of fooling someone. This device was used many times by Molière, Marivaux, Beaumarchais and Sheridan, and in Russia by Shakhovskoy, Krylov, and countless writers of vaudevilles. It is one of the variations on the theme of the "comedy of errors"—a deliberate attempt to pull the wool over people's eyes, which originates in a conspiracy, usually followed by changes of clothes or facial disguises. Gogol, however, never once uses this particular device for comic purposes. He employs the traditional device of substitution with great skill. Not only does he avoid revealing the off-stage element in the conspiracy, but never once does he hint at the outcome. Young Glov—who is a fake and himself is fooled—reveals that his old father and the treasury clerk are also substitute characters, and this is just as much a revelation to the audience as it is to Ikharev, the card-sharp who has himself been robbed.

The plot of *The Gamblers* is remarkable in yet another aspect. In *The Order of St. Vladimir,* there is a rudimentary love-intrigue, which perhaps would have ended happily; in *The Inspector General,* the love-intrigue is parodied; in *Marriage,* love itself is parodied; but in *The Gamblers,* there is not only no trace of a love-intrigue, but not a single female role. This represented a decisive break with tradition; I know of no precedents in the Russian comedy.

We can draw the following conclusion about the relationship of Gogol's comedy to tradition. It is a comedy of comic *action,* which developed out of the Molière tradition, with its underlying element of farce. It is also a comedy of *characters*—not conventional personifications, nor portraits of ordinary people, but artistic caricatures, intensifications of types drawn from life and refracted through the author's mind. The tradition thereby underwent modification. Gogol draws extensively on traditional plots and comic situations, but makes them psychologically convincing. Both artistic and moralistic considerations prompted him to abandon traditional methods of structuring plot (which were calculated to work an edifying effect on the audience). He eschews virtuous heroes and their triumph, in order to present "the contemptible and the insignificant," with "terrible, almost caricature-like intensity." In this he sees his moral and social mission.

At the same time that Gogol was writing his comedies, he was also expressing his views about the comedy in general. These are found in the article entitled "The Petersburg Stage in the 1835-36 Season," part of which was incorporated into "Petersburg Notes of 1836," published in 1837, and in his review of Zagoskin's comedy *The Dissatisfied Ones (Nedovol'nye).* He harshly condemns the melodrama and the vaudeville (the melodrama even more so), which then reigned supreme on the Russian stage, and he demands that writers should disregard convention and cease to be imitative. Instead of heroes who are "completely lacking in a definite passion or a sharply-defined physiognomy," writers should create "Russian characters...our rogues, our eccentrics." In short, he calls for a theater based on national principles. He assigns the theater specifically moralistic tasks: it is "a great school," a "rostrum from which a living lesson can be read to the entire crowd at one and the same time." These same articles already foreshadow Gogol's views of the nature of "laughter"; they are given fuller expression in "Leaving the Theater" (1842). There are various kinds of laughter, he says (seemingly by way of reply to the myopic critics who found nothing in him except "jesting of the sort typical of Little Russians"). There is "light" laughter. There is "banal" laughter. There is another kind of laughter—an "electric, vivifying laughter," which is "born out of calm delight and is produced only by a high intelligence."

This contrast is not very sharp in "Petersburg Notes," but it is developed six years later in "Leaving the Theater." Gogol no longer speaks of *banal* laughter; he never had any real sympathy for it. But now, along with "light laughter," he does mention "bilious" laughter. Both these kinds were exemplified in the works of Khmelnitsky and V. F. Odoevsky respectively. They existed in Gogol as well: light laughter is the kind of laughter found in *Evenings on a Farm Near Dikanka;* the laughter of *The Order of St. Vladimir* must have been "bilious," for he referred to the play as "a comedy containing malice, laughter, piquancy." Both possible kinds of laughter are now contrasted with laughter "which wings up out of man's bright nature, which gives depth to a subject and makes what would otherwise slip away stand out in sharp relief; without its penetrating power, the triviality and emptiness of life would not frighten man so much."

Gogol associated his vision as a moralist with this kind of laughter, which he went on to call "good" and "bright." But he reached full understanding of it only later, and then even the laughter in his own works revealed new aspects to him. Meanwhile (in the mid-1830s), he was relying mainly on the power of "a high and subtle intelligence" which was to create "electric, vivifying" laughter, dispense "refreshing delight to the nerves," and, through its esthetic efficacy, work a moral effect: the reform of man.

CHAPTER VII

NEW ESTHETIC MANIFESTOES

The end of 1835 and the beginning of 1836 were for Gogol a period when he finally abandoned attempts to accomplish his mission in some other way than through writing. The impetus from without was provided by his dismissal from the University. New hopes arose in conjunction with two projects. The first was to write a comedy and have it staged. In this way he would be speaking from a new rostrum, more reliable than the one he had just tried at the University. From it he would be able to read "a living lesson to the entire crowd at one and the same time."[1] He was disappointed in this hope; actually, it was his exaggerated expectations that were disappointed.

The Inspector General met with the same fate that awaits any major event: "enraptured praise" on the one hand, and "the judgment of the fool" on the other.[2] The legislators of the literary market-place, Senkovsky and Bulgarin, could not forgive Gogol for departing from tradition, and in fact attempted to reduce the entire play to nothing but a rehashing of "tiresome" traditions. The public simply failed to understand the play, and grumbled: why was there so much farce, so little "truth to life," so much "dirt" and so little moral edification? Most important, why were there no honest heroes? P. A. Vyazemsky, writing in *The Contemporary*, attempted to turn these objections aside. V. P. Androsov, the critic of *The Moscow Observer*, showed a rather acute understanding of the main tasks Gogol had set himself: they were moral ("this laughter has all the sanctity of virtue"), social (the comic element is not embodied in the idea of power, but rather, in characters who are scoundrels and for whom this idea is just a mask), and artistic (the play cannot be characterized by "the traditions of poetics," for it contains not the truth of the actual but of the possible, not portraits but *essences,* and therefore "life is depicted more vividly, more sharply, more intensely").[3] But Gogol was stunned and hurt by even the possibility that people would accuse him of wishing to slander Russia. The actual performance left him dissatisfied and added to his impression that all his hopes had been shattered. He imagined that "all the estates of society" had risen up against him (letter to M. P. Pogodin, May 10 [o.s.], 1836). Evidently he was expecting some exceptional recognition, perhaps even more, some exceptional result. At least, he later recalled that he had failed in his attempt to exert a beneficial influence on society. Hence the inevitable conclusion that "a prophet has no honor in his own country" (*ibid.*). Subsequent statements notwithstanding, such sentiments do crop up in the letters he wrote in the spring of 1836, and provide an explanation if not of the immediate reasons why he left Russia, then certainly of the way he felt when he left a month and a half after the premiere of *The Inspector General.*

But Gogol had yet another project and another hope: journalistic activity. He went to work for *The Contemporary,* where he was supposed to be Pushkin's closest collaborator, particularly as a critic. Later he even represented himself as having "implored and persuaded" Pushkin not to give up publishing the journal. It is important to note Gogol's statement that Pushkin found in his articles "a great deal that could impart a journalistic sparkle to the publication, which he [Pushkin] did not acknowledge in himself."[4] Pushkin trusted Gogol to such an extent that while out of the city he arranged for the journal to print an article by Gogol that he himself had not read. Gogol was given the responsibility of writing an article that was supposed to be a militant statement of policy (a survey of journals); he was also put in charge of the entire review section. Furthermore, "An Official's Morning," "The Carriage" and "The Nose" (which had been rejected by *The Moscow Observer*) were all accepted for publication in *The Contemporary.*

But Pushkin's hopes for Gogol, and Gogol's for Pushkin, came to naught. The two had an apparently serious disagreement. Gogol not only left Russia without saying goodbye to Pushkin, but, in a letter to Zhukovsky written en route to Italy (June 28, 1836), did not even include Pushkin among those to whom he sent regards, merely confining himself to the remark that "I did not even have time to say goodbye to Pushkin, and I could not; however, he is to blame for that." The reason for the disagreement must be sought in their relationship on *The Contemporary.* Pushkin was dissatisfied with Gogol's article on current journals, and apparently made changes in it. In the third issue he made it clear that he did not share all the opinions expressed in it, and that it was not a statement of policy as far as *The Contemporary* was concerned. Some of Gogol's reviews were not published at all; those that were published were cut, toned down, and in general changed, and Pushkin did apologize to Pogodin for one of the reviews that had appeared. Gogol was always very sensitive about anyone's making fundamental changes in his writings.[5] Besides, it became obvious that the close collaboration he had dreamed of was impossible.[6] This must have been a fresh blow not only to his self-esteem but also to his hopes of finding in St. Petersburg a "rostrum" where he could accomplish his mission through literary activity. Neither the theater nor *The Contemporary* became such a rostrum for Gogol. Meanwhile, the writing of *The Inspector General* and enthusiastic support by a few who could appreciate him boosted his sense of self-importance to unprecedented heights. And so he went abroad (not yet knowing for how long, but foreseeing that it might be for a long time indeed), with a mixed feeling of disappointment and depression over his failures, and elation stemming from an unwavering faith in himself.

On June 6, 1836, Gogol boarded a ship and left Russia. Only twice did he interrupt his twelve-year residence abroad, each time for eight months (1839-40, 1841-42). On this first trip, he traveled through Germany to Switzerland, then to Paris, and then to Rome. The letters he wrote en route are filled with an intense self-awareness, a sense of confidence in being one of the elect. The writing of *The Inspector General* and its reception had planted this idea in his head, and it was nourished by yet a new project: *Dead Souls*, which he had begun writing while still in St. Petersburg. This new project became the focus of all his missionary aspirations and cast all his earlier works into the shadow. He wrote Prokopovich: "And if a moth should appear and suddenly eat up all the copies of *The Inspector General,* and along with them *Arabesques, Evenings on a Farm Near Dikanka,* and all the rest of that nonsense, and if nobody should write or speak a single word about me for a very long time, I would give thanks to fate" (January 25, 1837). In June of 1836, he wrote Zhukovsky: "I swear I'll accomplish something no ordinary person is capable of. I feel the strength of a lion in my heart." And on November 12 of that same year he wrote (also to Zhukovsky): "Someone invisible is writing with a mighty staff before my eyes. I know that after I die my name will be more fortunate than I myself am." At the same time (and in the same letter) he was thinking about creating "yet another Leviathan" in addition to *Dead Souls,* and he felt a "holy quivering" in anticipation. He was aware that he was one of the elect, and he explained his mission as a reflection of the will and complicity of higher powers, "great providence," "someone invisible." Such expressions are clearly the first shoots of what was to blossom into a mystical interpretation of mission (although they are rather vague, because he had not yet consciously formulated the idea at which they were hinting). Still and all, they are firmly rooted in the proud self-awareness of an esthete and individualist. This attitude was also expressed in a letter he wrote to Pogodin after arriving in Rome: "I am homeless, I am battered and tossed about by the waves, the only thing with which I can steady myself is the anchor of self-esteem that has been lodged in my breast by higher powers" (March 30, 1837). Here Gogol is speaking of his self-esteem as a man, but he could also have been speaking of self-esteem as a writer too. Higher powers are invoked to support and reinforce this keen awareness of self.

An esthetic faith was at the very foundation of Gogol's sense of life. Now it spread and flowered in even greater abundance, and for the time being choked off other seeds that were beginning to sprout, such as moralism, which had only recently pushed its way above the surface. Italy began to attract Gogol as the environment where estheticism could best flourish, and where in fact it did flourish, more and more with each passing day. Even before Gogol reached Italy, he had some difficult moments to endure: he learned of the death of Pushkin. It is only in the context of the personal relationship between the two writers—a relationship which has not yet been fully explored—that we can understand the pain Gogol felt when he learned of the death of the man who had dominated his thoughts as an adolescent and as a young man, his first mentor, from whom he had departed so coldly, without having achieved the intimacy he had wanted, and without knowing that he was departing forever. Now this entire past, everything connected with Pushkin's name and personality that he had experienced with such joy and such torment, rose up before him in an idealized form, as a "beautiful dream," radiant and spotless. And it seemed to him that the writing of *Dead Souls* (whose plot had been suggested by Pushkin) was the legacy left him by Pushkin. Pushkin's tragic fate gave him yet another reason not to return to Russia, to the "assemblage of enlightened ignoramuses,"[7] not to share "the eternal lot of poets in their own land," but rather, to find something in common between Pushkin's fate and his own, and to seek a new native land, while continuing to love the old one, perhaps indeed loving it even more. Italy became that new native land.

"You fall in love with Rome very slowly, gradually, and then for life. In short, all of Europe is only for looking, whereas Italy is for living." So Gogol wrote the very first months after his arrival; and from that time on, he spoke of Italy with unflagging enthusiasm, of "darling, beautiful Italy," which in fact seemed to him like a beautiful, vivacious woman, "dark-skinned, gleaming, with big, big black eyes, wearing a dress so scarlet it hurts the eyes, and a shawl white as snow." Such were the Italian girls whom Gogol now admired, such was Italy itself. Gogol looked "as one in ecstasy" at its skies, which he often called "gleaming" and silvery; he was completely engrossed in its colors and in its odors, along with which "at least seven hundred angels fly into the nostrils." And he specifically called Italy his native land. "I was born here. Russia, Petersburg, the snows, the scoundrels, the government office, the university chair, the theater—all that was but a dream. I have again awakened in my native land." There is good reason why the word "scoundrels" has been inserted between a geographical and an autobiographical reference: these were the "existers" who had oppressed him, and in rejecting them he had plunged into the "bottomless sea" of estheticism. "I look and cannot get my fill of looking," he says more than once in his letters. "Heaven and paradise are in my soul...I have never been so happy, so content with life."[8]

To Gogol, Rome not only represented the beauties of nature but was also a museum of beauty, and he undertook a slow, attentive "reading" of the city and its art treasures (see his letter to Pletnyov of November 2, 1837). He made friends with the Russian artists who lived there. "The entire earth smells and breathes of artists and paintings," he wrote in his very first letter to his mother from Rome (March 28, 1837). And he himself did some painting. When Zhukovsky came to Rome at the end of 1838, Gogol wrote Danilevsky that he himself "held a brush in my hand more often than a pen...making quick sketches of the best views of Rome" (February 5, 1839); and after Zhukovsky left, Gogol ordered some paints from Paris. He also plunged into Italian literature, and discovered writers he had not known before—lyric poets and authors of comic epics. And he developed a fascination for Italian opera.

For Gogol, Italy was drenched in the perfume of estheticism, and he breathed it in as an esthete, not as a student of ancient history. While he was attracted by ancient Rome, it was really the modern city that was dear to his heart: "It is splendid by virtue of the fact...that one half of it gives off the aroma of the age of paganism, the other half the age of Christianity, and both are the two greatest ideas in the world." This statement (and others like it) has conveniently enabled scholars to speak of the coexistence of "paganism" and "Christianity" in Gogol at the end of the 1830s, or of a conflict between these same principles.[9] There are no grounds for either view. Certainly Gogol did state on more than one occasion that in Rome a person "is a good mile closer to the divinity" (letter to Pletnyov, November 2, 1837), and that *only* in Rome was it possible to pray. Certainly he was fascinated by the Catholic churches. Nonetheless, as Kotlyarevsky had rightly noted, these churches for him were primarily temples of art which provided impressions and experiences that were primarily esthetic. We know that representatives of the Polish Resurrectionist order tried to win Gogol over and had hopes of success. If they are to be believed that Gogol was leaning in the direction of Catholicism, then this could be explained by the powerful esthetic attraction of the Catholic liturgy, coupled with his indifference to matters of dogma as such. (He tried to reassure his mother, in a letter of December 22, 1837, that "both our religion and the Catholic are exactly the same, and therefore there is no need to exchange one for the other.") Statements like the following are typical of Gogol in 1838: "I am more prepared to forgive someone who puts on the mask of piety and hypocrisy...than someone who puts on the mask of inspiration and sham poetic feelings" (letter to M. P. Balabina, April, 1838).

The first three years abroad saw a predominance of estheticism in Gogol's general sense of life. For the most part he lived in Italy, absenting himself only for a brief spell in Switzerland, which he did not like, or in Germany, which he made fun of. When he returned to Rome he felt he was returning to "the native land of my soul" (letter to M. P. Balabina, April, 1838). During this same three-year period, he broke off work on *Dead Souls* to give artistic expression to everything that was associated with Rome in his own experience. The result was the tale entitled "Rome," which should be regarded as his esthetic manifesto.

In story-line it is unfinished. Yet it does have a certain finished quality, because the most important thing is not the story but the all-pervasive lyricism. This explains the choice of rhythmic periods, which are brought together into a lyrical monologue. (Belinsky made a rough and not quite accurate comparison of the elevated style to Marlinsky's.)[10] It relates the life-story of the main hero, a prince, more in terms of internal than external events. It is framed by two scenes in which the beautiful Italian girl Annunciata appears. After the second of them, the story itself is supposed to begin,

showing us the efforts the prince makes to get to know Annunciata. Instead, we find leisurely sketched genre-scenes and character-types, which end with the "shining panorama" of Rome; and here too ends the story as a whole.

The prince returns to Rome after living in Paris, a city which at first fascinates and then disappoints him. Paris is depicted in romantic, fairy-tale hues, as was St. Petersburg in "Nevsky Prospect," but without any touches of the demonic. "In the magic light of the gas lamps...all the houses suddenly became transparent...the windows and panes in the shops seemed to have disappeared"; in the bookshops the letters looked like hieroglyphics, the black vignettes on the volumes looked like spiders; other shop windows displayed huge red salt-water crabs and multicolored fish; the shop girls and the fair-haired heads seen through the windows are depicted in all their feminine charm and fascination. But these are superficial charms; they strike both Gogol and his hero as devoid of substance.[11] The life of society at large, which is not valued by the esthetic sensibility; Romantic literature, with its prevalence of melodramatic effects for which Gogol by now felt no sympathy; and finally, the vaudeville, which characterizes the tase of the public—all these, in the hero's mind, merge into an impression of something outwardly striking but inwardly trivial, a "dreadful kingdom of words instead of deeds." The French seemed to him, as they did to Lermontov, a pitiable and empty people: "The entire nation was somehow pale, incomplete, a trivial vaudeville created by the nation itself."

Genuinely deep impressions (and only esthetic impressions could be such for Gogol during this period) the prince finds in Rome. There he holds everything dear, as did Gogol himself: "the ancient world that stirs from beneath the dark architrave," and the "mighty Middle Ages," and the "present age that clings to them," as well as art and nature, for whose depiction Gogol chooses words with greater care and delicacy than in his letters: mountains that are about to fly off into the sky, a sky that on this occasion is not silvery but "of the indescribable color of spring lilacs," a field that bursts into flame at sunset. The prince's prayer "by the magnificent marble columns" in Genoa, a prayer whose only purpose is to express joyfulness of heart, also belongs among esthetic impressions of this same kind. We know what importance Gogol attached to the expression "the nurturing of the soul" during those later years when he was genuinely religious. In Rome the prince is also surrounded by objects "which stir and nurture the soul," but this is an esthetic nurturing, and these objects are objets d'art. On the very same page, we find something that points not toward Gogol's future but back toward his past. The contemporary world is characterized as follows: "The icons have been removed from the temple—and the temple is no longer a temple: it is inhabited by bats and evil spirits." These icons are of course esthetic objects, but the fate of the desecrated esthetic temple presents itself to Gogol's mind in the same images he employed to describe the church at the end of "Viy."

Italy is an esthetic paradise, and the mere thought of it makes a person beautiful. "And this marvellous assemblage of worlds gone by, and the delight of their combination with eternally flowering nature—all this exists in order to awaken the world, in order that this south should at times present itself to the inhabitant of the north while he is still half asleep, in order that this vision should wrench him out of the surroundings of a cold life devoted to tasks that callous the soul"—let us recall "the snows, the scoundrels, the government office, the university chair, the theater"—"in order that he might be a beautiful person at least once in his life." This vision of the beautiful person begins to tinge Gogol's attitute toward disgusting persons, or "existers." To be sure, he finds existers in Rome too, and he depicts them humorously though inoffensively: an abbot who loves to eat, Italian ladies who love to gossip; Peppe, who dreams of getting rich. These are all echoes of character types in earlier stories, and of characters he was creating at the very same time for *Dead Souls*: Sobakevich, the provincial ladies, Chichikov. But against this background of ordinary life there appears a figure who is all-powerful esthetically and *only* esthetically: the beautiful Annunciata. She is the same Alcinoë as in "Woman," the same mysterious stranger created by Piskaryov's vision in "Nevsky Prospect," the same Polish girl as in "Taras Bulba," only dressed in Italian costume, a variation on Pushkin's "beautiful lady," in whom "all is harmony, all is wonder," in whose presence everyone involuntarily comes to a stop (in Gogol, "they came to a stop, as if rooted to the ground"), "devoutly reverential before the sacred object of beauty."[12] In Pushkin they merely stop; in Gogol they either prostrate themselves, as in "Woman," or they ought to do so, as in "Nevsky Prospect"; and in "Rome," "all should have prostrated themselves—both the believer and the non-believer should have fallen before her, as before the sudden appearance of a divinity."

In the first draft, Annunciata comes even closer to the idealized sensuous female figures of Gogol's earlier work: "Oh, how boldly, how deftly did the gown embrace her powerful, beautiful limbs! But better had it not embraced her fully. Away with the coverings, and then all would have seen that this was a goddess." Which is more powerful, the beauty of a woman or the beauty of nature? That we do not learn from "Rome." At the beginning of the story, woman is more powerful; nature is subordinate to her beauty. When she appears, "the marvellous lines of the hills of Albano recede, lighter and lighter, into the distance, the depths of the Roman sky are darker blue, the cypress soars more erect...everything, it seems, exists for her, to show off her triumphal beauty." At the end there appears a panorama of Rome "in inscrutable purity," where "the transparent hills, light as air," become at sunset "even more blue and phosphorescent," and this fascination makes the prince forget "even the beauty of Annunciata, and the mysterious fate of his people, and everything that exists in this world." But then, Gogol thought even of nature as a beautiful Italian woman, as an Italian peasant girl (see his letter to N. Ya. Prokopovich, June 3, 1837). Female beauty and the beauty of nature combine to create a single esthetically powerful influence—which also includes the impressions stemming from art—and this influence either shapes all other possible workings of the conscious mind, or else pushes them into the background and destroys them.

"Rome" was written during Gogol's first three-year stay abroad, but was not published until 1842. A few months later (after *Dead Souls* had come out), another esthetic manifesto appeared in print: the new version of "The Portrait." Presumably Gogol began reworking the story during that same three-year period. The plot is different now, as is the basic concept. Originally it was a story built on the mythic subject of demonic powers entering into the work of one artist and the life of a second. But now that Gogol's awareness of the esthetic had reached such an intense pitch, the subject proved inadequate, and it had as yet found no new correspondences in his mind. Now he threw virtually all the elements of demonism out of the first part of the story of Chartkov (who replaced the "Chertkov" of the old version).[13] The portrait itself no longer has "malicious, sharp, caustic" features. There is none of the old fatalism involved in Chartkov's purchase of the portrait: he is looking for pictures by old masters, the shopkeeper presses him to buy, and when he settles up he forgets that he is spending all the money he has left. There is nothing miraculous about the appearance of the portrait in the room; Chartkov simply takes it there himself. Chartkov's nightmares obviously occur when he is asleep, and the old man does not try to tempt him in any way: in this new version, Chartkov has long since experienced everything that the Antichrist uses to try to tempt Chertkov in the earlier version.

Unlike Chertkov, Chartkov has never been an idealist or an enthusiast. His professor has long been apprehensive about the glaring colors in his work, which suggest a fashionable painter in the making: Chartkov prefers nineteenth-century painting to the old masters, and is envious of painters who have grown wealthy. The decisive change leading to his downfall has already been prepared, and no diabolical temptations are necessary for Chartkov to begin his downward slide once he lays his hands on the gold that falls out of the picture frame. There is not even any need for the fateful appearance of the first customer, who mistakes Chartkov's drawing of Psyche for the portrait of her daughter. After a brief struggle, the philistine mentality, with its dreams of high times, comfort, and fame bought with money, wins out over the visions of the artist. Chartkov is the one who makes his own publicity, and he deliberately reworks his Psyche-drawing into a portrait of the young society lady. Thus, the change within him is explained psychologically; and it continues to determine his life until an inspired young artist appears on the scene—significantly, from "the majestic breeding-ground of the arts," "wonderful Rome." The despair and the ferocity displayed by Chartkov at the end are the same in both versions (the only thing now missing is the miraculous disappearance of the portrait). Here too he is compared to a demon incarnate, except that it is not a mythic demon, as was the case in Gogol's earlier work, but a psychological one, as in Pushkin ("that dreadful demon depicted by Pushkin in 'The Demon' "). That is, it is the principle of negation and destruction which resides in man himself.

Thus, the portrait contributes to the change in Chartkov only by virtue of the fact that it puts gold into his hands. The same holds true in Part 2 of the story. The moneylender is still a demonic figure, but more vaguely and enigmatically so now. He is not the Antichrist, he does not impose particularly terrible conditions on anyone, but *all* who have anything to do with him are doomed. He does not enter directly into the life of the painter; rather, after the painter works on the portrait, feelings of envy and a desire to compete with the young artist awaken in his heart. And then, demonic features—the eyes—appear in the portrait he has painted (quite contrary to his conscious intentions, as often happens in Romantic reworkings of the portrait theme).[14] But the demonic power of the eyes is now explained differently, and the theme itself is thereby changed: it is no longer mythic, but has become esthetic.

The artist tries to determine why the eyes should have such strange power. The first explanation given in both versions is: an overly faithful imitation of nature (or "slavish," "literal," as it is termed in the second version). But in the first version, this "crossing of the boundary set for art by the imagination" is terrible simply by virtue of the fact that it reveals a *terrible reality,* that is, a reality which has fallen under the sway of the unclean power. In the second version it is put differently: "Or if you choose a subject apathetically and insensitively, without feeling any sympathy for it, will it inevitably appear *only* in all its terrible reality, *unilluminated by the light* of some incomprehensible thought that lies hidden in everything?" And a new question is asked: "Why then does simple, lowly nature appear *in a certain light* in the work of one artist, and you do not feel any sense of degradation.... And why does this very same nature, in the hands of another artist, seem lowly and sordid, even though he has been just as faithful to nature?" (Stresses supplied.)

In the final version of the story, Gogol seeks an answer to the question as to whether *any* material can be used by the artist. He replies: yes, provided it is illuminated "in a certain light." Originally, this seemed to have been the light cast by the esthetic sensibility. But we cannot say that Gogol rejects reality in the first version and accepts it in the second. The portrait in the first version proves to be a specimen of "terrible reality" not because its subject as such is lowly or sordid, but because it is the portrait of the Antichrist. This is, in fact, spelled out in Part 2. But *naturalistic* devices in the making of art—a slavish, literal imitation of nature—are condemned in both versions. In the second, they are even given a special significance, inasmuch as they eliminate the possibility of depicting nature "in a certain light." And the failures of the painter in Part 2 of the new version are explained by the fact that he "tried to force [himself] to be true to nature, by stifling everything in his heart. *It was not a work of art;* therefore, the feelings that are aroused in all who look at it are stormy feelings, agitated feelings, *not the feelings of an artist,* for the artist exudes peace even in agitation." (Stresses supplied.)

It is clear that Gogol *wishes* to explain the secret of the portrait esthetically, by the fact that the artist is not a complete artist. He *wishes* to, but does not entirely succeed, inasmuch as the demonic figure of the moneylender remains at the beginning of the story, which means that there also remains the possibility of a supernatural rather than a psychological explanation of everything that happens. This duality is also particularly evident in one statement made by the artist who has become a monk. Here both possible explanations are mechanically fastened together, and the reader is invited, as it were, to choose either one: "This was indeed some kind of diabolical manifestation. I know that the world denies the existence of the devil, and therefore *I will not speak of him; I will only say* that I painted him with revulsion." (Stresses supplied.) But even if there is no consistency of ideas in the story, Gogol's very intentions are important. And these intentions are obvious: art, regardless of the subject it treats, is *light,* and in this light there is a power which had no equal of which Gogol was aware, as of the time of writing. It is also important that the artist-turned-monk is now primarily a painter. Only a brief account is given of his monastic life, and the pages describing his religious experiences are omitted completely: he discusses the meaning of art with his son, and this does not exist in the earlier version.

"The Portrait" was being completed in 1841. It also reflected something of Gogol's new experiences. This accounts for the great complexity of ideas in it. There are vestiges of the first version which, with its "mythic" plot, moves toward a religiosity that Gogol had not at that point personally experienced. The esthetic ideal that held sway in Gogol's mind at the end of the 1830s is stronger here too. Finally, the story also reveals elements of moralism, which had been temporarily stifled but were beginning to stir once more as the 1840s opened. Gogol's awareness of the esthetic led him to conclude that *art is light,* which illuminates terrible reality, and that this light is the highest value in this world. But this conclusion is now given greater complexity by a fresh purpose: that of making this light necessary not just to the artist but to all people ("because it is for the sake of calming and reconciling all men that the lofty creation of art descends into this world"). A year later, Gogol would return to this idea in "Leaving the Theater," where the bright, illuminating principle is perceived in *laughter.* At the same time, this idea summed up everything he had personally experienced, and represented a first step in a new direction. Only "Rome" gave full expression to that extreme intensity of pure esthetic awareness as it was experienced by Gogol in the second half of the 1830s.

Gogol's three years abroad did more than add to his experience of the esthetic. From that time on he began to make friends. Until the end of the 1830s, his relationships with other people had never been close. At school in Nezhin, his only intimate friend was G. I. Vysotsky; he never managed to get close to Pushkin; he was not as yet on an equal footing with Zhukovsky. If he did love any women (and there are only hints of that), his feelings were evidently not reciprocated. Although he left Russia in the company of his friend Danilevsky, inwardly he was alone.

However, his encounters with other Russians abroad sometimes developed into close personal friendships, which were a new experience for him. The habit-patterns of the reserved and proud individualist were still in evidence; there may well be a grain of truth in Iordan's rude remark that Gogol behaved like an "oracle" toward the Russian artists in Rome.[1] A new experience was the close friendship he formed with Iosif Vielgorsky at the beginning of 1839, and the young man's death shortly thereafter. The despair he felt at this loss was not merely esthetic—that is, not merely despair at the death of something beautiful—but almost existential as well. The lyrical pages entitled "Nights at a Villa" reflect these experiences. Of course, this is a literary work, as A. I. Kirpichnikov points out, and is only roughly autobiographical;[2] but besides lyrical pathos it also contains plain statements showing that Gogol had grown extremely fond of his dying young friend. What he says in the conclusion is also important: "To me there returned, fleetingly, a fresh fragment of the days of my youth, when the young heart seeks friendship and brotherhood... Did this fresh breath of youth suddenly waft over me only that I might suddenly and immediately sink into an even more deadening coldness of feelings?..." These allusions to friendships experienced in early youth, then to a coldness of feelings and a momentary return of youthful stirrings of the heart are in general confirmed by the events of Gogol's life. In this same year he finally formed a close friendship with Zhukovsky. His more complex relationship with Pogodin during that period was marked if not by depth, then certainly by warmth. He also developed a certain closeness to Shevyryov, and his trip to Moscow added the Aksakov family to the list of good friends. Gogol could have said by now, as he did later, that "my family grows larger the further away it is" (letter to A. O. Smirnova, December 24, 1844).

It would seem that this new feeling of affection for people should have displaced the earlier egocentrism and individualism. But for the moment, something different happened: those old attitudes took on a distinctive kind of complexity.

Gogol's visit to Russia between the autumn of 1839 and the spring of 1840 had little importance in his life: he was caught up in family and financial fuss at that time. The ground had already been laid for a rapprochement with the Slavophiles and with semi-Slavophile circles by his encounters with them in Rome and by his exaggeratedly low opinion of West European culture, which developed, by way of contrast, out of his deeply esthetic love-affair with Italy, a country he perceived as being the synthesis of all ages, and as essentially ageless itself. In Russia he pined for his paradise, Rome, and made haste to return; but on the way back he stopped over in Vienna for the entire summer.

Those summer months were for Gogol what the Boldino autumn had been for Pushkin.[3] Here he worked on a tragedy based on the history of the Zaporozhian Cossacks, a significant part of the new version of "Taras Bulba," "The Overcoat," and three new chapters of *Dead Souls;* and he polished what he called the "society" scene from *The Order of St. Vladimir.* All this was accomplished in the course of little more than a month. No finished work resulted, and some things, such as the tragedy, were abandoned altogether. But the psychological significance of this intense creative activity in very different directions was enormous (settings in the Ukraine, Petersburg, the Russian provinces; tragedy, comedy, novella and novel; humor and lyricism). It constituted a review of Gogol's own creative potentiality. His health gave way under this relentless work. The serious illness and the threat of death which followed heightened his awareness of what he was capable of accomplishing. And his recovery struck him as miraculous. He wrote: "This miraculous healing I have experienced fills my soul with ineffable comfort; therefore, my life is still necessary" (letter to P. I. Raevskaya, end of 1840/January 1841). And in the same letter comes the following significant statement: "only the wondrous will of God has resurrected me." In two letters written from Rome at the end of 1840 (to M. P. Pogodin on December 28, and to S. T. Aksakov the same day), this surmise becomes a certainty, and we can guess what prompted it. Both letters exude a proud sense of artistic self-confidence. The first volume of *Dead Souls,* on which Gogol had been working for so long and with such difficulty, had been completed in rough draft. This proud awareness of the "longed-for moment," when "the work of many years has been completed" and a joyful new period of "making changes, refinements," and of reworking, was beginning—this awareness intensified Gogol's sense of individualism (which had been esthetically substantiated) to the point where it seemed divinely ordained. The first volume was completed, and Gogol had already conceived the sequel, which he described as being something "colossal" by contrast with the "insignificant theme" of the beginning. At that time the completion of *The Inspector General* and the idea for *Dead Souls* had filled him with a sense of being almost prophetically inspired. The same was true now, except that on this occasion he was speaking not of lofty Providence or of someone unseen, but of God as such. In essence it came to the same thing. The feeling was much more intense now. His self-esteem had never been higher; it stemmed from his artistic achievements, and was symptomatic of his profound conviction of being marked out as an individual. The religious element in his words and his style does not as yet reflect any inner experiences, but rather is the form in which his individualism has invested itself in order to show that it has gone as far as it can. Individualism is bathed in a providential light. To himself, Gogol seems a prophet; he has no doubt about the holiness of his work and almost none about the holiness of his person. "I now must be cherished not for myself—no...a treasury is now contained in this vase" (letter to S. T. Aksakov, March 5, 1841); "I swear, it is a sin, a terrible sin, a grievous sin, to distract me! Only one who does not believe my words and who is inaccessible to lofty thoughts is permitted to do that. My work is great, and my deed is salutary" (letter to S. T. Aksakov, March 13, 1841).

From here it is but a step to a belief in the holiness not just of the literary word but of *any* word he utters; and Gogol takes precisely this step when he bids Yazykov, in Biblical style, to believe his words, when he assures Danilevsky that "my word is invested with a higher power," when he writes to Ivanov, at the end of 1841, in the same resolute manner: "he who remembers me bears strength and fortitude in his heart."[4] The examples could be multiplied. Evidently the heightened awareness of a self to which he assigns a great mission, inspired from on high, generates the expectation and then in fact the demand that others too should bend all their efforts to the same end. The demand that each person do his duty is typical of Gogol in various periods of his life; but during these years of heightened self-esteem it becomes especially importunate. He wants to raise others up to his own level, and he measures everyone according to himself. "We are sent here in order to carry out a mission that has been imposed upon us by the One Who has sent us," he writes in the spring of 1841. Who are the "we" he has in mind? Writers, artists? No, this is written to his sister Anna, when she seems on the point of neglecting her household duties. He addresses a prophetic-sounding adjuration to Danilevsky—"doubly authoritative for you is my word, and woe unto him who does not heed my word"—with the aim of persuading him to attend to the business of the village on his estate. It is clear that Gogol was trying to pour into others the forces that seethed within him, in hopes that his great deed would challenge others to do great deeds, and that everyone together would serve the good in the objective sense of that term. Gogol was becoming a resolute *moralist:* estheticism was a thing of the past; religion had not yet come; moralism now was predominant.

Gogol was now consciously moving out of himself toward others. The groundwork had been laid in the late 1830s and early 1840s by the efforts he made to form closer attachments to people. At first a sense of *personal* mission predominated, and in summoning others to do a great deed, he in essence was trying to raise them to his own level. But little by little, the moralism that was directed at others began to be directed at himself. From the end of 1841 thoughout 1842, he spoke of his "colossal design" and continued to see it as a great deed—in fact, as a *moral* deed, a deed on behalf of a good which he could bring to others through his own efforts. The meaning of the deed became clearer and, as it were, more accessible to all; the blinding radiance in which this design originally appeared to him now seemed to spread. It is natural to expect a moral imperative to turn back upon the initiator. That is what happend with Gogol: the need to form others was unwittingly complicated by the need to form himself above all.

The clearest expression of this is to be found in a letter written to Zhukovsky on June 26, 1842: "Much labor and travel and nurturing of the soul still lie ahead. My soul must be purer than the mountain snows and more radiant than the heavens, and only then will I acquire the strength to initiate great deeds and a great career, only then will the riddle of my existence be solved." The words "nurturing of the soul" became a favorite expression of Gogol's. From that time on, he was no longer blinded by the splendor of a great deed awaiting him; on the contrary, he was afraid that he would be "called fearfully to account" if he should undertake it unprepared. "*My* great deed" becomes "my *great deed*." But this did not mean that he had put the cult of his own personality behind him completely. That would not be accomplished immediately, but only as the result of a great struggle.

The turn in the direction of moralism was also evident in the reworking of earlier writings that Gogol undertook at this time. Sometimes it came out directly, through the introduction of moralizing passages, and sometimes indirectly, through a change of attitude toward the heroes, the so-called "existers," whom Gogol up to now had always found repellent, as "lampoons of mankind," in Belinsky's term. (An exception—and, as we have seen, it is a significant one—were the old-fashioned landowners.) Leaving aside *Dead Souls* for the moment, let us take a look at the stories which were first published in the collected works of 1842: "The Overcoat" and "Taras Bulba." Gogol worked on these during the productive summer of 1840 in Vienna, and he continued working on them afterwards as well. In this respect, "The Overcoat" is particularly revealing: the initial draft of 1839 underwent a fundamental change by the very next year.

Minor clerks appear as heroes in the works of other writers of the 1830s; but Gogol's "Diary of a Madman" proved a further stimulus to this theme.[5] In particular, the motif of a clerk's love for his boss's daughter was picked up by other writers, although they treated it in the spirit of the sentimental and melodramatic tradition, rather than with Gogol's special coloration. But the ordinary life of the minor clerk, both at the office and at home, was also depicted. The clerk-theme had become traditional by 1839, when Gogol wrote the draft entitled "The Tale of a Clerk Who Stole Overcoats," from which "The Overcoat" ultimately emerged. Gogol's own originality vis-à-vis the tradition was bound to stand out. Two basic themes intersected in that tradition: the sentimentally moralistic theme of the "poor man" (not necessarily a clerk) who has been lacerated by fate; and the didactically satirical theme of the insignificant clerk, along with all those facile and shallow comments that Gogol waxes ironic about at the beginning of "The Overcoat." Characteristic of the first theme is V. A. Ushakov's story "Iona Faddeevich," which appeared in 1832 (*Syn otechestva*, Vol. 154);[6] and it could well have provided the first *literary* stimulus for Gogol's "The Overcoat," with which it has some points of coincidence.

Ushakov's story begins with the grandmother, "who was foretelling her grandson's destiny," and who "advised against giving him too common a name, such as Ivan or Peter, instead calling him Akaky or Mamont, for distinction's sake. But the priest...took matters into his own hands and named the newborn child Iona." The boy was born hunchbacked and was utterly disfigured by smallpox, which had pitted his face, made him squint-eyed, and left bald patches on his head. In military school and later in the regiment his fellow soldiers laughed at him, but he bore their gibes courageously. "Iona Faddeevich did get angry when one wag called his bald patches the Aleutian Islands." He did not grow angry when another dubbed his face "this cow-flap from the town of Poshekhonya." The story ends idyllically, with marriage and a happy family life.

Ushakov's moralistic theme had not yet become a social theme: his hero is lacerated only by nature itself. Gogol's predecessors in the theme of the poor clerk were Bulgarin and Grebenka. Bulgarin was one of those who "gibed and jeered" to his heart's content at people who were unable to bite back. His "Lament of Deacon Pankraty Fomich Tychkov Under the Overarching Code of Laws" (in his *Collected Works* of 1836)[7] depicts a bribe-taker and drunkard, whose palmy days are over when a new code of laws is issued. His story "A Government Mushroom, or, The Life, i.e., the Existence and Great Deeds of My Friend Foma Fomich Openkin" (*ibid.*) gives a picture of the domestic and office life of a poor clerk, generally painted in the same hues as the life of Akaky Akakievich's office-mates in Gogol's story. In "Openkin" the office workers get together to drink tea, smoke tobacco, and play boston; they also go to restaurants, parties and the theater. For this they have to dress decently, but they manage to get the money by writing letters for people, giving lessons, etc. The clerks with their scratching pens envy their superiors, and strive for higher things, sometimes successfully; but those who do break out of the common mould remain mushrooms even "on a silver dish," retaining the same coarse habits which are the target of Bulgarin's satire.

The hero of Grebenka's story "Luka Prokhorovich" (1838) is a provincial secretary, "a great master at mending pens" and by no means poverty-stricken: quite the contrary, now and then he makes some new acquisition. He is ridiculed for his philistine insignificance, which is responsible for a tragi-comic misunderstanding that has led him to marry his cook: he thinks she has won a hundred thousand rubles in the lottery, not knowing that her ticket has long since been sold. But this same Grebenka, at the beginning of "Gorev" (1840), depicts a poor man who is out of work and has lost his last coin. The ending is melodramatically happy and the story itself bears the subtitle "A Theme Perhaps Suitable for a Melodrama." And in "Diary of a Student" ("Zapiski studenta," published in its entirety in 1841), he gives a picture, no less sad than Gogol's, of the fate of a hero who gradually sinks into poverty, is deceived by everyone, including various persons of consequence, and dies of consumption.

Knowing what we do about Gogol in the 1830s, it is natural to expect that once he had rid himself of his esthetic impressions of Italy and turned his creative talents to "Russia, the snows, the scoundrels, the government office," he would depict a clerk that was all of a piece with the heroes of *Dead Souls*, which he was then writing, and with the civil-servant types of an earlier vintage: Barsukov, Zakatishchev-Sobachkin, Podkolyosin, Yaichnitsa and Khlestakov. That is, he would depict an "exister" and would subject him to ridicule. And that is exactly what happened. In "The Tale of a Clerk Who Stole Overcoats," which was begun in 1839 in Marienbad, Gogol sketches a portrait of the kind of self-satisfied loafer which is so common in his work. "He was satisfied with his job and with the rank of titular councilor.... Deep down he was a very kind-hearted beast, and what is called a loyal person, for actually, nobody ever heard either a bad or a good word from him....His salary was 400 rubles a year. On this salary he (obtained for himself a multitude of pleasures), he ate something like cabbage-soup or ordinary soup....he would lounge in bed to his heart's content, and he paid for having patches put on his trousers, on virtually one and the same place." The disdainful, mocking comments continue to the end of this fragmentary sketch: fun is made of his nose, which looks like a doughnut, and of his frock-coat, which is the color of a cowflap.

We do not know how the original idea for the story continued; but in the new versions of 1840-42, we see something different.[8] Akaky Akakievich here too remains "at the ultimate stage of shallowness," to use Apollon Grigoriev's phrase, but the quality of self-satisfaction has been eliminated, and the "kind-hearted beast" has thereby been turned into a pitiable man, and farce into social tragedy. For the second time (after "Diary of a Madman"), Gogol depicts a man who has been wrenched out of the social norm—not by a combination of social and psychological factors, as in the earlier story, but by harsh, naked economic factors. There is also a defense of people who are "unable to bite back," as well as the celebrated "pathetic" passage about the young man who hears "other words—'I am your brother' " echoing in the timid words of Akaky Akakievich. To be sure, this passage—like everything in art—is subordinate to the overall artistic design; and it creates an effect of contrast, as does the conclusion of "The Two Ivans." But *this particular effect* could have appeared in Gogol's work only when he had been psychologically prepared, both by the personal experience of forming close attachments to people and by the moralism that was developing within him at the beginning of the 1840s. If Gogol in 1839 was still closer to the "mockers and gibers" (Bulgarin, and perhaps Polevoy), now, in the early 1840s, he had made contact with the sentimental and moralizing version of that same tradition, as represented by the stories of Ushakov and Grebenka, and he himself provided the stimulus for its further development. It soon produced Dostoevsky's "Poor Folk" ("Bednye liudi," 1845); and according to A. G. Tseitlin, some 150 stories about poor clerks appeared in the 1840s.[9]

Although the theme of "The Overcoat" closely resembled a literary tradition which had already come into vogue, the story differed from its predecessors by virtue of its unique style and structure.[10] By the beginning of the 1840s, Gogol had already achieved complete mastery of the rhythms of the epic monologue, which sometimes developed into pure lyricism and sometimes parodied lyrical rhythms for comic purposes. In the structure of the story, a special place is occupied by the fantastic ending. (It must in fact be regarded as fantastic.) The censorship committee made the reassuring conjecture that "naturally, the rumor [of the dead man's appearance] was spread by thieves." Unfortunately, it is not only school textbooks that have been responsible for fostering this notion.[11] For anyone familiar with Gogol's penchant for creating fantastic episodes and weaving them into plots dealing with everyday life, such qualifying statements are strange and unnecessary. Besides, in an earlier draft, Akaky Akakievich, while lying delirious just before dying, threatens the general in no uncertain terms and vows to take his overcoat away from him. The artistic task of highlighting the "ultimate degree of shallowness" through an excursion into the supernatural goes hand in hand with morally directed tasks, as is the case with the no less effective ending of *The Inspector General*. We witness the punishment of vice, as represented by the "significant" exister (i.e., the Person of Consequence), who fails to remember his obligation to perform a "great deed." His perception of that obligation is only momentary, but no perception at all would be possible on any but the fantastic level.[12] The punishment of the general represents the triumph of the degraded Akaky Akakievich; the general is not Peter the Great, and there is no reason for Akaky Akakievich to humble himself before him, as does Yevgeny in Pushkin's *The Bronze Horseman*. The parallel between Gogol's story and that earlier poem not only reminds us that Pushkin himself had picked up a theme that was then becoming traditional, but also calls to mind the very frequent appearance, in Pushkin's works, of "superhuman" figures from beyond the grave who utter reproaches and often bring revenge: the drowned man, the river maiden, the commander. In Gogol this motif is first adumbrated in the surviving fragment of *The Hetman*, where Glechik tells the story of the deacon who was hanged and even after his death persecuted his murderers.

A new and powerful wave of moralism also emerged in the reworked version of "Taras Bulba." During the final months of his stay abroad, Gogol returned to the history of the Ukraine. Then, in his own words, he had a "clairvoyant vision of the past." This vision was buttressed by an attentive study of historical sources and the reading of Ukrainian songs and ballads ("ringing, living chronicles"). At first, Gogol's enthusiasm for the Ukrainian past was tied in with the idea for a tragedy, on which he had worked earlier while in Vienna. But nothing came of it, just as, somewhat earlier, nothing had come of the idea for a tragedy based on English history (*Alfred*). *Alfred* was abandoned; the Ukrainian tragedy was also either abandoned or burned;[13] only isolated fragments remain, as well as scraps of dialogue and sketches of the plan for the whole, which make it clear, incidentally, that for the first time, Gogol was to have depicted the jealousy of a woman for a "villainness," a rival. But an imagination now bent toward the past found an outlet in the reworking of "Taras Bulba." Gogol's historical studies gave the story a density and unity; matters that were only hinted at in the first version unfolded into broad canvases; the work grew in scope and took the form of a smoothly flowing epic. It also acquired a rhythmic unity which is virtually unbroken throughout. In some places, as in the battle and death scenes, the rhythmic and stylistic sources of the story are evident: i.e., the Ukrainian ballads and the Russian heroic poems, *The Igor Tale,* the Bible, and Homer. All are synthesized into a form that is purely Gogolian.

The central character, Taras, also underwent a transformation. In the earlier version, he was all of a piece with "the carefree nature of the reckless ages" in which Gogol was still thinking of setting his projected tragedy as late as 1839. Now, however, Taras is not only outwardly heroic, but also (as Gogol put it in those years) a "man endowed with divine prowess," despite his cruelties, which are not played down but are tacitly justified by the historical significance of his task. He makes two speeches before his men, and in both cases, what he says is "authoritative," just as Gogol wanted his own words to be authoritative when he was giving advice to people close to him. Moreover, the speeches are directly connected in subject matter and style with those of Gogol's later writings which are thoroughly moralistic, and with his concern for giving cheer to people whose spirits have flagged. The first speech is made in order to banish despondency. This is also the purpose of the speech by Kukubenko, who prefers to utter a "consoling word" to offenders, rather than a "reproachful" one; and for that he is praised by the leader in Biblical style ("blessed is the father who begot such a son"). Taras's second speech, which is made "not in order to encourage and reinvigorate them" but simply to "express everything in his heart," is a speech about comradeship, about the sacred nature of the comradely bond, and about the spark of humanity that can set off a moral revolution "in the worst of scoundrels": "and the hapless wretch will let his arms fall in despair, will clutch his head and loudly curse his vile life, and will be ready to expiate his shameful deed with torments."

This attitude toward the "worst of scoundrels"—the recently despised "exister"—was new for Gogol; and it determined the moralistic conception underlying the continuation of *Dead Souls*. But this moralistic hope is tinged with something which was never so strongly expressed (even in Gogol's later writings) as in "Taras Bulba": moral regeneration is possible only for one who has "a grain of Russian feeling"; only Russians can be "akin in soul"; and finally, "No, lads, to love as the Russian heart can love, love not with the mind or with anything else, but with all...that is within you...no, no one else can love like that."[14] Here we detect an echo of Gogol's personal and ideological proximity to the Slavophiles at the beginning of the 1840s, which had been prepared by the estheticism of his Roman period. Although he would long cherish the idea of the advantages of the "Russian soul," his Slavophilism in the years thereafter would not be so single-minded. Prophecies about Russia and eulogies of Russian strength can also be heard in the words Taras utters just before he dies.

In reworking the essay entitled "Leaving the Theater," Gogol had only to fan the sparks of moralism which glowed in the sketches made in 1836 but which had been temporarily left to smoulder by his rampant estheticism. There he had written: "Oh, you do not yet know how greatly moral and powerful is the laughter that has permeated the work." In the new version of the essay, the word "moral" is not mentioned in the author's monologue; but he does speak of the same illuminating and reconciling power of *bright* laughter. More than that: the theme of the moral significance of comedy is included in the conversations of the public, along with the esthetic themes, and two characters—"a Very Modestly Dressed Man" and "Mr. B."—express the author's ideas as to the way in which laughter helps overcome "sinful inclinations," and as to the necessity of "the heart's soaring far above that which is contemptible in life," as well as his belief that social evils must not be concealed if such things are to happen. The closing words of "Leaving the Theater"—"he who often sheds tears from the depths of his heart seems to be the one who laughs more than anyone else in the world"—also ended the collected works of 1842, for which this particular piece served as the epilogue. The artist's laughter is the moralist's tears. Tears, as well as laughter, originate in "man's bright nature" and should illuminate everything that is "contemptible and insignificant."

But the "bright laughter" which illuminates frivolous and bilious laughter and is its opposite was not so much a self-definition on Gogol's part as it was a fond hope. And soon the tears of the moralist would strike him as being a more direct and sure way than the laughter of the artist. Meanwhile, in 1842, he had not yet lost hope that they could be joined inseparably. He still aspired to be not "an artist *and* a moralist," but "an artist-moralist."[15]

CHAPTER IX

THE POEM

Gogol worked on the first part of *Dead Souls* for about seven years. According to "An Author's Confession" (1847), it began as a project for a "full work" in which "various types of characters and personalities" would appear, and in which both "comic" and "affecting happenings" would intermingle. He had no more "detailed plan" than that. He had been advised by Pushkin to use the adventures of a buyer of dead souls for a large work. Pushkin himself had been intending to make "something like a long poem" out of this "plot." We can suppose that it was Pushkin who suggested the idea of a gallery of character-types, a novel of *characters* rather than events (whether external or psychological). At least, Gogol reported him as saying: "And with this gift for recognizing the essential man and presenting him all at once in a few strokes as a living human being—and with this gift, not to undertake a large work! That's simply sinful!" ("An Author's Confession.") But even so, the very nature of Gogol's art made it imperative for him to devote himself to character-drawing rather than to a depiction of manners and mores.

It is curious that as material for a large work Gogol chose a way of life with which he was least familiar from direct experience: that of provincial Russia.[1] Evidently he relied on his ability to "recognize the essential man." In 1835, the same year he began working on *Dead Souls,* he made a stab at depicting provincial life in his story "The Carriage." The local-color scenes offer nothing new beyond what is to be found in *Mirgorod,* and the character-types are drawn from military life. There is almost nothing specifically "provincial" in this story. The most valuable thing about it is the comic effect created by the discovery of someone who has concealed himself; this comes from the tradition of the farce and the vaudeville-comedy. Gogol had no first-hand knowledge of the Russian provinces. That was noted long ago, and underscored fairly recently by S. A. Vengerov.[2] He himself never tried to conceal the fact, admitting that "the provinces are already growing dim in my mind" and that only the life of St. Petersburg could supply his art with material based on personal observations. But prior to the early 1840s, his art was moving in another direction—that of "intellection," as he put it, of "recognizing the essential man," as Pushkin put it.[3] To be sure, in a letter to Pushkin he had said that he was "looking for some snitcher that I could become close friends with" (October 7 [o.s.], 1835). But in the very first letters from abroad, he had forgotten all about that and said instead that he wanted to rely only on the *imagination* of his fellow-writers. He wrote as follows to Zhukovsky: "Couldn't you think of some situations that might arise in connection with the buying up of dead souls? That would be a marvellous thing for me, because whatever else, your imagination will have a true picture of something mine will not. Tell Pushkin about this, perhaps he too will find something" (November 12, 1836).

Up to that time, Gogol's work could have moved in one of three possible directions. The first was to create idealized worlds divorced not only from contemporary life but from real life in general. There are flashes of this in a few of the fascinating and incorporeal phantoms that flit through *Evenings on a Farm Near Dikanka.* The second was to idealize and romanticize reality. This could be done by depicting exceptionally colorful phenomena of the past (the Middle Ages, the Cossacks) and the present (Italy)—and Gogol was nudged in this direction by the Romantic literary tradition—or by depicting even ordinary phenomena of the present (as in the ending of the first idyll, *Hanz Küchelgarten,* all of the second, and later, the third as well)—and Gogol was being summoned in this direction by the commanding voice of the tradition of socially engaged literature. The third possibility was to set his own personality in opposition to real life (whether "amusing" or "terrible"), which he had transcended, and from this vantage point of self-awareness to depict the phenomena of life as "amusing or terrible caricatures." This was the way of the realist, but the realist who, in his very realism, did not cease being a Romantic. The fact that Gogol's romanticism did not move either in the first direction (idealistic) or the second (sentimental and idyllic) but rather, in the third (realistic), can be attributed to many factors: his ties with the tradition of Ukrainian comedy, his own psychological quirks, the influences—recognized or unrecognized—of Pushkin's personality and Pushkin's art (particularly his prose fiction).

Dead Souls, like *The Inspector General,* is based on a migratory anecdote which grew out of real life itself. Several stories about people who actually bought up dead souls have come down to us. Ukrainian landowners of the first three decades of the nineteenth century resorted to this subterfuge in order to qualify for a license to distill spirits. Mentioned among them is a certain distant relative of Gogol's;[4] and Vladimir Dahl told of one such case involving a Russian in a secondary episode of his tale *Vakh Sidorov Chaikin,* which was published virtually simultaneously with *Dead Souls.* Here a certain Vasily Ivanovich purchases some two hundred dead souls, registers them as living in one small bit of swamp, and then mortgages an estate of two hundred souls with the Registry Board. The author of the present book knows of one prototype of Chichikov from a legend that has come down in his own family.[5]

We have no evidence that allows us to conjecture just *how* this story got to Gogol and Pushkin, whether through Dahl or someone else. The important thing about Pushkin's idea, as suggested to Gogol, was not the anecdote itself, but rather the fact that it could serve as the basis for a large literary work with a variety of characters and episodes. The anecdotal origin also predetermined which literary traditions the narrative was to draw upon: the travel novel *(Reiseroman)* and the picaresque novel *(Schelmenroman)*. *Don Quixote* stood as a brilliant example of the combination of these two traditions; and it is significant that in Gogol's account of his conversations with Pushkin—which dealt specifically with a "large work"—the name of Cervantes is mentioned.[6] It is more difficult to point to models in Russian literature: the "sentimental journeys" of Radishchev, Karamzin, Vladimir Izmaylov and others were primarily lyrical and did not take the form of novels. M. M. Kheraskov's novels were shaped by a tradition that was already outmoded, and the tradition represented by Goethe's *Wilhelm Meister* and its Romantic progeny did not put down roots in Russian soil. If ideas of this kind did materialize, as in the case of V. F. Odoevsky, they were not fully developed.

The picaresque novel took deeper root. Its earliest Russian version is the seventeenth-century *Tale of Frol Skobeev (Povest' o Frole Skobeeve)*, which became available to a wide circle of readers only after Gogol's death but was circulating in limited manuscript and printed collections as early as the eighteenth century. At the beginning of the nineteenth century, a conscious imitator of Lesage's picaresque novel appeared: Vasily Narezhny, who in 1814 published the first three parts of *A Russian Gil Blas*. At the beginning of the 1830s, Gennady Simonovsky's *A Russian Gil Blas (Russkii Zhilblaz)* was published, and even earlier, in 1829, came Bulgarin's *Ivan Vyzhigin*, which created a tremendous sensation.

These novels (and others like them) are connected with *Dead Souls* only in the most general way. First of all, Gogol omits any love-intrigue, as he does in his comedies too. He does not dispense with didacticism, at least not in the final version of Part 1. It is not reflected in the development of the narrative, however, but comes out in skilfully interjected passages which interrupt the main line of the story. He does dispense with the intricacies of plot required by the adventure tradition; and *Dead Souls,* which was conceived as an adventure novel, ceased to be such in the realization, and instead became a novel devoted to a *single adventure,* with no others strung onto it. The stringing device itself was retained, but the episodes that are strung onto the hero's picaresque journey are static rather than dynamic in nature, consisting mainly of character sketches and impersonal genre pictures. In pre-Gogolian literature, something similar is done by Narezhny in part of his novel *Aristion, or Reeducation (Aristion ili perevospitanie,* 1822). Kassian, who is responsible for "reeducating" Aristion, acquaints him with life by taking him around from one neighboring landowner to another. There are three examples of "vice," and the last landowner visited represents "virtue." The negative characters are Silvester, a sluggard who spends the entire day hunting, lets his peasants do what they will, and neglects his estate; Tarakh, a miser; and Paramon, a dissolute reveller. Each visit ends with a didactic conclusion drawn by

Kassian. This book could have influenced the way in which the plot of *Dead Souls* is structured. However, Gogol had nothing to learn from Narezhny, and we must look to the West for his teachers in prose-epic construction.

Here we must limit ourselves to conjecture, inasmuch as the problem of Gogol's teachers and models in the West has not yet been studied as fully as it deserves. Cervantes might be too general a model, although he is undoubtedly a tempting one. There are even fewer grounds for proposing Laurence Sterne—that is, Sterne specifically as the author of *A Sentimental Journey*. Clues must be sought in statements made by Gogol himself. As early as *Arabesques* (1835), he speaks of the ideal historian of the future and requires of him the "dramatic interest" of Schiller, the "absorbing way of telling a tale" of Walter Scott, and the "art of developing large traits of character within narrow limits" typical of Shakespeare. After going abroad, Gogol reread Shakespeare, Molière, and Scott, and mentioned Scott in an article in *The Contemporary*.[7] That particular name was never mentioned again, but others were. In the drafts of *Dead Souls* written abroad, Gogol made one very important statement which has come down to us in three variants. He speaks of ladies who demand a hero "without the slightest blemish"; and in reply to the "fool's judgment" that he foresees, he says: "he [the author] does not have the habit of looking around while he is writing. If he does raise his eyes, it is only to look at the portraits of Shakespeare, Ariosto, Fielding, Cervantes and Pushkin that hang before him; they reflected nature as it was, and not as certain people wished it had been."

The list is no less significant than the "Petrarch, Tieck and Aristophanes" in Hanz Küchelgarten's library. Cervantes and Pushkin are the least unexpected names here. We can guess that Shakespeare was the model of "the art of developing large traits of character within narrow limits," which Gogol had already noted. (Cf. the third letter on *Dead Souls* in *Selected Passages from Correspondence with Friends*, where Gogol, paraphrasing Pushkin, defines his own art as "the ability to sketch the banality of a banal person with such power that every small detail which slips by unnoticed looms *large* in the eyes of all.") We can guess that Gogol valued Ariosto not only for his brilliant style but also for his skill at constructing a truly epic, *retarded* narrative, which was brought up in Galich's esthetics and which Gogol was not equal to in the early version of *Taras Bulba*. Between these two pairs Gogol places Fielding. He mentions the same name in the rough draft of this textbook on the theory of literature, along with Cervantes, as an example of a writer of "the lesser epic genres," which, "although they are written in prose, can nonetheless be included among poetic works."[8] Fielding's novels had been known in Russian translations since the end of the eighteenth century. A reviewer in *The Loyalist (Blagonamerennyi)*, writing in 1824 (Part 7), lamented the fact that there were so few Russian novels, but consoled himself with the hope that "our own Fieldings, La Fontaines and Walter Scotts will appear." There is good reason why Fielding is listed in first place here; and

116

Fielding was the only Western novelist besides Cervantes that Gogol named; he hung his portrait on the wall (of his imagination), hereby acknowledging him as one of his five mentors and inspirations. The relationship between the English novelist and Gogol still requires study.[9] Be that as it may, the manner in which Gogol asserts authorial control over the action—through a continuous commentary consisting of humorous and lyrical interjections—could have been suggested not only by Sterne but also by Fielding, particularly during the time when it was his intention to intermingle "comic" and "affecting happenings" in his work.

Dead Souls was not from the outset created in the form we know today. With reference to the chapters he had read to Pushkin while still in Petersburg, Gogol said: "If anyone had seen the monsters that emerged from under my pen at first for my eyes only, he certainly would have shuddered." The reading made a painful impression on Pushkin: he "finally became extremely gloomy" and "said in an anguished voice: 'Lord, how sad is our Russia.' " Gogol continues: "This astonished me. Pushkin, who knew Russia so well, did not notice that this was all a caricature and of my own devising."[10] And so, originally *Dead Souls* was conceived even more as a caricature. We do not know whether much of it was composed in Petersburg. In October of 1835, Gogol wrote Pushkin that he had stopped in the third chapter; thereafter he was preoccupied with *The Inspector General*. There is only a fragment which we can ascribe to this early version with any certainty. It is from the eighth chapter, and was written after Gogol had gone abroad, as is evident from the text. We are struck first of all by the much more *personal* tone, compared with the later versions: the author speaks of himself in the first person, gives vent to a whole gamut of emotions, ranging from irony to bitterness ("I am stubborn, I don't want to see faces that should be spat upon"), and he carries on a relaxed conversation with the reader in a tone that is very different from the rhetorical pathos of the final version ("and so, let's be on familiar terms, my merry and openhearted reader; I don't stand on the slightest ceremony with you"). In this fragment, Gogol's manner of character-depiction reaches a degree of caricature it never had in his earlier work. He does not depict normal human faces but ugly mugs, which in turn become animal-like: "And in fact, look at the kinds of faces we see in this world! Whichever mug you take, it's certain to be unlike any other. On one person the nose carries out the duties of commander, on another it's the lips, on another the cheeks, which have extended their domain even at the expense of the eyes and even of the nose itself, which as a result is no bigger than a waistcoat button; this man has such a long chin that he has to keep it constantly covered with a handkerchief so as not to drool on it....And how many there are who don't look like people at all. This one is a perfect dog in a tail-coat, so that you are surprised to see him carrying a stick; it would seem that the first person he meets would seize...." Here the manuscript breaks off.

In his review of *Dead Souls,* S. P. Shevyryov resorted to zoological metaphors: Manilov is a hoopoe, Korobochka a squirrel, Nozdryov a dog, Sobakevich a mixture of bear and pig, Plyushkin a mole, Petrushka a goat. All the metaphors except one (Sobakevich) were the products of his imagination. But he did come close to Gogol's original (if not final) idea: to depict, in S. T. Aksakov's phrase, "an assemblage of freaks," as in a zoo.[11]

After telling of the occasion on which he read *Dead Souls* to Pushkin, Gogol goes on to say: "From that time on, I began to think only about ways of alleviating the painful impression that *Dead Souls* might create. I perceived that many vile qualities were not worthy of malice; it was better to show all their insignificance...." It would seem that the expression "from that time on" is not to be taken literally. But as is evident from the surviving drafts that were written abroad, the new plan for *Dead Souls* was characterized by an absence of malice, by a less direct expression of personal feelings, and by a certain refinement in the caricatures, which had been too stark. Out of this developed the version on which Gogol worked mainly in 1840, and which he was polishing in 1841. Everything he put into it, except for a few details, is known to us from the final printed version. But after returning to Moscow toward the end of 1841, he subjected *Dead Souls* to still another revision: the basic text was what he had written abroad, but now it was amplified. His self-esteem, which had grown to such intensity in 1840 and had taken on greater complexity by virtue of his moralistic concerns, needed to find expression; and this personal need coincided with the artistic tasks he faced in working on the structure of *Dead Souls*. He now studded the novel with "pathetic" passages, which provided some respite from the hyperrealistic passages and conferred a lyric and epic unity on the entire work.

In his textbook on literature, Gogol devotes a separate chapter to the "lesser genres of the epic." He describes them as falling "somehow between the novel and the epic; the hero may be an ordinary, unprepossessing individual, yet one who is significant...to the observer of the human heart. The author takes him through a series of adventures and changes, in order to present, along with them, a true-to-life, faithful picture of everything significant in the mores and characteristic features of the time he has chosen...." The definition that follows—the demand for an "almost static" picture of abuses and vices—reflects the artistic tasks that Gogol was to set himself later (the "textbook" was written between 1844 and 1846). But there is an unmistakable allusion to *Dead Souls* in the sentence that reads as follows: "Many of them may be written in prose, but can nonetheless be numbered among poetic creations." The final version of *Dead Souls*, in fact, is not a novel but a "lesser genre of the epic," and therefore was called a "poem" by Gogol. As far back as 1835, Belinsky had called "Taras Bulba" an "immense picture, enclosed in a narrow framework, worthy of Homer"; and this may have exerted some influence on Gogol's own understanding of himself as an artist, and on Konstantin Aksakov's over-enthusiastic drawing of a straight line from

Homer to Gogol, with specific reference to *Dead Souls*.[12] (Belinsky hastened to dissociate himself from that.)

But the "narrow framework" of the first version of "Taras Bulba" opens out in the second; in *Dead Souls* it is further expanded, and the narrative is subject to the "laws of retardation." The purposes of retardation are served not only by the interpolation of highly rhetorical passages, but also by the extended comparisons in rhythmic prose (the ball is compared to flies on sugar, Nozdryov to a lieutenant on the attack, etc.), whose "Homeric quality" was pointed out by A. A. Potebnya.[13] The same purposes are served by the "epic digressions," which Gogol introduces into the new version as generously as he did the "lyrical digressions,"' perhaps out of a still vaguely felt need to saturate the "poem" with material drawn from everyday life, even on the most tenuous grounds. Some passages, such as the collective portrayal of provincial society, existed in the version written abroad. New material was introduced into the Moscow version: the stories about Nozdryov's bailiff, about the life of the provincial civil servant (which was tacked onto the reflections about the landowner's life, in Chapter VI), and about the "lazybones and stick-in-the-muds." The barge hauler Fyrov is added to the company of the already existing peasants who were the subject of Chichikov's reveries; we are shown Selifan and Petrushka on a spree in the taverns; new too are Ivan Antonovich the Pitcher-Snout and, most important of all, the detailed account of Chichikov's childhood and school years. The poem took on a form which Shevyryov compared to a pie that had been over-stuffed by "an ingenious gourmet who has bought the ingredients without calculating how much he will need, and who does not spare the filling."[14]

The "law of retardation" is also at work in the time-structure of the novel. The first chapter is a prologue, which covers the first two weeks of Chichikov's stay in the provincial town. Thereafter the author follows Chichikov day by day, and in the space of *six* chapters he depicts *four* such days. Beginning with Chapter VIII, this scheme breaks down: there is no longer a symmetrical time-pattern. Gogol reproached his critics for "lacking the habit of closely examining the construction of a work," and he himself found faults in the structure of the second half; "major and important   situations are compressed and abridged, unimportant and secondary ones are expanded... the diversity of the parts and the fragmentary nature [of the work] are glaringly obvious."[15] Subsequently, Gogol attempted to correct these defects; for example, he developed the questions asked of Chichikov by Sobakevich and Korobochka.

The first half of the book is a gallery of portraits. Here Gogol takes as his point of departure "thematic traits," which sometimes develop into grandiose hyperboles. In the earliest of the surviving versions, most of these thematic traits were lumped together in one general formulation: after Chichikov had left, "he saw in his mind's eye, on a narrowed and reduced scale...the society of the town, the governor and the ball, the joke-cracking postmaster, the *bear* Sobakevich, the *sugar cube* Manilov, the wretched inn, the endless games of whist that lasted until dawn...," etc. Gogol uses a thematic trait, such as "bear" or "sugar cube," to join together a character's outward appearance and personality. The critic M. P. Sorokin, writing in *The St. Petersburg Register,* aptly characterized Manilov as a man "with the heart of a calf and a philosophy dating from the times of poor Liza."[16] As early as Chapter I, Gogol notes that Manilov's eyes are "sweet as sugar," and, in Chapter II, "it seemed that too much sugar had been added to this sweetness." Further on, his facial expression is compared to a sickly-sweet mixture. The touches that were added in the final version are fully consistent with the theme of "sugariness": the list of peasants made on paper with a pretty border and tied with a pink ribbon. There is good reason, of course, why Gogol shows Korobochka as utterly lacking in any outward appearance, any *face:* he speaks of the flannel wrapped around her neck, and the cap on her head, and that is all. On the other hand, the small details of the furnishings and the household are carefully drawn; they fully define not her personality but her lack of personality.

For Nozdryov, models already existed—partly in Narezhny's Paramon and Bulgarin's Glazdurin *(Ivan Vyzhigin),* partly in Gogol's own Pirogov ("Nevsky Prospect") and Ikharev *(The Gamblers);* and there is something more closely resembling a description of external appearance. Innokenty Annensky noted the wonderful luxuriance of Nozdryov's side-whiskers as an expression of his "creative corporeality."[17] On the other hand, Sobakevich, for whom there were no obvious prototypes, is depicted with deliberate emphasis on one thematic trait: the *bear.* His tail-coat is the color of a bearskin; his name is Mikhailo Semyonovich;[18] the bureau in his room is "a perfect bear," and in general, all the furnishings "bore a certain strange resemblance to the master of the house himself" (this sentence occurs in the final version), every chair seemed to be saying "and I too am Sobakevich"; even the thrush in the cage resembled him. Plyushkin is characterized by the image of something *rent:* the rent in his dressing-gown (which is Chichikov's first impression) exists in all the versions. In the final one, the following sentence appears: "everything [in his household] was becoming torn and rent, and he himself had at last turned into a rent on the cloak of humanity." The Plyushkin of earlier years was not miserly but thrifty, and "ran like an industrious *spider,* bustling but efficient, from one end of his household web to the other." Evidently the new image of the *rent* induced Gogol, as the chapter progressed, to discard the image of the bustling efficient spider; to describe the Plyushkin of later years, there remained only the spider attaching its web to the clock whose pendulum had stopped; and the whole picture of the room became unified in immobility and dustiness.

The miser-type itself goes back to a very ancient tradition which was constantly being renewed with fresh materials. The parallels that have been noted between Plyushkin and the characters of Maturin, Narezhny and Kvitka are of the most general nature.[19] Shevyryov said of Chichikov that "he outdid all the animals in trickery and only thereby did he maintain the glory of human nature." Pereverzev was right in recognizing Chichikov as a synthetic type: he combines all the "fervors" of Gogolian heroes (see the following chapter) by virtue of that "mediocrity" in which—according to D. S. Merezhkovsky—utter banality is manifested not only in its extreme instances but also in its demonic significance. "Not handsome, but not ugly in appearance either; not too fat but not too thin either; you couldn't say he was old, but neither could you say he was very young." He loves his own body and his own nice mug, he loves food, good clothes and comfort, he gets along with everyone and mesmerizes everyone, precisely because those elements of banality that are distributed among the other characters come out in him in full force.

Such are the central figures of the work—"a few ugly landowners," as Gogol puts it. No less ugly are the serfs: hardly anyone would be moved by Selifan's human qualities, as was Shevyryov; and the stink of Petrushka, the idiotic Mityay and Minyay, along with the "two Russian peasants" introduced at the beginning of Chapter I, all add to the gloomy impression created even by the final version of the book, which is toned down in these respects. Belinsky wrote that *Dead Souls* "relentlessly tears the covers off reality"; and here he was reacting essentially to the *final* version in the same way that Pushkin had reacted to the *first*.[20]

The second half of Part I offers no new large-scale portraits, only collective ones. These create a backdrop in which the characters are not even given names but are referred to in general terms: a government official, ladies, lazybones and stick-in-the-muds. The second half is significant mainly for its dynamic quality (in contrast to the static quality of the first half). Dynamism of this kind was nothing new in Gogol's works: the critics, whether hostile or sympathetic, had been as one in noting the similarity of *Dead Souls* and *The Inspector General* in this respect. It is a dynamism created by mystifications and errors, and it closely resembles *The Inspector General* even in specifics: everyone is awaiting a new governor-general and is prepared to believe that Chichikov is the one; but everyone is thrown off that particular track by newly arrived letters which speak of a mysterious counterfeiter and brigand, who people think must be Chichikov. The commotion set up in this world of freaks, in this "fantastic" (Shevyryov's term) town, is supposed to appear absurd; and Gogol himself does not seem to be denying this even when in Chapter X he insists on the symbolic significance of this apparent absurdity. As in *The Inspector General*, the "poem" takes on greater complexity by parodying both a love story and the action of an adventure novel. The fascination that "the not too fat and not too thin" Chichikov feels for the youth and purity of the governor's daughter might very quickly have turned into a parody of feeling; but the imagination of the townspeople credits Chichikov with a plan to abduct the girl—an action that is appropriate for the hero of an adventure novel, but not for him. With a leap back into the past *(Vorgeschichte)*, the story-line itself is brought to an end.

The process by which Part 1 of *Dead Souls* was created makes one thing clear: that besides "stuffing" the book with materials drawn from ordinary life, Gogol increasingly felt the need to arrive at something resembling a naturalistic description of manners and mores. But it is also clear that this need, in general, found no deeper expression than descriptions drawn in terms of hyperbole and caricature. A significant number of "strengthened" images were discarded in the Moscow version—cockroaches the size of rye bread, Nozdryov's dream about Kuvshinnikov's marriage to a dog, the comparison of Sobakevich's female relative to "spots or dots on an object," the comparison of Plyushkin's village to a rag. Some remain: the "vendor of hot mead, with a copper-red samovar and a face just as red as the samovar, so that from a distance you might think there were two samovars in the window, if only one of the samovars were not wearing a beard black as pitch." Some new images were introduced, in the most hyperbolic of the chapters (on Sobakevich): one of Bobelina's legs (in the picture) now proves to be larger than the torso of a dandy, and "a turkey the size of a calf" appears. The comparison of the faces of Sobakevich and his wife to a melon and a cucumber remained; and, perhaps in keeping with this last image, Feodulia Ivanovna's hands have been washed in cucumber brine as well. Along with the deliberate intensification of realistic traits, we also find unintentional departures from realistic accuracy. These evidently did not bother Gogol much at this point, although they certainly would later on. The action takes place at an unspecified time of year; to all appearances it is summer, but this is counterindicated by the heavy bearskin coats that Chichikov and Manilov are wearing, and by the sheepskins the peasants are wearing.[21] And after awakening as late as ten o'clock in Korobochka's house, Chichikov is on his way before noon. Aksakov also drew Gogol's attention to inaccuracies which bespoke a poor knowledge of the life of provincial civil servants and of office work.

At this period in his life, too, Gogol felt the need of getting out of the stifling world of freaks into the fresh air. However, he does not counterbalance the "freakish" qualities of his characters with more human impulses or different types of characters, but only with the intense emotion that "wings up out of" himself. First of all, he gives his reader guidelines by passing judgment on his heroes, even defending some of them at this point. In this way he seems to be carrying on the didactic tradition of the earlier novel. But the rhetoric is different from Narezhny's: it is more refined and at times develops into lyrical pathos, as in the chapter on Plyushkin. There are as yet only faint suggestions of something radiant in the heroes themselves; but there is a more ringing expression of hope for something radiant in the Russian character generally, in Russia herself as a phenomenon of symbolic significance. The earlier version of Chapter V contains a digression criticizing aristocratic drawing rooms, but in the final version it ends with a passage, in rhythmic prose, on the "word" that distinguishes various people, and on the Russian "word" as something that bursts forth from the heart itself. Chapter XI breaks off with an eerily mysterious half-doubt and half-prophecy that is addressed both to Russia and to the writer himself. And at the very end of the book, Chichikov's troika is replaced by a symbolic troika—Russia—which soars in "terror-inspiring movement," makes no reply when asked where it is going, yet overtakes other people and other states.

If we can detect echoes of Slavophile ideas and influences of the Aksakov family in these prophecies, we must also note that Gogol's forebodings (for which he himself would probably have been unable to give a rational explanation) contained elements of tragic pathos that were foreign to the Slavophiles. That is why, after all, it was not they but Belinsky who reacted to this enigmatic prophecy "with a holy tremor, hair standing on end." The introductory sections to two of these chapters are also distinctive: lyric and epic in Chapter VI, lyric in Chapter VII. The latter did not come to Gogol straightaway. The first version of it to be written after he had gone abroad (1836) maintains the same self-assured personal tone that characterized the surviving passages of the earliest draft of the novel (1835). This tone answered to Gogol's sense of his role as a writer whose task was to bring "the contemptible and the insignificant" to light (and, as we have mentioned, it grew in intensity in 1840). Here he was being true to his zeal for exposé. "Repulse the servile request, people's thirst for self-oblivion. Do not befog the mind...they will call you ignoble, insignificant...but keep walking along this road...." In the second version of this passage, also written abroad, there is an expression of hope that the poet of the future will detect the pathos that lies hidden in the exposé, that "these lowly pages will then appear in a light which is now unseen," and that this future poet "will pause before them in perturbation; an awesome storm of inspiration will envelop his head, and songs unheard will refresh the world." And finally, in the Moscow version we are given to understand—although Gogol does not come right out and say so—that the "awesome storm of inspiration" will envelop the author of the "lowly pages" himself, and that people will hear from him "in confused trembling the mighty thunder of other words." And in the last chapter, by way of reply to the ladies who demand a virtuous hero, the narrator does not point so proudly as before to the portraits of writers "who reflected nature as it was, and not as certain people wished it had been." Rather, he promises to depict "in this very same story" a man endowed with divine prowess or a wonderful Russian girl.

Dead Souls arose out of a passion for what we might call exposé, except that Gogol was not interested in exposing the historical and social forms of Russian life, but rather, the individual "existers." This passion in turn had its source in Gogol's awareness that he was superior to the "existers," and it developed from estheticism into moralism as he worked on the book. Contrary to what he intended, the book did become "a social, public and historical phenomenon," as Belinsky at once perceived. The censors perceived it clearly too. The suspicions of the "Asiatic censors," as Gogol called them, that "the author [was] taking up arms against immortality" ("The Adventures of Chichikov" was added to the title as insurance), or that he was instigating people to commit some criminal act, can be regarded as a historical curiosity. Yet the fears of the censors that "this [was] therefore against serfdom" were not so very curious: of course it was not Gogol's basic concept that represented a threat to Russia's social structure, but rather, the impression created by the book. With the help of the "European censors," who also uttered a lot of nonsense, agreement was reached on thirty-six passages that had met with objection;[22] and only one interpolated episode, which Gogol cherished very much—"The Tale of Captain Kopeikin"—was seriously affected.

"The Tale of Captain Kopeikin" represents a distinctive stylization of colloquial speech. (This roused the indignation of Polevoy, who was accustomed to the decorous cliché.)[23] Gogol's original plan in fact called for a satire with social significance. The figure of the seasoned veteran who is the victim of bureaucratic arrogance and negligence was also known in earlier Western literature (LeSage's *Gil Blas*) and in Russian satire of the eighteenth century.[24] But Gogol combined this motif with the folksong motif of the brigand Kopeikin, and created something more impressive. The hungry Kopeikin can get nothing out of the government minister; the latter at first refuses him, and then, when "hunger spur[s] Kopeikin on" and he announces he will not budge from the spot, the minister summons the courier and orders Kopeikin sent into exile. But Kopeikin escapes and organizes a band of men who rob for the sake of an idea. They are brigands of the Schiller type, who steal only money belonging to the state. Finally he escapes to America. The ending is a happy one, to be sure: the Emperor receives a letter in which Kopeikin tries to persuade him to act solicitously toward disabled veterans; he takes it to heart, calls off the pursuit of Kopeikin's confederates, and establishes a fund for veterans.

But from a political viewpoint, this ending also showed more ambiguity than loyalty. Gogol did not venture to submit it to the censor, and he watered it down considerably: Kopeikin, reassured by the Emperor's promises, hits the bottle and squanders all the money. Then, spurred on by hunger, he begins to comport himself in a rude manner. In other words, he himself is to blame in some measure. The story breaks off with the appearance of the robber-band. The censors rejected even a version as innocuous as this. Gogol was extremely discouraged by their reaction. But since he set great store by the style of the story, he sacrificed its social content; and in place of a character closely resembling the tragic figures of Poprishchin and Bashmachkin (men who are wrenched out of the social norm), he carelessly substituted yet another variation on the "exister" type that is so familiar in his earlier works. Kopeikin was hereby denigrated, and the government whitewashed. In this version, people do everything possible for Kopeikin, and it is still not enough —he dreams of going to the theater and dining on delicate foods. The new version weakened the social significance of the book as a whole, but could not destroy it entirely.

Dead Souls was greeted by a discordant chorus of criticism. Both "Westerner" and "Slavophile" critics took the book as a whole when they read it, with all its extremes of realism and rhetoric, and judged it accordingly. (A "predominance of subjectivity" and "lofty lyrical pathos" were just what fascinated Belinsky more than anything else.) But there were cautious reservations: Belinsky, a "Westerner," noted the "too easy" judgment passed on other nationalities; conversely, Shevyryov, a Slavophile, noted with displeasure that the Russian people were shown as being slow-witted. But the johnny-come-latelies of Romanticism and eclecticism understood nothing, accepted nothing, and outdid themselves in abuse and mockery: lack of taste, gaucheness, barbarous language, lower than Paul de Kock (Grech), a salacious palette unworthy of an artist (Masalsky), utter filth and childish rhetoric (Senkovsky), and finally, the simplest condemnation of all: rubbish (Polevoy).

This was how *Dead Souls* was branded by Russian writers of Gogol's own time (and not bad ones, either). Polevoy held to a theory of moderate Romanticism and could not forgive Gogol for his Romantic hyperbolism. He demanded realistic verisimilitude: "But how can you depict man by making a collection of freaks?...Who is requiring you to depict a virtuous man? All people require is just *man*, and they reject the absurd caricatures you are giving us." Nor could he forgive Gogol for the rudiments of naturalism that he found in the work, and scornfully rejected the "disgusting details," the "dirty trivia," the "words that belong in the mouths of servants and in taverns." At the heart of Polevoy's criticism lay a demand for an ideology of Romanticism, a demand that Gogol "reconcile for us the visible disharmony in reality by means of the beautiful idea of art, which has grasped the secret of life." Shevyryov was also interested in the question of the possibility of such a reconciliation, but in Gogol he detected a Romantic of a different type, the Romantic dualist, although he did not use that term. To quote him: "The lower, coarser, more material, more bestial the physical world depicted by the poet...the higher, more aloof and more free of it should be his subjective self.... It is as if two beings are visible from his novel....His poetry is not all of a piece, not unitary, but rather, is of a double nature, bifurcated." Shevyryov did appreciate Gogol's use of hyperbole and saw the town in *Dead Souls* as "a fantastic town" in which "the demon of confusion and stupidity" seemed to be running riot. He knew Gogol personally, and to him the roots of the writer's duality were obvious: a belief in esthetics as an ideology. As he put it: "at the same time when in flights of imagination he [Gogol] sees nightmares in which characters such as Sobakevich and Nozdryov figure," it was essential that "his eyes come to rest...on the wonderful azure of the Italian skies."[25]

Better than anyone else, Belinsky appreciated *Dead Souls* as a literary

125

event; but Shevyryov came closer than anyone else to discerning the artistic *tasks* that Gogol had set himself. These tasks, however, were not definitive ones. The first part of *Dead Souls* was a summing-up of the past, not the beginning of a new direction. Gogol did not sustain the ideological or artistic duality of the work. Rather, he tried to effect a personal reconciliation with that world which for the time being he still saw in terms of an insoluble tragedy, as "the dreadful murk of life," "the emptiness and the impotent sloth of life," which are followed by "death, opaque and unspeaking,"[26] and he filled in the drawing on the cover of *Dead Souls* with emblems of death. The psychological turning-point was to determine an artistic turning-point as well: a search for new artistic devices.

CHAPTER X

AN ASSEMBLAGE OF FREAKS

The first part of *Dead Souls* and the collected works of 1842 represented Gogol's last appearance in print as a writer of fiction. The final ten years of his life were years of great inner struggle, which were directly related to his plan for the continuation of *Dead Souls* and his reevaluation of all his earlier work. But even while making this reevaluation, Gogol continued to feel a tenuous personal tie with the world of his fictional heroes: he called his art the history of his own soul, and his heroes nightmares that had oppressed his soul. Now the time had come to sum things up, to take a close look at his character-types and at the system they had formed (whether he liked it or not) by the time he made that statement about the nightmares.[1]

To characterize the world he had created, Gogol often resorted to general formulations, such as "insignificant people," "a few freakish landowners," "strange heroes," "banality," "the terrible staggering morass of trivia," "the dead insensitivity of life," "the dreadful murk of life." We might also recall his definitions of the heroes of Fonvizin and Griboedov (certainly with his own heroes in mind too): "incontrovertibly dreadful ideals of coarseness" (with reference to Fonvizin's *The Minor*), and "a collection of society's freaks" (with reference to Griboedov's *Woe from Wit*).[2] The expression "an assemblage of freaks" is S. T. Aksakov's; the expression "dreadful ideals" with reference to comic character-types had already been used by Galich in his treatise on esthetics, when he spoke of "comic hyperboles, caricatures, the dreadful or amusing ideals of spiritual life."

As the critics hostile to Gogol understood it, "caricature" was a term of censure; but Gogol himself often used it in an entirely positive sense when he spoke of his works as artistic caricatures.[3] For instance, in the conversation between Two Members of the Audience in "Leaving the Theater," one of them asks the following question: "Why, in analyzing any action, character or personality-trait in isolation, do you see that it is all true, lifelike, and taken from nature, yet at the same time it seems to be something enormous, exaggerated and caricatured?" The other replies: because "the setting and the scene of action are imaginary. Otherwise the author would not have perpetrated such blatant inaccuracies and anachronisms." And in the concluding monologue, the author, in speaking of "laughter's" characteristic ability to deepen a subject and "throw into sharp relief that which would otherwise slip past," adds that otherwise "the contemptible and the insignificant...would not grow before our eyes with such terrible, almost caricature-like intensity." In the letters on *Dead Souls* in *Selected Passages from Correspondence with Friends*, Gogol says virtually the same thing: that the book has "cut many to the quick with its mockery, and truth, and caricatures." In a letter written to Pletnyov in 1846, he observes of himself: "Any teacher who advises his students to study the art of writing...from me will be acting thoughtlessly; he will have them producing caricatures....I have never aspired to echo everything or to reflect in myself reality as it exists around us." And a sympathetic Vyazemsky called *Dead Souls* "caricatures in the manner of Holbein."[4]

Later the term "caricature" was replaced by the more precise "hyperbole." Apollon Grigoriev was the first to apply it to Gogol, in an article entitled "Russian Literature in 1851" ("Russkaia literatura v 1851 godu"), where he spoke of Gogol's humor as "a passionate, hyperbolic humor." In the article "Russian Literature in 1852," he developed this suggestion. Reality, in Gogol, assumed "those colossally comic dimensions which were imparted to it by an inflamed and irritated imagination. For that reason, Gogol's works are not true to reality, but rather, to the general sense of a reality that is at variance with an ideal...in this respect only Shakespeare is similar to Gogol, and in this sense Shakespeare is just as unnatural as Gogol." Grigoriev's point of view elicited no response until forty years later, in an article by V. V. Rozanov. He resurrected the forgotten word "caricature," but in a patently hostile sense. Since then it has gradually come into literary criticism and scholarship.[5] In 1909 Valery Bryusov was publicly hissed for his modest attempt to repeat the ideas of Grigoriev and Rozanov on Gogol's tendency toward hyperbole. But nowadays no one is surprised by the idea that Gogol is a hyperbolic realist; and little by little, set themes for pupils' compositions, such as "*Dead Souls* as a Mirror of Russian Life," are disappearing even from the secondary schools. We are justified in calling Gogol a realist—until the term, like the majority of our scholarly terms, is accurately defined—in the same sense we call Shakespeare, Swift, Rabelais, Molière, and V. F. Odoevsky realists. But the interrelationships between Gogol's own prose and the prose that came after him cannot be determined simply by reference to "Gogol's influence." The prose of the Natural School is certainly indebted to Gogol in many ways; but in general it moved in a different direction. The problem is further complicated by the fact that Gogol himself began to lean in this same direction toward the end of his career.[6]

Through his artistic devices, Gogol turns his world of existers into a veritable "assemblage of freaks." His persistent return to the same thematic traits enables us to observe a system of types in operation, despite all the individual variations.

In Gogol's world of banality, we can distinguish static banality—the absence of movement—and the dynamic banality of movement as such. There are two circles, as it were: one lower, and one that is comparatively higher, but only comparatively so. The lower circle represents the lowest depths to which people can sink. The type belonging to this circle can be defined as the essence of self-satisfied visceralness and self-satisfied sloth. Well-fed, warmly dressed, surrounded by domestic comfort, along with its inevitable attribute, "a little woman," he aspires to nothing and does nothing if he can possibly help it. Gogol speaks, in Chapter IX, of the "lazybones and stick-in-the-muds" whom "it was impossible to entice out of their houses even with a pressing invitation to partake of a fish chowder costing five hundred roubles, made with sterlets two yards long and served with all sorts of pies that would melt in your mouth." The *even* in this sentence is significant: in Gogol, even dogs are sometimes capable of gastronomic reveries; but in the lower circle, nutrition amounts to "a process of satiation." This last expression comes from "The Dread Wild Boar," in which the gluttonous Ivan Osipovich is depicted. Gluttony of the same sort is seen among the seminary students in "Viy," in the scribe in "The Two Ivans" (who eats nine pies at one sitting), in Sobakevich (a foe of German cuisine), and in "the gentleman of middling means" whose appetite and stomach are envied by Gogol at the beginning of Chapter IV of *Dead Souls*. The "process of satiation" is almost identical in the case of the old-fashioned landowners (in the story of the same name). They are the most attractive of the characters in the lower circle, living as they do at its very top. The most repellent of them—living at the very bottom —is the "dreadful Plyushkin" (an expression that is found in the sketches for *Dead Souls*). He is dreadful by virtue of the fact that the lower circle, to which the others have simply grown accustomed, has for him become a desirable end in itself: though a caricature of stinginess, he too is secretly greedy for food. The visceralness of the "lazybones and stick-in-the-muds" is inseparable from their sloth, which is a manifestation of the same emptiness of life.

Stylistically, this emptiness is pointed up by the use of the word "pursuits" with reference to the idleness of the characters, and by the mock-serious tone in which the narrator recounts the "pursuits" of Ivan Fyodorovich Shponka (he cleans his buttons, reads the fortune-telling book, sets mouse traps, or lies on his bed), of the two Ivans (one lies on his porch, the other on his stoop), of Major Kovalyov, in "The Nose" (he strolls along the Nevsky Prospect), and finally, of Kovalyov's servant, who, "lying on his back, was spitting at the ceiling and hitting one and the same spot rather successfully." The "official," Ivan Petrovich, spends his morning trying to tie a piece of paper to his dog's tail, evidently thinking that this is mere sport by comparison with his real business—the game of whist that provokes a quarrel with his guest ("An Official's Morning"). In Chapter I of *Dead Souls*, the guests "sat down at the card table and did not get up again until supper time. All conversation ceased completely, as is always the case when people finally devote themselves to a really important pursuit." Here Gogol resembles V. F. Odoevsky, who was an implacable foe of card games. Idleness comes in for special emphasis in the case of the Manilovs, a couple lacking any "fervor" whatsoever. The smoking of a pipe and the displays of affection toward the wife, the opening of a sweet little mouth to receive a tasty morsel, the preparation of surprises, long and languid kisses—these are the only things that lend variety to their static existence (*Dead Souls*, Chapter II).

Self-satisfaction is characteristic, in varying degrees, of everyone who belongs to this lower circle. The world of the old-fashioned landowners is one in which "not a single desire wings its way over the fence that surrounds the small yard." Ivan Ivanovich expresses this in his own way in "The Two Ivans": "What don't I have? Fowl, buildings, barns, everything I want, distilled vodka; pear and plum trees in the orchard, poppies, cabbage and peas in the garden....What is there that I don't have?...I'd like to know what there is that I don't have." The only thing Ivan Ivanovich has omitted from his list is Gapka, "a healthy wench with fresh calves and cheeks." And we must suppose that his well-being is essentially no different from that of the Manilovs, or of the Chertokutskys ("The Carriage"). Chertokutsky "had married a rather pretty woman, and with her had gotten a dowry of two hundred souls and several thousand roubles in cash. The cash was promptly spent on a team of six truly splendid horses, gilt locks for the doors, a tame monkey for the house, and a French butler." The terms of endearment—"lovey-dovey," "give me your cheek, sweetie-pie, I'll kiss you"—represent the first signs of what later, in *Dead Souls,* would become Manilovism. Just as self-satisfied are the hero of "The Tale of a Clerk Who Stole Overcoats" (the first version of what eventually became "The Overcoat"); Schiller, in "Nevsky Prospect," who has mapped his whole life out, down to the smallest detail, and has become ossified within the boundaries he has drawn for himself; and Korobochka, in *Dead Souls,* who is completely immobile within the mindless domestic life she leads. All levels of society are as one in this dedication to self-satisfaction— the small Ukrainian landowners, the large Russian landowners, the officials of Petersburg, important and unimportant. And only the "dreadful Plyushkin" has no place in this circle, because of his way of life and his personal obsessions. The hapless Akaky Akakievich, who has replaced the self-satisfied clerk of "The Tale of a Clerk Who Stole Overcoats," cannot fit in here either; and this fact makes a social tragedy out of a story that was originally intended to be comic.

In the chapter on the Manilovs in *Dead Souls,* there is an indication of yet another circle, one that is not completely immobile. "Every man has his particular fervor: one man's fervor is directed at wolf-hounds; another fancies himself a great lover of music, and is wonderfully sensitive to all the profound passages; a third is an expert at dining with gusto; a fourth feels that he can play a part in life ever so slightly higher than the one allotted him; a fifth, with more modest aspirations, sleeps and dreams of promenading with some aide-de-camp, in order to show himself off before friends, relatives, acquaintances, and even strangers; a sixth is endowed with a hand that feels a preternatural desire to turn down the corner of an ace of diamonds or a deuce, whereas the hand of a seventh itches to set things aright somewhere, to get under the skin of a stationmaster or coachman."[7]

Leaving aside the music-lover, who evidently was stuck in between the dog-fancier and the gourmet only for comic effect (he does not exist in earlier drafts), we find the familiar "fervors" of Gogolian heroes: the fourth, fifth, and seventh go together in their hankering for ambition and power; the fervor of the card-player (who is often a card-sharp in Gogol) is closely related to the fervor for enrichment; and there is a whole gallery of "experts at dining with gusto" in Gogol's works. We learn about still another fervor from an earlier work, *Evenings on a Farm Near Dikanka:* "Things are wonderfully arranged in our world. Everybody who lives in it, everybody strives to ape and imitate everyone else. In the old days the judge and the mayor were the only ones in Mirgorod who wore cloth overcoats lined with sheepskin in the winter, while all the lesser officials wore just plain sheepskin; but nowadays the assessor and the reeve have gotten hold of new cloth coats lined with Reshetilov astrakhan. The year before last the office clerk and the district clerk got themselves some dark blue duck at sixty kopecks a yard. The sexton had some nankeen summer trousers and a vest of striped worsted made. In short, everybody's trying to be somebody!" ("Christmas Eve.")

As things turn out, everything that is an essential appurtenance of the lower circle can become the object of a fervor, the object of a dynamic force. Satisfaction with food, clothing, domestic comfort, a "little woman," rank, money—each can develop into a "fervor": elegant eating, dandyism, elemental eroticism, the pursuit of rank and money. These are not *passions,* which might have been capable of creating real dynamics and developing into tragedies. They are *fervors,* which create an illusion of being dynamic. Such dynamics are the essence of Gogol's brand of comedy.

Elegant eating and dandyism are the lower stages of that dynamic process which, in the static circle of existence, finds its counterpart in the "process of satiation" and the process of dressing the body in warm clothing (something that costs Akaky Akakievich so dear). They are elemental forms of a purely physiological estheticism, which is the only kind these "existers" can possibly know: the odd color combinations in the clothing reflect a simple need to irritate the optic nerves, just as elegant eating gratifies a need to irritate the taste buds. A very elemental sociology, based on a unique kind of customary law, is interwoven with this physiological estheticism; and the elementalness is further emphasized by the devices that are characteristic of Gogol's art: hyperbole always combines easily with primitivism. The dynamic possibilities inherent in the theme of elegant eating had already been suggested in those parts of *Evenings on a Farm Near Dikanka* that deal with everyday life, especially where we find Rudy Panko exclaiming: "My Lord, what dishes there are in this world! As soon as you start eating then, it's a real treat, I'm telling you—delicious beyond description!" To the mentality of the lower circles, even heaven seems the ultimate in gastronomical desires: "May he rest in peace, may he eat in the other world only wheat cakes and poppyseed cakes in honey." Ukrainian national cuisine is depicted in every detail in "Ivan Fyodorovich Shponka"; and in "Old-Fashioned Landowners," insofar as the story remains within the realm of the comic, the only hint of dynamics (rather, a parody of dynamics) comes in connection with good eating.

Khlestakov's gastronomic fervor, in *The Inspector General,* is naive and simple-minded. Like all his fervors, it finds its expression in fluent and inspired yarn-spinning, when his imagination conjures up quail costing a thousand roubles, a hot meat pie with ice cream (in the first draft), or soup that has come straight from Paris. D. S. Merezhkovsky rightly emphasized the significance of Khlestakov's statement: "I love to eat. After all, man lives in order to pluck the flowers of pleasure."[18] Among the blandishments of St. Petersburg that the mayor dreams about after he is suddenly galvanized into motion are sea-eels and smelts. In addition to the crudely self-satiating Sobakevich and the delicately self-satiating Manilov, *Dead Souls* adds to the list a wonder-working police chief and the tragi-comic figure of Kopeikin. Strictures imposed by the censor forced Gogol to endow Kopeikin with a gastronomical fervor too: he dreams of a cutlet and French wine. The Italian abbot who is the tutor of the hero of "Rome" also takes his place in the company of Gogol's Ukrainian and Russian gourmets. The high point in this whole gallery of gourmets is represented by Pyotr Petrovich Petukh, in Part 2 of *Dead Souls.*

The dandies belong to the same lower dynamic circle as do the gourmets. Gogol owes little to the tradition of the dandy unmasked (male and female), which had its beginnings in the satirical literature of the eighteenth century and passed over into the nineteenth. He employs the same stylistic devices as he does to depict elegant dining: ultra-refinement in the choice of colors (as in the choice of taste-sensations). For example, with reference to food: "a sterlet chowder with burbots and soft roe...followed by an open-top pie or a pie with sheat-fish tail filling" (*Dead Souls*); with reference to clothing, "a brown frock-coat with blue sleeves, or a tail-coat of scintillant whortleberry hue" (*Dead Souls*). Typically, this fervor undergoes comparatively little development; there is a touch of the dandy, as a secondary characteristic, in Ivan Ivanovich Pererepenko ("The Two Ivans") and in Chertkov ("The Portrait"); it is much stronger in Khlestakov (in the first version of *The Inspector General*) and in Chichikov.

As *The Inspector General* underwent revision, the dandy-element in Khlestakov was toned down. In the first version, he discourses on the way provincial "enlightenment" differs from that of the capital ("after all, these piggish landowners, I know, wear sacks instead of tail-coats," etc.), and in the boasting scene (Act III), he lets his imagination run on about the way tail-coats and trousers can be made in Petersburg without any delay. In the 1836 version, all this has already been abridged; and in the final version, the only thing left is the sentence: "No, it's better to go hungry if only you can arrive home in a suit made in Petersburg." Evidently Khlestakov is meant to combine all the fervors, not to embody any one in particular. But the pronouncement on "enlightenment," which Gogol took away from Khlestakov, was given to Ikharev, the hero of *The Gamblers*: "I can undertake something that promotes education....I will go to Moscow, I will dine at Yar's. I can dress in the style of the capital, I can become equal to others, and perform the duty of an enlightened man." The exaggerated seriousness of tone is a favorite comic device of Gogol's. Podkolyosin is serious, in *Marriage,* when he makes a connection between rank and the colors of tail-coats: "I'm of the opinion that black tails are some how more dignified. Colored ones are much more suitable for secretaries, titular councilors and other such small fry—there's something of the milksop about them." The "conversation between two ladies," in *Dead Souls,* has become a classic: they talk about the latest fashions as something very significant and mysterious. In Chichikov the dandy-fervor reaches its greatest intensity: Part 1 delineates traits which in Part 2 will undergo development in those scenes where he is buying cloth and examining ready-made clothing.

The fervors of the dandies are set in higher relief by the tragic figure of Akaky Akakievich Bashmachkin, who feels drawn to that minimum which has been given as a birthright to the "exister" of the lower circle. Something resembling a dynamic force stirs in Akaky Akakievich as well: "The most bold and daring thoughts even flashed through his head: shouldn't he really have marten-fur put on the collar?" His tragedy consists in the fact that he is *unable* to dream in any other way. The psychological contrast with those who *do not want* to dream in any other way is strengthened by a repetition of the same stylistic devices: Bashmachkin's new overcoat is described in the same deliberate detail as is Chichikov's new dress suit.

In Gogol's heroes, a yearning for tasty food and for good clothing is sometimes combined in a more general yearning for *comfort.* As with other instances we have mentioned, this is most fully developed in two mutually complementary characters: Khlestakov and Chichikov. Khlestakov's ideals remain hidden in the final version of the play, which omits his descriptions of the houses in Petersburg with their columns and vases, their pools and cascades; but his dream of acquiring one of the famous Iokhim carriages is still present. Zakatishchev and Sobachkin, in *The Order of St. Vladimir* (evidently they are one and the same character), dream of acquiring a carriage. And interest in a carriage is what sets the comic situation in motion in the story of the same name. Yaichnitsa, in *Marriage* (and particularly in the earlier version entitled *The Suitors*), strives after domestic comfort and material well-being in various forms. Comfort of one kind or another is the object of conscious and intensive efforts on Chichikov's part. With it in mind, he undergoes a "prolonged fast" in his youth, and at the very first opportunity acquires a good cook, fine Holland-linen shirts, a splendid suit, and "soap that imparts a smoothness to the skin." Even later, he continues to dream of acquiring a "substantial household." Connected with this is another fervor which, because of its intensity and the possibility that it might at any moment turn into tragedy, can actually be called a passion. This is the passion for gain; and Gogol himself uses the word "passion" in this sense precisely when he is speaking of Chichikov.

On one occasion, in a casual jotting, Gogol called gold—wealth—a "terrible gift." Twice he depicted it as the gift of an unclean power: in "St. John's Eve" and in "The Portrait." He was not always able to treat it comically, except when it was acquired for purposes known to be insignificant, or when it did not actually fall into someone's hands. Khlestakov, who almost instinctively stuffs his pockets in the vague hope of acquiring a suit from Ruch's and a carriage from Iokhim's, is comic. So is Peppe ("Rome"), who "was firmly convinced that he would be a rich man," and ended up with nothing, after spending all his money on the lottery. Ikharev is doubly comic: he has failed with "Adelaida Ivanovna" (as he calls his pack of cards), and has therefore had to give up his dream of "dressing in the style of the capital... performing the duty of an enlightened man." The successes and failures of Chichikov are depicted as comic, because both are determined by paltry aspirations; it is only in Part 2 that the comic aspect undergoes erosion, for special reasons that lay deep in Gogol's personal and artistic development. The passion for enrichment enters the realm of insignificant daydreaming when it is the means for creating comfort. The word "comfort" is not Gogol's: as a general term it was used somewhat later by Alexey Pisemsky (in the novel *A Thousand Souls* [*Tysiacha dush*, 1858]), but in precisely the same sense in which we have been talking about a dynamic force of the lower variety, the "fervors" of Gogol's heroes.

Comfort, in the form of a cozy domestic life, is not complete without a "little woman"; and the yearning for such a woman takes its place in the catalogue of fervors, inasmuch as it is predetermined by a primitive psychology, combined with a no less primitive sociology ("it's a Christian deed, even one that is essential for the fatherland"). In Khlestakov, Pirogov, Kovalyov, and Nozdryov, comfort is a vague instinct rather than a fervor. Khlestakov can gratify his fantasy equally well with "two pretty merchants' daughters" who, he thinks, are in love with him, and with "pretty little shop attendants on the Nevsky Prospect." He instinctively swings back and forth between Maria Antonovna, the mayor's daughter ("so fresh, such rosy lips...and she wears such nice calico"), and Anna Andreevna, the mayor's wife. The examples and quotations here are taken from the first version of the play. In the later ones, this particular fervor is toned down, as are the others, although a fresh play of fantasy by association is added: "You'll go up to some pretty little daughter...."[9] Similarly, Kovalyov ("The Nose") is attracted by Podtochina's daughter and by a pretty girl he encounters; Nozdryov and Lieutenant Kuvshinnikov (*Dead Souls*) have their fun with women; and Pirogov ("Nevsky Prospect") almost instinctively rushes off in pursuit of a pretty blonde, just as Kopeikin (*Dead Souls*) trots off after a stately English girl. Even Akaky Akakievich, after having a champagne supper, "was on the point of breaking into a run, Lord knows why, after a lady of some sort"; but he stopped himself at once, "feeling surprised at this impulse that had appeared out of nowhere." But fatefully, he is unable to move even into the realm of elemental physiological fervors. Gogol employs a device of style to depict the physiological nature of this yearning for women: it is linked with elegant eating. At the beginning of "Leaving the Theater," the first few members of the audience who emerge switch the topic of conversation from a young actress ("not bad-looking, but there's still something missing") to the fresh green peas at a "new restaurant," from green peas to trousers, from trousers to cards. And Nozdryov, after telling about Kuvshinnikov's philandering, recalls that "a lot of marvellous fish and sturgeon were brought in."

There is another type of erotic fervor, in which dreams of a "little woman" are inseparable from dreams of a cozy domestic life generally. For instance, in *Marriage* Kochkaryov paints the following picture by way of trying to arouse Podkolyosin's interest: a couch, a dog, a siskin, needlework, "and suddenly a little woman will sit down right beside you, such a pretty little thing, and she'll put her little hand...." Podkolyosin, whom Kochkaryov "keeps in a state of sensual intoxication," promptly agrees: "Damn it all, certainly when you come to think of it, what nice little hands there are, why, my friend, they're just like milk."[10] It is only in the intensity of their fervor, not in its essence, that four of the heroes in this play differ in their attitude toward the "little woman": Kochkaryov, Podkolyosin, Zhevakin ("a great lover of female amplitude") and Yaichnitsa (who peeks through the keyhole with just as much curiosity as the others, but who is essentially more interested in houses and droshkies).

And finally, Chichikov, the brilliant synthesis, the combination of all the fervors, is even less capable in his daydreams of separating the "little woman" from all the other items essential to a happy existence. After his first meeting with the governor-general's young daughter, he begins to think of having a "nice little woman": "Well, if this girl were to be given, let's say, 200,000 roubles or so in dowry, she could make a very, very *tasty little morsel*" (stresses supplied). Usually he dreams of "a life with all the contentments, all the comforts: carriages, a splendidly built house, tasty dinners"; but after he snacks and drinks at the house of the chief of police, one more temptation appears: "a blond bride with a blush and a dimple on her right cheek." And in his concern with "posterity," these same dreams also take on a tinge of very elemental sociology.

Among the special fervors as such is the pursuit of rank and sometimes decorations. Here the connection with general material well-being is the most remote: ranks are not a means but an end. The very substitution of an illusory goal for goals that are potentially genuine ("benefit to the state," coming from the lips of the mayor in *The Inspector General*, can only sound like irony) creates a dynamism that is comic in nature. Purely physiological fervors did give some hint of dynamism, but did not as yet make for the kind of true dynamism capable of shaping the structure of a story or play. Dynamism of this kind is possible only where there are social overtones. Gogol consciously made social dynamics the criterion for his own comedy, and said so in "Leaving the Theater," where he set "the electricity of rank, money capital, a profitable marriage" in opposition to the love-intrigue. He showed the physiological characteristics of insignificant people, and in addition, their view of the world, which amounts to a fixed belief in social barriers and clichés that have been established by others. Insignificant daydreams also flow in well-worn channels. Hence the inevitable misunderstandings between insignificant people and those with a broader outlook. For Maria Alexandrovna (in "A Fragment"), her son's fiancée is a strumpet simply because her father has no position; Mr. P. (in "Leaving the Theater") is honestly bewildered as to "how an actual state councilor can be a silly goose." The words of A Gentleman of Weighty Position (also in "Leaving the Theater") make it evident that the Table of Ranks is at the basis of their view of the world: "Today he'll say: such-and-such a councilor's no good, and tomorrow he'll say that God doesn't exist. After all, its just a step from one to the other."

This view of the world is what determines the statics and dynamics of this circle of society. The Important Personage, in "The Overcoat," feels comfortable only in a society where everyone is "of almost the same rank." An "unimportant" Russian has "a strong passion for making the acquaintance of someone who is even only one rank higher than himself." In "The Nose," Kovalyov finds it gratifying to call himself both a major and a state councilor. In Chapter I of Dead Souls, Chichikov says "Your Excellency" by mistake to the vice-governor general. Khlestakov's fantasy runs in ready-made channels too, particularly in the final version of the play when, in Act III, Scene 6, he begins with a very modest fabrication, and then his imagination soars higher and higher, with incredible rapidity, through the following stages: (1) maybe you think I'm nothing but a copy-clerk; no, the head of the department is on a friendly footing with me; (2) they wanted to make me *even* a collegiate assessor, but I thought: what for?; (3) I played a game of whist with the ambassadors; (4) there were counts and princes in the anteroom, sometimes a minister too; (5) on packages addressed to me they sometimes *even* write "Your Excellency"; (6) once I was *even* head of a department; (7) the State Council itself is afraid of me; (8) tomorrow I'm being promoted straight to field marshal. This symmetrical structure is largely the achievement of the final version. In the earlier ones, time and again Khlestakov tries to curb his own flights of fancy, but to no avail: before long he begins to contradict himself, and goes to extremes as he tells about the decoration he has received and about heading a ministry.[11] In the flush of inspiration, he unwittingly expresses the same hopes and aspirations as the mayor, who in the last act starts dreaming of becoming a general and wearing a blue ribbon across his shoulder. The insignificant Khlestakov twists the insignificant officials around his finger merely by means of the "electricity" of decorations and of the Table of Ranks.

This is comedy. And still within the realm of comedy are the director, in "Diary of a Madman," who is laughed at by his own dog for coveting a decoration, and Barsukov, in the surviving fragment entitled "An Official's Morning," who is also trying to get himself a decoration. But another possibility glimmers in the basic idea underlying *The Order of St. Vladimir*: an absurd view of the world, when taken to the extreme, produces an absurd outcome, which is no longer funny but terrible. Barsukov loses his mind. "Diary of a Madman" ends the same way: in Poprishchin's delirious mind, the absurd image of the King of Spain is a hyperbolization of the Table of Ranks with which Poprishchin is familiar: "There is a king in Spain....I am that king....I don't understand how I could have thought and imagined that I was a titular councilor." Here psychological comedy is completely overshadowed by social tragedy, yet the tragedy is also psychological, because Poprishchin does not belong entirely to the world of insignificant people: his love for the director's daughter is not the same as a simple attraction to a "little woman."

Gogol's approach to physiological and social fervors was anything but psychological. The term "the physiological tendency" appeared in the 1840s with a somewhat different meaning: of those who included themselves in the "Gogol School," Pisemsky was undoubtedly "physiological" in the same sense as Gogol. Gogol was being physiological and not psychological when he created caricatures; by reducing psychology to physiology, he made his primitive characters particularly striking and all of a piece. Vasily Rozanov, who was fascinated by Dostoevsky's psychological approach, could not forgive Gogol for this particular technique.[12]

But Gogol is not always a physiologist, because he is not always a purely comic writer. Time and again he takes us to the very limits that the comic can go: psychology triumphs over physiology; elemental sociology takes on greater complexity; and the possibility of tragedy appears. Just where these limits are has not yet been established by the critics, who have been mesmerized by the formula of "laughter through tears," which supposedly applies to everything in Gogol's work.[13] Apparently the comic goes as far as it can without ceasing to be comic when: (1) feelings that cannot be reduced to "fervors" arise in an insignificant mind, as in "Diary of a Madman"; (2) social concerns push physiology into the background, as in "Diary of a Madman" and "The Overcoat"; (3) the fervor itself, or an insignificant existence as a whole, appears in a different light to the author himself: he feels drawn to this other world (as was the case in the first two idylls), or else he tries to find some meaning in the world of insignificant people and even in their fervors. Hereby he strives to find some justification for these people, as well as for the attraction he unconsciously feels toward them. This is the case with Gogol's third idyll.

CHAPTER XI

THE THIRD IDYLL

After returning to Russian for the second time, in 1841-42, Gogol again left for six long years, deep in the grip of a spiritual crisis, which was aggravated by external factors as well: his painful struggle with the "Asiatic censorship." The moralism which had grown out of a heightened self-esteem he now began to direct more and more toward himself, toward the "nurturing of his soul"—a term which dates from 1842 and becomes a favorite of his from then on. At the same time, he gained greater experience in the whole matter of forming closer ties with other people. He made new friendships, with Yazykov, with A. O. Smirnova, with A. P. Tolstoy, with the elder Sheremeteva (who called herself Gogol's spiritual mother), and with the Vielgorsky family. (Gogol had especially tender feelings for Anna Vielgorskaya, whom he later intended to marry, in 1848 or 1850, according to a not entirely trustworthy story.)[1]

By this time, the esthetic fascination of Rome had worn off. Now Gogol lived more often in various towns in Germany, in Ostend, and elsewhere, for reasons of health, to be sure, but obviously with no real regret either. And whenever he returned to Italy, he chose Naples, not Rome. He had now completely outgrown the phase of estheticism; his extreme individualism had assumed a moralistic form; and he was moving in the direction of religion. He proceeded with uncertain steps, feelings of hope alternating with a despairing sense of failure. At first, particularly in 1843, he buoyed and, as it were, mesmerized himself by reading Russian Orthodox Church literature. Later, from the end of 1844 onward, he saw that he actually had achieved something in his personal life. Gradually he was overcoming the individualism that was of such recent vintage, but he was not moving in a straight line: there were fresh waves of self-doubt, followed by waves of self-satisfaction with what he had achieved. A writer who had entertained such fond hopes of "nurturing" himself began to think he was entitled to "nurture" others. The details of Gogol's religious development do not fall within the scope of this book, nor does a study of his mental illness; as V. V. Zenkovsky rightly noted, an interest in the latter merely complicates the biographer's task.[2] The only thing about which we have no doubt is that the agonizing periods of melancholia (which had organic bases) created in Gogol's mind an aura of gloom, which he felt must be dispelled by light, and that he found this light in religion. There was no abrupt turning-point; there was an evolution; but it is only from the first half of the 1840s onward that we can speak of a religious period (in the narrow sense of the term) in his life.

A new complication was created by the serious illnesses he suffered in 1845 and 1846. As in 1840, he regarded his recovery as miraculous. This again produced waves of pridefulness and self-satisfaction with what he had achieved, and again convinced him that he had been specially chosen and was entitled to teach others. The recovery made him look on the "nurturing of his soul" as having been completed, and it turned him back onto the path of moralism. He left Russia with two projects in mind: to complete *Dead Souls*, and to make a pilgrimage to Jerusalem. In his mind they competed for priority: one seemed a necessary condition of the other. Both were bound up with his hope of attaining a new stage in his inner life, when it would be possible to make a summing-up of his entire past. From the very beginning, his plan for the continuation of *Dead Souls* bore a tinge of moralism. But now, in 1845, with moralism once again intensified, this plan underwent a complete transformation. A moral feat, Gogol thought, should consist of showing people neither the disgusting (as he had been doing in all his work, including Part 1 of *Dead Souls*), nor the beautiful, but rather the paths to the beautiful. This purpose was not yet evident in the version of Part 2 of *Dead Souls* that was written between the end of 1843 and the beginning of 1845. Apparently he burned this version during the crucial summer of 1845, precisely because, as he later explained it, the paths to the beautiful had not yet been disclosed to him.

We know nothing about the lost chapters.[3] After Gogol burned them, however, *Dead Souls* had to be cast in a different manner. But just when was that to be? Even before destroying the version of *Dead Souls* in question, he had conceived the idea for "a small work whose unsensational title will create no stir in present-day society but which is necessary to many," perhaps fearing that death would cut him down before he could produce anything. The plan was temporarily shelved, but he returned to it after recovering from his illness of 1845, when "[he] imagined that...[he] had reached higher stages" (letter to N. F. Pavlov, before August 24, 1848). And he began trying to hasten the onset of this new stage, in which he placed such high hopes. He imagined it would begin in Jerusalem, where he had formerly hoped to go after completing *Dead Souls*. "Seeing that it would be some time yet before I could gain mastery of my *Dead Souls*," he wrote S. T. Aksakov (August 28, 1847), "I hastened to begin speaking of those matters which were preoccupying me and which I was preparing to develop or create in living images and characters." Thus, exactly one year after Gogol burned *Dead Souls*, a book appeared that was unsensational in title but unexpectedly sensational in its reception: *Selected Passages from Correspondence with Friends*.

Gogol did not avail himself of any "correspondence with friends"; only a very few of the articles were variations on ideas that had gone into actual letters. It is a purely literary work, consisting of a series of articles, most (though not all) of which are cast in the form of letters, some addressed to real people, some to fictional ones. As a literary work, the book has some definite traditions behind it. These have not yet been established.[4] It is written in that same rhetorical style which was beginning to take form in "A Terrible Vengeance" and which reached full development in *Dead Souls*. There is a tendency toward rhythmic sentences and toward a distinctive word-order which is not infrequently found in the rhetorical passages in Gogol's letters proper, and which seems to be either a direct stylization of Biblical syntax, or a stylization of his own earlier stylizations. The abstract theme required dryness and simplicity, rather than a profusion of images, as was the case in the prose fiction. This manner, when combined with the solemn rhythm and phraseology, sometimes seems like nothing more than rhetoric. Perhaps this is what struck Belinsky when he wrote—with both the substance and the style of the book in mind—that Gogol had been abandoned by both "intelligence and talent" (letter to Gogol, July 15, 1847).

For readers who had missed the moralistic touches in "The Overcoat," *Dead Souls* and "Leaving the Theater," and who had had no idea of the direction in which Gogol had been developing, this book came as a complete surprise. People had been expecting humorous works. There had been rumors of something called "Diary of a Russian General in Italy," which supposedly had already been written and was very funny—and suddenly there appeared a collection of confessions, exhortations, and prophecies. People had been accustomed to thinking of Gogol as a social satirist, because of such works as "Diary of a Madman," *The Inspector General,* and *Dead Souls*—and suddenly there appeared a defense of autocracy and even serfdom. Gogol's contemporaries were entitled to feel indignant about the unexpected betrayal of what they regarded as an obligation to society. From today's vantage point, it no longer seems unexpected: the book is in line with all of Gogol's development as a man and artist. The book actually grew out his own awareness of this fact.

Selected Passages was not a full spiritual confession on Gogol's part. For all his arrogance at that point, for all his inflated sense of achievement as far as "higher stages" were concerned during the writing of the book, he did not presume to represent for Russia as a whole what he wished to represent in his personal life for certain of his friends (notably A. O. Smirnova and A. M. Vielgorskaya): a teacher of religion. He contented himself with playing the role of a teacher of morality (which, to be sure, included esthetics, sociology and politics). Only in certain passages did he betray his recent agitation, more in those which gave evidence of lyrical excitation and bordered on despair than in those which were self-confidently didactic. In general, the book was more closely linked to his past than to his present.

S. T. Aksakov noticed in Gogol a sense of "the need to escape from this dreadful assemblage of human freaks, the need for reconciliation."[5] This problem shaped Gogol's new plan for *Dead Souls* and was raised in *Selected Passages* as well. In one of the articles in the latter, he put it explicitly: "Everyone has forgotten one trifling thing: everyone has forgotten that the paths and ways to this *bright* future lie hidden precisely in this *dark* and *tangled* present....But lead me, for one, into a knowledge of the present. Do not be troubled by abominations, and give me any abomination!...since I have begun to look more closely at abominations, I have brightened in spirit: exoduses, means and paths have begun to open up before me..." ("What Is the Wife of a Provincial Governor"). When "exoduses from abominations" were found, then what Gogol calls "the work of his soul" would be completed. In another passage he wrote: "My heroes have not yet detached themselves completely from me...but I do not like my abominations and I do not hold their hand, as my heroes do....I have already delivered myself from many of my nasty qualities by transferring them to my heroes" (third letter on *Dead Souls*). But this was not enough for him. The business of ridding himself of his own abominations by representing them in exaggerated form in his heroes was now replaced by a new task: that of giving a psychological account of all the good and bad possibilities that lay within him and his heroes both. The old world of freaks was being subjected to re-examination and re-evaluation.

The main "abomination" that was brought to light in *The Inspector General* was bribe-taking. Behind this lay a long literary tradition, going back to Sumarokov and Novikov in the eighteenth century. But by 1842, Gogol was interpreting the play in such a way as to *justify* the mayor. The mayor, he says, is not bad by nature; he is only weak in the face of the temptations offered by life and the environment. "He has had no time to take a harder look at life...he has had no malicious desire to oppress people...he is even thinking about repenting some day." In 1844, Gogol advised S. T. Aksakov's two sons to "adopt a kindlier attitude toward bribe-takers": "sometimes they are not at all bad, there are even some who can be moved by a well-intended admonition."[6] In *Selected Passages,* Gogol now looks for the reasons for bribe-taking, and finds them in the extravagance of wives. This particular instance is generalized: all one's associates, all the "good" people are to blame in general because they have pushed the "ignoble" people away. "Perhaps some one of them [the ignoble] was not born dishonest...perhaps one drop of love would have been enough to return him to the strait and narrow path" ("Easter Sunday"). In short, "there are no guilty people in the world." This is so because there are no innocent people: all are equally guilty of evil because they do not wish to fight against it. "We are summoned here to do battle," Gogol exclaims in the article "Parting Words"; but to his mind, this battle is a matter, as it later is to Tolstoy, of bringing influence to bear on each person individually. He naively believes in the power of moral persuasion, even for the eradication of social ills. It is enough to tell an "honest but myopic rich man" that his wealth is a temptation to others and to paint him a picture of hunger, and "his hair will stand on end." It is enough to explain to fashionable ladies that they are the cause of bribe-taking, and "the thought of a hat or a fashionable dress will not enter their heads" ("It Is Necessary to Travel Through

Russia").

The people who only recently were "freaks" now proved at bottom to be good. One must know how to bring this good to light; one must "sense in the freak the ideal which the freak has come to caricature." Everyone should buckle down to the task of general reform. A woman ought to encourage, reform and direct her husband; the landowner should do the same for his peasants, the superior for his subordinates, the writer for his readers. This work should yield fruit, because within each "freak" lies *hidden* good or *distorted* good, or both at the same time: "If you recognize a cheat not only as a cheat but also as a man, if you recognize all the spiritual powers which have been given to him for the good, and which he has turned into evil or has not used at all, then you will be able to hold him up to reproach for himself, and in such a way that he will find no place to hide for himself...and only then will you sense how noble is our Russian nature even in a cheat." Along with the "noble cheat" Gogol names another similar combination of contrasts: "the honest bribe-taker."[7]

The turning of *distorted* qualities toward the good has a special significance in Gogol's theory and practice of reform. What he says about the theater is equally applicable to human psychology. "My friend, we have been called into this world not to shatter and destroy but...to direct everything toward the good—even that which man has already corrupted and turned into evil" ("On the Theater, On a One-Sided View of the Theater, and On One-Sidedness Generally," in *Selected Passages*). In this idea of not denying but transforming the world of freaks lie the roots of Gogol's ethics, social theory and politics. His ethical views develop entirely out of his re-evaluation of "fervors." *Ambition* is the "fervor" of the Important Personage in "The Overcoat," of Barsukov in *The Order of St. Vladimir,* of the director in "Diary of a Madman," of the mayor in *The Inspector General.* Now this particular fervor proves to be one of the useful "weapons of incitation," which has simply been defiled by man (letter to A. O. Smirnova, December 24, 1844). In the article "On *The Odyssey,* as Translated by Zhukovsky," one of the signs of the times is identified as "an unaccountable thirst to be something other than what one is; perhaps this comes from a beautiful source [which incites man] to be better." Gogol wishes to find such "beautiful sources" for every "abomination," if the abomination is not merely a matter of physiology.

The *passion for gain,* with all its accompanying features—cheating and miserliness—is also traced to a "beautiful source": energy, resourcefulness in practical matters, love of reason, and the running of an orderly household. These qualities play an enormous part in the idyll of a reformed world of freaks which Gogol pictures in his imagination, and he is therefore specially persistent in searching for this "beautiful source" in the heroes of his recent works. Such a re-evaluation is indicated in the sketches for *Dead Souls:* "He [Chichikov] did not even stop to think why it was that Manilov, who was good and even noble by nature, lived a futile life in the country...whereas Sobakevich,

142

a cheat, a man who was anything but noble in spirit and in feelings, nonetheless did not bring his peasants to ruin and did not allow them to be drunkards or idlers; or why Korobochka, the widow of a collegiate assessor, who had never read any books at all except the Book of Hours—and even that not very carefully—who had not learned any of the fine arts expect perhaps fortune-telling with cards, nonetheless knew how to fill trunks and boxes with roubles, and to do this in such a way that order of some sort was nonetheless preserved in the village: souls were not mortgaged, and the church, though not wealthy, was maintained." It is clear that Gogol sets greater value on the distorted good in Sobakevich and Korobochka than on the good in Manilov, even though he does note the latter's kindness and nobleness. The regeneration of Chichikov is conceived of along these same lines, according to the plans for Part 2, where it makes its appearance, and Part 3, where it was evidently meant to be accomplished. He, and perhaps Plyushkin as well,[8] were supposed to become ideal proprietors and householders. There is already a hint of this in Part 1: "And perhaps in this very same Chichikov the passion that draws him on no longer comes from within, and perhaps his cold existence contains that which later will cast a man down into the dust and on his knees before the wisdom of the heavens. And it is still a mystery why this figure has appeared in this poem that is now coming forth into the world" (Chapter XI). Little by little we are beginning to get to the bottom of this mystery.

Gogol had long been thinking of using the ideal of the "beautiful person," the "epic hero" (bogatyr'), to set off the world of freaks. He had found such a hero in past times, when he was writing "Taras Bulba." But now, in Part 1 of Dead Souls, we find the narrator dreaming of a contemporary epic hero, "a man endowed with divine prowess": "Is it not here, is it not in thee [Russia] that a limitless idea will come to birth, since thou thyself art without end? Is it not here that an epic hero will appear, here where there is room for him to develop and stride about?" This is the dream. It is also present in the article on Russian poetry in Selected Passages (which was written, by Gogol's own acknowledgment, "at three different stages" in his life), where he speaks of Derzhavin's use of hyperbole: "The mind is at a loss to determine whence came the hyperbolic sweep of his speech. Is it a residue from the legendary times of our Russian epic heroes, which soar above our land to this very day in the form of some dark prophecy, prefiguring something higher that awaits us?"[9] But this very same book contains lines which betray a new attitude toward the image of the "epic hero." They occur in the second letter on Dead Souls, which is devoted to an interpretation, and in essence, a re-evaluation of Gogol's recent Slavophile vision.[10] The painful anguish and the frenzied prophecies have given way to a moralistic didacticism: "In Russia one can now become an epic hero at every turn. Every calling and every position require heroic qualities. Each of us has so disgraced the sacred nature of his calling and position that heroic energies are required to elevate him to his lawful height." In this new concept, the epic hero is not to overshadow the freaks, but is himself to rise up out of the world of freaks, in an office in the government bureaucracy. The ordinary sort of freak was defined by "fervors"; the ordinary sort of epic hero should be a product of these same fervors, now transformed. Chichikov stood at the center of Gogol's satire; the same Chichikov was to stand at the center of Gogol's idyll.

In his first two idylls, Gogol betrayed an unconscious attraction to the world of "existers," which he himself ridiculed. This was evidence of the strong ties that still bound him to the milieu that had nurtured him. Generally speaking, he was in the process of rising above this milieu during the years of estheticism and incipient moralism: any feelings of attraction to his native soil at that point were experienced as temporary escapes from himself. Now he was in the process of creating his third idyll. He was painting a picture of the idyllic domestic, social and political life of morally transformed people. He returned—but now consciously—to his native soil, to the old traditions, and made the idealized old-fashioned farmstead a stronghold in the battle against evil. And he gave his return an ideological foundation. This happened at a time when he was reading intensively in *ascetic* literature, which one might think would have impelled him to deny material well-being instead of idealizing it. But the social tradition proved more powerful than all the others, although we must remember that there was also a definite literary tradition which corresponded to the social tradition, and that *Selected Passages* did not represent the final phase of his ideological development in every respect.

Thus, the new "epic hero," no longer a folk-tale figure but an ordinary person, was to be an idealized *proprietor*. "The household of the soul" is a very common term in Gogol's writings in those years. He considers it possible only insofar as it is based on "the domestic household." The connection between the two is established in *Selected Passages,* in the article whose very title makes his purposes clear: "What a Wife Can Be for Her Husband in the Simple Domestic Life, Given the Present-Day Order of Things in Russia." Gogol thinks that his prescription should be relevant to his own times and accessible to all, and he does not suspect that he is creating a new utopia. Here the regulation of domestic life gradually prepares the way to an overcoming of "fervors": Gogol advises the wife to divide money into seven piles and to "cut down on the expenditure of each pile," so that something will be left over for the poor. The same pedagogical tone can be heard in his actual correspondence during those same years. He often gives his sisters and friends advice on how to regulate their time, their way of life, their households—all in the same hope of indicating a very easy and sure path leading to the transformation of their personal lives. But his appeal to the *housewife* to maintain a well-run household and encourage her weak-willed husband has a special significance. An essential condition of material well-being for a philistine of the "lower circle" had been a "little woman." Yaichnitsa, Podkolyosin and Chichikov cannot separate their desire for such a woman from their desire for comfort generally. If the household itself is to undergo transformation, then so too should the "little woman"—into an ideal housekeeper.

After the idealization of the well-run household[11] came the idealization of wealth. The very defense and advocacy of the well-run household presupposed the possibility of wealth. No matter how strongly Gogol recommends economy as a salutary practice, with something put aside for the poor, he still considers expenditures "for replacing furniture, for the purchase of a new carriage" entirely legitimate, and he thinks of the most modest way of life in terms of "having no more than one carriage and a pair of horses... four courses at table" ("What a Wife Can Be..."). In Part 2 of *Dead Souls*, which is supposed to indicate "paths to the beautiful," Kostanzhoglo starts out as an ideal household manager and, by an absolutely imperceptible process, attains to wealth; and Murazov represents the ideal of a rich man. Gogol's notebook for 1846 contains the following fragment: "Men of wealth, remember above all that you possess a terrible gift. Remember what the Gospel teaches about the dangers of riches and the difficulty a rich man has in achieving salvation. But riches have been given to you, and you do not have the right to refuse. You should remember that you are stewards of God." At a superficial glance, this is an advocacy of denial, but in fact it is a justification of wealth. Here Gogol is not only selecting what is most convenient for his own purposes from examples in the Gospels; he is also making an arbitrary intepretation of what he has selected, as for example when he says "you do not have the right to refuse." This particular justification of wealth was confined to the notebook. In the article entitled "The Russian Landowner" in *Selected Passages,* Gogol provided another justification, which makes wealth merely a reward for piety: "in every village that has been touched by the Christian life, the peasants are shovelling up silver." But here too he indiscriminately brings in a phrase from the Gospels—"all these things shall be added unto you" —which certainly does not refer to the shovelling up of silver.

One more step and the idealization of any household leads to the idealization of a landowning, serf-based economy. For Gogol this transition was utterly painless. Strange as it may seem, the ground on which he based his defense of serfdom was mainly the smooth functioning of the established norm, the harmonious operation of the system. The main thing he saw in the serf-system was good household management. Hence his sympathy for Korobochka and Sobakevich, who "did not bring their peasants to ruin." A didactic moralism also comes into play here: the landowner ought to be a center and source of personal influence; each landowner can "regenerate" his peasants to a better life. Finally, once he set forth on the path of transforming rather than denying what existed, Gogol had to proceed logically, step by step. His approach to the social structure was predetermined by the general direction in which his moralistic utopian system tended, and by those factors of environment and tradition which shaped the direction and would make themselves even more strongly felt as time went on. Gogol had only to provide all this with a religious underpinning as well; and he did so with particular indiscrimination on this occasion. The Russian landowner is exhorted to do something that must have filled even the most moderate liberals of the time with indignation: "Tell them [the peasants] ...that you are compelling them to toil, because man has been condemned by God to earn his bread in toil and sweat....And everything you say, reinforce at once with the words of Holy Scripture, point out to them with your finger the very letters in which this is written, compel each one to cross himself before it," etc. ("The Russian Landowner"). Now Gogol is no longer appealing to the spirit but to the letter of the words, since he is referring to peasants and there is no need to stand on ceremony. But even the spirit of the text he cites has its own history in Russian literature. Satirists of the eighteenth century had mocked landowners who thought that "peasants are not human beings" and that "it is precisely peasants of whom it is said: in the sweat of your brow earn your bread" (*The Drone [Truten']*, 1769, pp.23-24). Gogol did not in the least suspect that he was interpreting the Bible in the spirit of Novikov's Bezrassud when he said that it was precisely the peasants who must toil in the sweat of their brow, and the landowners had only to compel them to do so. [12]

Gogol affirms that every man has a right to a small household on condition that it is in a state of equilibrium with the "household of his soul" and has been established in the name of the "heavenly household." This same state of equilibrium is also required of the landowner's household, in the name of the requirements imposed by the "heavenly landowner." (This last image is very characteristic of Gogol and is taken from the fragment entitled "Landowners.") And he bids the landowner concern himself not only with the "household of his soul" but with that of all his subordinates as well. Furthermore, the landowner is to provide guidance for "his" local priest and act, as it were, as the highest local spiritual authority. This theocratic oddity was set forth in all its details, which were thrown out by the frightened censors (to wit, the priest must not only choose his sermons at the landowner's behest, but must also accompany him "in the capacity of an assistant" as he goes about his work).

Karamzin had already hinted at the same kind of thing in his reactionary idyll entitled "Letter of an Inhabitant of the Country" (1803). It is significant that Karamzin's name appears in *Selected Passages* and later in "An Author's Confession." The idea that the landowner should concern himself with the "earthly household" of his peasants and with the performance of his duty as a landowner was anything but new in Russian literature. Besides Karamzin, we find it in Marlinsky's story "The Test" ("Ispytanie," 1830), where a well-born lady abandons polite society and follows her fiancé into the country-side, in order to try to alleviate the lot of the peasants. We also find it in Rossiyaninov, the ideal landowner in Bulgarin's *Ivan Vyzhigin* (1829), and in Pushkin's unfinished *Novel in Letters (Roman v pis'makh)*. [13] The death-blow to these naive dreams of perfecting the structure of serfdom from within was delivered by Leo Tolstoy in "A Landowner's Morning" ("Utro pomeshchika,"

1856). But Gogol did not merely take over a traditional and at bottom Sentimentalist theme; he also made it part of a more general one: the conversion, through moral efforts, of all given forms of life, from small to large, into a form he regarded as ideal. The result was a utopian fantasy,[14] like those pictures of a "golden age" to which the Sentimentalists dreamed of returning. Gogol does not make specific mention of a golden age, but in essence he is thinking of the same thing when he holds up the patriarchal relationships in *The Odyssey* as an ideal for his own time. He does lay a specific commandment on the landowner: "Be a patriarch." The patriarchal landowner should be a preceptor, a preacher, a judge ("Rural Justice and Punishment"). He also wishes to build the state along the same patriarchal lines.

As far back as 1837, Gogol knew very well "what sort of people all councilors are, from titular ones all the way up to the actual privy kind" (letter to M. P. Pogodin, March 30, 1837). With an eye to the censor, he had populated his world of freaks mainly with provincial civil servants, being very cautious in his treatment of more important personages. However, in his notebooks for 1840-41, he made a detailed enumeration of "the bribes of the public prosecutor," "the bribes of the governor-general," and all the "masks put on by the governor-general." This was the real Russia. But he also felt compelled to paint an idyllic picture. Corresponding to the ideal landowners in his idyll are ideal civil servants, who have taken "their positions" in order to save their souls and their country. "It is on the ship of his position and his service that each of us must now escape the whirlpool....And each of us must now serve not as he would have served in the old Russia but in the heavenly State, the head of which is Christ Himself" ("The Fears and Terrors of Russia"). But this ideal "heavenly state" is thought of in terms of the already existing forms of the bureaucracy of Nicholas I; and Gogol's fond hope is not to alter them but transform them from within. He even stands amazed at "the organism of government in the provinces," "the wisdom of the founders," but of course he has in mind not real "provinces" but an unreal, patriarchal structure, where all the gentry are close friends, where the marshal of the nobility exerts a "moral influence" on them, and where the governor nips all abuses in the bud. The public prosecutor is the eye of the law, "an individual independent of all"; he stands up for justice even when "the governor himself may be guilty of sins" ("To One Who Occupies an Important Place"). At the same time, the ideal governor's wife is also in league with the priests, trying to reform the behavior of people who belong to every estate of society: some she influences by personal example, others by persuasion.

At the top of this utopian hierarchy stands the ideal governor-general, who establishes "the proper limits of each position, and instills in each official of the province a full knowledge of his position," and in the gentry, "a true knowledge of their calling." He suggests to the gentry that they should look on the peasants "as fathers do on their children," bring them up properly, and make them "a model of this estate for all of Europe," inasmuch as

Europe, supposedly, is also giving serious thought to "the ancient patriarchal way of life, whose features have disappeared everywhere except in Russia." He should not only encourage the landowners to be patriarchs, but should himself become a patriarch. To the question of how to eliminate abuses, Gogol replies: "In Russia, every governor-general can get matters under way...and so simply: by doing nothing more than making his own life an example. By his patriarchal way of life...he can root out fashion, with its empty labels," restore Russian customs, etc. Gogol not only exhorts the governor-general to be "a true father to all the officials who are subordinate to you," but he utters a warning as well: "Also, see to it that there is no weeping when people take leave of you."

All this comes very close to the ideas expressed in Karamzin's *A Memoir of Ancient and Modern Russia (Zapiska o drevnei i novoi Rossii,* 1810-11): that "the art of choosing people...is of primary concern for the sovereign of Russia," and that fifty good governors-general can do everything. But Karamzin resolutely renounced his own youthful dreams of a "golden age," and in general was satisfied with the prevailing state of affairs. Gogol does attempt to idealize the *forms* of his own time, but it is clear that he wishes to fill them with a new content which is lacking in contemporary life. The Sentimentalists dreamed of a golden age in the future, when something that had been lost would return. And Gogol, in creating his patriarchal utopia, indicates an ideal in the past—*The Odyssey,* in which "our nineteenth century will hear a strong reproach directed at itself," and which will remind the contemporary world of "much that is youthfully beautiful, which (alas!) is now lost, but which mankind should recover as its lawful heritage...a great deal from patriarchal times, with which the Russian nature has such an affinity, will spread unseen over the face of the Russian land" ("On *The Odyssey,* as Translated by Zhukovsky").

Gogol's utopia is topped off by the figure of the ideal monarch, who, "loving everything in his state, every last individual in every estate of society and every rank...will acquire [the] all-powerful voice of love" ("On the Lyricism of Our Poets"). The love with which Gogol hopes to fill his idyllic hierarchy "should be communicated upward, from one superior to the next...so that in this way it may reach its lawful source and so that in the sight of all the beloved Tsar may triumphantly communicate it to God Himself" ("To One Who Occupies an Important Place"). The images of heavenly landowner, heavenly provider and heavenly commander crop up in various places in *Selected Passages;* and the ultimate is mentioned in the article entitled "On the Lyricism of Our Poets": the monarch should be "the image on earth of Him Who Himself is love."

Gogol crowned his socio-political utopia with an apologia for autocracy. This did not become fully known to the readers of his time: the censors threw out all of "The Fears and Terrors of Russia," "What Is the Wife of a Provincial Governor," and "To One Who Occupies an Important Place," and made drastic cuts in "The Russian Landowner" and "On the Lyricism of Our Poets." But the remarks that did remain were suggestive enough to provoke an angry rebuke from Belinsky.[15] In itself, a religious idealization of monarchy was nothing new either in Russia or in the West. At the end of the eighteenth century and the beginning of the nineteenth, this same theme was developed in Novalis's "Faith and Love as King and Queen," a Romantic utopia very similar to Gogol's. Novalis's friends in the Romantic movement—Friedrich Schlegel and Schelling—soon became apologists for reaction; literary echoes of the ideas of the Holy Alliance and even its official literature adopted the Romantic style.[16] But coming as it did after the revolution of July, 1830, in Europe, and on the eve of the February, 1848 revolution, such ecstatic monarchism was bound to frighten off not only Belinsky and Herzen, but the Slavophiles as well.

Gogol regarded himself as outside parties, above parties; he was constantly appealing to a "desired mean"; he believed that his book contained "the germ of general reconciliation, not discord"; he reproached both the Westerners and the Slavophiles for being one-sided; and he counted on his ideal "heavenly state" to unite and reconcile everyone. In fact, he opposed the Slavophiles from the right, not the left, and gave voice to the reaction that was spreading across all Europe toward the middle of the 1840s. At a time when Herzen was fleeing from a "dead" Paris, Gogol could find support only from extreme reactionaries. The fantastic Alexander Ivanov, in his *Thoughts on Reading the Bible (Mysli pri chtenii Biblii)*, which was being written at the same time as *Selected Passages,* went even further than Gogol and openly compared Nicholas I to Christ.[17]

Gogol is perceptibly different from his Sentimentalist predecessors in that he endows his idyll with patently utopian characteristics. He does not conceal the fact that his dream of introducing Christianity into domestic, social and political life is still far from realization. On the contrary, he vehemently denounces the formal Christianity of his own times. "Oh, Christian! They have driven Christ out into the streets, into the infirmaries and hospitals, instead of summoning Him into their own homes, under their own roofs, and they think that they are Christians!" ("Easter Sunday.") And that is not all. There are two aspects of Gogol's utopia. One runs along the same lines as the Slavophiles' idealization of Russian national characteristics, their conviction that the Christian ideal could be realized only in Russia. But the other comes close to the utopian socialism of the 1840s. This is plainly and unambiguously indicated in the epilogue to the book, entitled "Easter Sunday": "It would seem as though this day were specially designed for our nineteenth century, when ideas about the happiness of mankind have become virtually the favorite ideas of all; when to embrace all of mankind as brothers has become the favorite dream of young men; when many dream only of ways of transforming all of mankind...when people have even begun to talk about the need to hold everything in common—both houses and land...." Of course

149

there is no outright expression of sympathy for socialism here; but there is a glimmer of hope that this utopia will satisfy everyone—Slavophiles, official monarchists, and socialists. Gogol's fond hope for such a synthesis can be seen in his correspondence with P. V. Annenkov, in his extremely upset reaction to Belisnky's indignant letter about *Selected Passages* (where he concludes that they are both wrong), and in his uncertain attempts to make friends with Herzen. But of course any possible combination of reaction and socialism proved illusory; the dream of "transforming mankind" was completely overshadowed by the idealization of autocracy and serfdom. Absolutely no one detected the utopian impulse that was at work here.[18]

The articles on poetry and the theater occupy a special place in *Selected Passages*. Knowing that Gogol's estheticism was already a thing of the past, and knowing the general purport of the book, we are prepared to find him subordinating art to religious or largely moralistic ends. But the nature of this subordination shows that he is wavering between two possibilities—making art an "imperceptible stage on the way to Christianity," that is, seeing something like a moral and religious nature in estheticism itself; or making art a "perceptible" stage, a means to moralistic ends.

The first possibility is evident in everything Gogol says about Pushkin, whom he calls an "imperceptible stage" of the kind we have been talking about. Now he not only does not play up Pushkin's personality, as he did in *Arabesques*; he even deems it elusive. "What can you grasp about the man himself from his writings? Just try to perceive his character as a man!... The reader detects only its fragrance; but what substances burned in the breast of the poet in order to emit this fragrance, those no one can detect." The article in which these words occur—"What, Then, Constitutes the Essence of Russian Poetry, and What Is Its Special Nature"—contains many scattered observations of a purely esthetic kind on the distinctive qualities of the poetic language of individual poets and the Russian language generally (sometimes to the point, sometimes astonishingly obtuse, as in the evaluation of Lermontov). " 'Euphony' is not such a trivial matter as people unacquainted with poetry think...with euphony...the wild passions subside and grow calm, imperceptibly, by themselves...." In a letter to Zhukovsky, which Gogol intended to put at the beginning of a second edition of *Selected Passages,* art is called a sacred thing. "A genuine work of art contains something soothing and conciliatory." The article was to have been entitled "Art Is a Reconciliation with Life."[19] That is to say, art, by its esthetic nature alone, and quite apart from its themes, "imperceptibly" exerts a salutary influence. But another idea then intrudes and takes over: art must serve morality through its *themes* as well. In the article on the essence of Russian poetry, Gogol reproaches poetry for "neither instructing society nor giving it expression," and he assigns poetry the task of "summoning man to another, higher battle...for our soul."

A number of tasks, now specifically moralistic, are assigned in the article addressed to Yazykov and entitled "Subjects for the Lyric Poet at the Present Time": reproach those who are downcast, appeal to the man who has beautiful qualities but who is slumbering, heap ignominy upon the usurer, extol the inconspicuous toiler, etc. It is not surprising that in the article "On the Theater, On a One-Sided View of the Theater, and on One-Sidedness Generally," Gogol picks up an idea from some ten years earlier and restates it much more forcefully: the theater is "a rostrum from which one can tell the world much that is good." And in his own work too, he was making an ever greater effort to create "perceptible" stages on the way to Christianity. To this end he wrote "The Denouement of *The Inspector General*," also in 1846. Here he does not rely on just the "electric" power of laughter which "wings up from the bright nature of the soul," or on esthetic influence alone. For the instruction of his readers he makes a didactic comparison between the town's officials in the play and the passions, between Khlestakov and the flighty, wordly conscience, between the genuine inspector general and the awakened conscience. And he requires of the audience, the reader and the writer himself that the "scourge of laughter" should be directed not against others, but against themselves. This is the context in which he was working on the continuation of *Dead Souls*.

CHAPTER XII

DEFEAT

After *Selected Passages from Correspondence with Friends* had been completed, Gogol's mood was one of intense self-satisfaction. He was elated by what he had achieved—or by what he took for achievement. Doubts did crop up, but they were short-lived, swept away in a new and even greater surge of elation. He believed that his book would not only explain the riddle of his own soul but would also "bring good to many other souls" and "reap a wonderful harvest." He talked of it in a prophetic tone and style that he had never employed at any time since 1840 in reference to his own works. Now he considered that "the household of his soul" had been put in order: "The most difficult thing of all is being taken care of, and now I can get down to everyday concerns" (letter to P. A. Pletnyov, December 12, 1846).

He set the date of his departure for Jerusalem for January, 1847. However, he kept putting it off, first for external and then apparently for internal reasons: he had an intense desire to wait and see what the reactions to his book would be. He would thereby feel confident that he was not only "preparing" himself for the journey for which he wished to be "prepared" (as he assured N. N. Sheremeteva in a moment of modesty), but that in fact he was prepared to reap the "wonderful harvest" of which he was already secretly certain.[1]

To be sure, he did foresee attacks "from all sides, from all quarters, and in every conceivable respect," as he wrote S. T. Aksakov (January 20, 1847). But he did not foresee the most important thing: the effect these attacks would have on him. Never had he risen to such heights of complacency as in the early months of 1847, while he was awaiting the reactions to *Selected Passages*. He wrote his mother and sister in a confidently didactic tone, accusing them of failing to understand the essence of Christianity, and almost openly asserting his own freedom from sin (e.g., January 25, 1847). A heightened sense of self-satisfaction can also be detected in the letters he wrote to people he considered his equals—Zhukovsky and Smirnova. If he wavered in his attitude toward *Selected Passages* and was prepared to admit to a "false tone" and "a tendency to inappropriate over-enthusiasm" (letter to P. A. Vyazemsky, February 28, 1847), he had in mind not the substance but the style; and even these self-deprecations appeared only after he had lost all hope of defending the book as a whole against the depredations of the censors. Gogol took these depredations very much to heart and spoke of them in images that consciously or unconsciously repeated motifs from "The Overcoat" and "The Bloody Bandore-Player." As he wrote in a letter to P. A. Pletnyov on February 6, 1847, "they are tearing off not only my shirt but my very skin as well...and you seem to think they are removing just my overcoat."

If we look closely at Gogol's correspondence for 1847, we are struck by the abrupt change in attitude toward his book which occurred in the space of just a few days. Beginning on March 4, 1847, there is a sudden, drastic modulation: no longer do we find the slightest trace of the old self-assurance, the old complacency. The same book for whose every line he had recently put up such a fight he now saw in a completely different light, as "a true mirror into which I must look in order to see all my slovenliness, and to sin less in the future" (letter to Zhukovsky, March 6, 1847). What had happened during these few days?

Gogol had received the initial reactions to *Selected Passages*. And these were the decisive ones: a blow from which he never fully recovered, despite later expressions of support from various people.

Gogol received three letters simultaneously, three blows: the first from S. T. Aksakov, the second from the wife of D. N. Sverbeev, and the third a letter from Sverbeev himself to Aksakov, which Aksakov sent on to Gogol.[2] Sverbeev's letter is written in a haughtily contemptuous tone: Gogol had put himself "outside all proprieties" and his words of advice were so importunate as to be ludicrous. Sverbeev also conveyed the opinion of a certain "desperate daredevil" who "within earshot of everyone declared that the author of the letters from now on ought to be called not Nikolay Vasilievich but Tartuffe Vasilievich." He passed on other such talk, and expressed his own opinion by proposing "three captions" for the book: "(1) self-disparagement that is worse than pride; (2) the pride of humility; and (3) fraudulence." The letter from Sverbeev's pious wife was written in a different tone; but she too found a "strange arrogance" in the book and only a "deceptive reflection of Christian humility." And she touched Gogol painfully to the quick by observing that Yazykov, just before his death, had been alarmed by Gogol's state of mind and felt apprehensive about the forthcoming book. Yazykov was a kindred soul by virtue of his religious and reactionary views, and Gogol had been counting on him more than on others. Aksakov, irritated and indignant, branded Gogol's pride demonic, and concluded: "Your book is harmful, it disseminates the falseness of your theorizings and your errors."[3]

Charges of eccentricity and hypocrisy did not have much effect on Gogol, but the charge of pride—and, what is more, un-Christian and even "demonic" pride—was a bitter blow. Although he expected attacks "from all quarters," he could not have expected them from this particular one, from people who were supposedly his allies. Here is where Belinsky's remark to the effect that Gogol was defeated with his own weapons would have been appropriate (instead of referring, as it did, to N. F. Pavlov's polemical phrasemaking).[4] Gogol replied to Aksakov with deliberate restraint. But in a letter to Pogodin, written on March 4, he let himself go: "Do you really think it is easy to hear accusations and evidence of that which brings dishonor here on earth and eternal torment in the life to come from people who are close to you and beautiful in soul, perhaps even saintly? That is far harder to bear than contempt from contemptible people." On that same day he wrote Zhukovsky a letter that was unmistakably repentant, describing the radical change that had taken place in him specifically as a *defeat*: "It has been my lot to have suffered defeats of every kind on the most sensitive cords of my soul.... I could not even have imagined how much pride, arrogance, self-love, self-importance and haughtiness still remained in me...it is now more painful for me to look into my book, everything there seems so pompous to me, so intemperate, so unrestrained, that I cover my face with both hands in anticipation. Oh, how difficult it is for me to manage the household of my soul!" Had it been long since he regarded this household as already having been put in order?

The statements Gogol made in subsequent letters were phrased in stronger and more graphic terms, but they only confirmed what he had confessed to Zhukovsky on March 4. In reply to an evasive, approvingly disapproving letter from Zhukovsky, Gogol wrote, in the same relentlessly repentant tone: "The appearance of my book was like a sudden slap in the face, a slap in the face of the public, a slap in the face of my friends, an even more violent slap in my own face....I cut such a Khlestakovian figure in my book that I haven't the courage to glance into it" (March 6, 1847). The same expressions—a slap in the face and Khlestakovian—are also repeated in other letters. The same sentiments are evident when he writes, less picturesquely: "It is my immaturity that is largely to blame for the numerous reproaches that have been brought against my book" (letter to N. N. Sheremeteva, March 20, 1847); or, even more plainly: "I imagined that I could teach others as well, I published a book that let me see clearly that I am the pupil" (letter to Matvey Konstantinovsky, May 9, 1847).

Despite such statements, Gogol did not repudiate his book in essence. Rather, he undertook a resolute reexamination of the path he had recently been following, made a personal act of submission, ceased to believe that he had found himself, and once more became a seeker. The conviction he had felt in 1836, 1840, and 1845, of having been chosen for a special mission and therefore having the right to be a teacher (of morality, if nothing else)—this he now put behind him once and for all. Even in his letters to his mother, he promised to stop giving advice and again called himself a pupil; until now he had always considered himself entitled to lecture her.

The change was so abrupt that even the sympathetic replies he received in April and May did not bolster his self-confidence. Vyazemsky published an article which attempted to dissociate Gogol from "his former admirers who are now his attackers," that is, Belinsky and like-minded people; but Gogol replied with a defense of his attackers. The reactionary Vigel crowed that

Gogol "has cast a heavy stone at those who are not with us"; but this did not tempt Gogol into a partisan quarrel. The most important of the published defenses of the book—an article by Apollon Grigoriev—did not register on Gogol's mind, and he spoke of it in an offhand manner that is incomprehensible. Fresh attacks erupted from two different quarters. From one, the voice of the clergy was heard—letters from Bryanchaninov, Innokenty, and Matvey Konstantinovsky; from the other, articles by N. F. Pavlov, A. D. Galakhov and Belinsky.[5] Reproaches by the clergy did not greatly trouble Gogol. Once he had recovered from the first blow and had regained a certain stability of mind, he was able to reply calmly to fresh and by now familiar accusations of pride. There is nothing to indicate that the first letter from Father Matvey, whom Gogol still did not know personally, had any greater impact on him. He replied to Matvey's denunciations in a self-possessed manner, bearing down on one important idea: his intention had been good, but despite his desire to be the teacher, he had turned out to be the pupil. He stated that after reading Matvey's reproaches, "[he] had remained in low spirits for some time" (May 9, 1847). But we cannot conclude from this that he was actually despondent; his reactions to Matvey's letters as expressed in his correspondence with A. P. Tolstoy are also rather restrained. N. F. Pavlov ironically called *Selected Passages* the work of the devil's hands, but this certainly did not produce the effect that Belinsky had hoped for: Gogol brushed irony aside with irony.[6]

But Gogol was upset by the irony in Belinsky's article in *The Contemporary,* the repressed and choked irony of a critic who was compelled, as he himself put it, to "purr like a cat and wave his tail like a fox and confine himself to little more than quotations and vague nods of the head." Through Prokopovich, Gogol initiated a correspondence with Belinsky, which has been studied in great detail but is still insufficiently appreciated.[7] In Belinsky's restrained article, Gogol sensed that a blow of no less force than the one he had already received was being delivered. That explains the inner turmoil that is evident in his first letter to Belinsky, where he has not yet put his finger on what was really dividing them, but simply comes up with an over-simplified explanation of Belinsky's irritation as wounded amour-propre.

Belinsky's reply to Gogol—the celebrated Salzbrunn letter—burns with genuine revolutionary ardor, and is so well known that there is no need to remind the reader of it in detail. If we disregard the personal accusations and the expressions of suspicion, some of which are entirely without foundation, if in general we disregard everything that bears on Belinsky's feelings about the "old" and the "new" Gogol, then the letter amounts essentially to an attempt at proving two ideas. The first is that Gogol is a reactionary, an apostle of the knout and of ignorance, a panegyrist of Tartar ways. The second is that Gogol is not a Christian. The reactionary nature of Gogol's book did not require proof; a mere selection of quotations was sufficient, and Belinsky had already done that in his published article (which had been subject to censorship). We do not know whether Gogol had sensed that this first idea was implicit in Belinsky's article; in any event, it had little effect on him even now, and he was able to respond to it in an almost Pilate-like phrase: "Where is our civilization?"[8]

The charge of not being a Christian was bound to have an entirely different effect on him. As Belinsky wrote in his letter: "It is impossible to remain silent when, under the cloak of religion and the protection of the knout, people preach falsehood and immorality as truth and virtue....[The church] has always served as the mainstay of the knout, but why did you have to mix Christ up in all this?...He was the first to proclaim to people the teaching of freedom, equality and brotherhood.....He who is capable of suffering at the sight of other people's sufferings, he who is pained by the spectacle of other people's oppression—he is the one who bears Christ within his bosom, and he has no need to make a pilgrimage to Jerusalem....It is not the truth of Christian teaching, but the morbid fear of death, the devil and hell that wafts from your book."

The reproaches from Sverbeev's wife hit Gogol hard, but they were made in the context of a view of life to which he was accustomed, and they did hold out the promise of hope. But Belinsky's accusations along the same lines caught Gogol completely unawares. More than anyone else, Belinsky defeated Gogol with his own weapons. He developed the suggestions that were contained in Gogol's own "Easter Sunday" (the last article in *Selected Passages*), drew conclusions from them, and showed that they stood in contradiction to the book as a whole. Gogol tried to raise objections to Belinsky, but was unable to do so.

The unfinished and unrevised drafts of Gogol's first reply, which were written at fever pitch while the impact of Belinsky's letter was still fresh, create an impression of irritation and perplexity at his own dim understanding of his opponent's basic view of things. Throughout, he feels that there is still hope of reaching agreement, even in matters such as the significance of the church and the merits of the clergy. All Belinsky has to do is to study the history of the church, which Gogol in all seriousness advises him to do. Then this whole whirlwind of misunderstandings and irritations suddenly died down. On August 10, Gogol wrote Belinsky in a composed and reconciled tone: only the words "my soul is exhausted, everything within me is shaken" remind us of the storm that has passed. Instead of raising objections, Gogol now refuses to argue, and he makes a vague concession: "Lord knows, perhaps there is an element of truth in your words."[9] Gogol felt exhausted and shaken; he could not muster the strength to frame replies to Belinsky's ideas that would be logical and to the point; yet he was still painfully aware that he had been accused of un-Christian behavior, and evidently decided to treat his opponent in as Christian a manner as possible. He reaffirmed this attitude two days later in a letter to Annenkov, with anxious inquiries about Belinsky's health.

Attempts have been made to show that Belinsky's letter had a direct effect on Gogol's ideas; but there is no convincing evidence.[10] However, there is no doubt about the psychological effect of this second decisive blow, which was followed by a prolonged period marked by an awareness of "defeat."

In January, 1848, Gogol finally went to Jerusalem. From there he planned to return to Russia. In fact, he did spend the last years of his life in his native land. From the end of 1847 to the day of his death five years later, he found himself beset by the same attitudes. They were: (1) an awareness of spiritual *callosity,* which set the buoyant humors of such recent vintage in even higher relief; (2) the renunciation of his teaching mission; and (3) the decision to dedicate himself to modest labor. Jerusalem worked no changes in these moods, but actually intensified them. "Never have I been so dissatisfied with the state of my heart as in Jerusalem, and after Jerusalem...never have my insensitivity, callosity and woodenness been so palpably evident to me."[11] Gogol left Jerusalem the same as he had left Italy: shattered in soul and tormentingly aware of a coldness in his soul instead of what he had thought of as fire. "And so, what I supposed to be all but *near* is *far away* from me," he wrote N. N. Sheremeteva on May 16 (o.s.), 1848, himself emphasizing the words "near" and "far away." This conviction was uppermost in his mind throughout all of 1848.

It might seem strange that in those same years of deep disillusionment Gogol was writing a work that was a kind of self-defense. Shevyryov gave it the title of "An Author's Confession." And yet it was a very limited self-defense. Gogol tried to prove, as energetically as he could, that *Selected Passages* was not a renunciation but a continuation of the labor of writing, and that a genuine "work of the soul" lay at its very heart. He did not reassess the achievements he had already made; he simply did not wish to under-assess them (here he addressed himself to those who did not share his opinions), calling himself a pupil who simply had "greater success in some things than another pupil." He summed up all the reactions to *Selected Passages* under three categories: unprecedented pride; delusion on the part of a good man; a truly Christian view of things. He acknowledged that each of them was justified "in part," and he did not consider any one of them—including the last—justified in its entirety. He did not deny pride, of which he had repented in his letters, but, as he put it, "where pride actually existed, no one noticed it." Again he categorically refused to be a teacher: "I am giving thought to my own formation...and I feel that even now I find myself far away from what I aspire to, and therefore I should not speak."

The four years that Gogol spent in Russia (mostly in Moscow), between his return and his death, look like one long and unrelieved stretch of "lazy and sleepy life,"[12] a period of despondency that he stubbornly tried to overcome, a period when concentrated work was his only way of moving toward the perfection that glimmered in the distance and remained unattainable. All the things he admitted to during those years—laziness, sleepiness, exhaustion, and (particularly insistently) callosity—were the result of the awareness of defeat which set in after the publication of *Selected Passages* and which was aggravated by his futile pilgrimage to Jerusalem. He no longer dreamed of attaining "higher stages," but simply of regaining a stability of mind; and this was largely dependent, as he saw it, on work. Work was an obligation, or, as he now liked to say, an "order" given from on high. Work and a religious life were now so inextricably intertwined that each conditioned the other: rebirth was necessary for work, but work was necessary for rebirth, or at least for stability. The image of the day-laborer recurs very frequently in the letters that were written in those years. "We are all day-laborers" comes up for the first time in 1848, in a letter to Danilevsky (October 29 [o.s.]), and it is repeated often thereafter. Gogol returned to it again several weeks before his death: "We are all day-laborers, obliged to work and work and direct our eyes upward: our reward is there" (letter to P. A. Vyazemsky, January 1 [o.s.], 1852). His new attitude toward his work found full reflection in this image.

Certain passages in the articles Gogol completed during those years round out our picture of his state of mind. In "On the Love of God and the Nurturing of Self" importance attaches to the struggle against the "spirit of despondency," which is now plainly called the work of the spirit of darkness. Gogol bids us "not to grow gloomy, but to become bright in soul." What he has to say about catechumens in "Meditations on the Divine Liturgy" is also a personal confession, as he sometimes literally repeats expressions that are common in the letters: "each one present, reflecting how *far* he is in faith and in works from the believers...seeing how, so to speak, he has merely talked about Christ but has not taken Him into the very center of his own life...still cold is his faith, and there is no fire of all-forgiving love for his brother which would eat away at the *callosity* of his soul; and reflecting that he has not *achieved* that regeneration of spirit without which his Christianity is worthless...he contritely numbers himself among the catechumens...." (Stresses supplied.)

The change in Gogol's view of himself brought about a change in his ideas as well—not a radical change, to be sure, but one that is perceptible nonetheless. He did not have the courage to repudiate the essential matter of *Selected Passages*. But the ideals set forth there were no longer so firm in his mind, and were in fact beginning to give way to others (none of which, however, could win the support of his opponents). External events—the revolutionary turmoil of 1848 in Europe, of which he learned when he returned from Jerusalem—could not help but have an effect on him. The effect was not of course direct, and he did not see the historical significance of this first instance of proletarian struggle against the bourgeoisie. He thought that those of his friends who took an interest in the proletariat in the West were letting themselves be carried away. Given the nature of his utopia, he should have idealized the bourgeoisie, placing it on the same level in his hierarchical system with the feudal aristocracy (which was becoming increasingly unreal even in Russia), and merging the two. But the revolution of February, 1848, in France was a graphic refutation of even the possibility that his utopias and his fond hopes for a "desired mean" could be realized. These ideals now depressed him, and with good reason. Earlier he had envisaged the transformation of the existing forms of the economy—in the home, on the landed estate, at the national level—although he could not help but idealize them underneath it all. But what he now had in mind was the ascetic ideal of renunciation. Here he was bolstered by the monks of the Optina Pustyn Monastery, with whom he had become friendly in 1850.[13] In particular, the year 1851 passed under the aegis of asceticism.

The most important evidence of this change is to be found in the kind of advice that Gogol was dispensing to others. He was having no trouble in putting his own "fervors" completely behind him. At the beginning of the 1830s, he had not been averse to the idea of seeking a philistine happiness in his *personal* life, even going so far as to dream of a little house of his own. But in the 1840s, he had become a homeless wanderer, and tirelessly reiterated the symbolic images of *apartments, lodgings for the night,* and *roads.* Even in the draft version of his letter to Belinsky he wrote: "I have come to love my poverty....I do not even have a corner to myself, and I am making an effort to lighten my small traveling case even more so that I will find it easier to take leave of the world." In the early versions of *Dead Souls,* he put the matter even more strongly: "[the author] loves his poverty, as a lover loves his beloved—strongly, ardently." And in "An Author's Confession" he wrote: "I have renounced everything else (except work), all life's enticements, and, like a monk, I have severed my ties with everything that is dear to a person on this earth."

So much for his personal life. In what he preached, however, whether directly or in fiction, Gogol indicated another path: that of transforming rather than renouncing those very "enticements"—the household, wealth, the civil-service hierarchy, and authority. And in the process he slipped, all too tragically, into an idealization of the freaks who had appeared in his own fiction and were now only slightly prettied up. The surviving chapters of Part 2 of *Dead Souls* are still cast in the earlier moralistic mold, the one exception being the figure of Khlobuev. But in Gogol's personal correspondence, especially dating from the final year of his life, we already begin to detect something that is different from the ideas in *Selected Passages.*

The letters to his mother and sisters written in 1851 speak of a struggle against the vanity of life (whether workaday, social or otherwise). At that time his mother was petitioning for a clarification of the family's status as hereditary gentry. He considered that "utter nonsense. As long as one has one's daily bread." With respect to household matters, to which he had only recently attached such salutary importance, he now quotes Scripture to the effect that "all these things shall be added unto you" (*Matthew* 6:33), but with quite a different interpretation than before. It is not surprising that he wrote of himself: "Prosperity in everything is harmful....Man has such a capacity for becoming brutalized that it is even dreadful for him to desire to live without want and in prosperity." Only recently he had been giving A. O. Smirnova advice on running her household; now he calls on her to live "like the birds of heaven, neither sowing nor reaping," hereby reminding us of the statements in the last chapter of *Selected Passages* which contradict the system set forth in the book as a whole. And he tries to persuade his sister Yelizaveta of the following: "My dear sister, love poverty. A great secret lies hidden in this word: he who loves poverty is no longer poor but rich."[14]

If we date the draft of the article "On the Estates of Society in the State" from this same period (it is not clear just when it was written), then it turns out that Gogol is now placing certain limitations on the monarchical and bureaucratic system set forth in *Selected Passages*. In that book, monarchy was affirmed as an absolute ideal; but now government is seen as something conditional, arising "imperceptibly, all by itself, out of the spirit and traits of a particular people, out of a locale—the soil on which a people lives, out of the history of a particular people...." Furthermore, "if a government has become completely monarchical," then the state has become full of bribe-takers and is verging on anarchy. Gogol asks the question which would have been impossible for him earlier: "Where, in what cases, should democratic participation on the part of the people be permitted?" And he replies with a new variation on his utopia, which in essence echoes the modest Slavophile dreams of setting up consultative bodies, and which outlines the organization of each of the social estates. Yet he does not reject the serf-system in essence, but merely states that the landowners have not lived up to their designated obligations and have "demeaned the calling of landowner." Did Gogol know that in the mid-nineteenth century he was repeating the babble of the eighteenth-century satirical journals (written under censorship), which also sighed over "virtuous landowners"?

But the idyllic relationship between peasant and landowner was nonetheless proving very shaky in Gogol's mind. In *Selected Passages* the Russian landowner was supposed to make the peasants work because it was precisely *they* who were to toil in the sweat of their brow. But in 1849, this same Biblical passage was applied to Gogol himself, to his own toil: "Oh, how salutary is work, and how profound is the first commandment given to man after his expulsion from Paradise: earn your bread in sweat and toil" (letter to S. M. Sollogub and A. M. Vielgorskaya, October 20 [o.s.]). Earlier he had raised this point in a letter to his mother and sisters: "Be that as it may, the poor peasants work for us in the sweat of their brow. But we, while eating their bread, refuse so much as to look at the labor of their hands. This is shameless.... Entire generations are cruelly punished when they forget that they are in the world for the purpose of earning their bread through their labors and tilling the soil in the sweat of their brow, and allow themselves to become kid-gloved shirkers" (April 3 [o.s.], 1849). This is now a reproach directed at kid-gloved gentry folk, although it is unclear what they should do in order to avoid that condition. In any event, it no longer represents Gogol's earlier attitude toward the peasants[15] or toward the gentry. And in another letter to his mother, he vaguely alludes to certain circumstances that are known only to him and to government officials (perhaps to rumors that the serfs might be freed), and then says: "If the gentry-folk do not abandon their habits and all these supposedly essential proprieties, then their lot will be most lamentable and pitiable" (September 2 [o.s.], 1851).

Gogol did not subject his past to a thoroughgoing re-evaluation. But the utopia was already shaky in his mind. Instead of those ideal forms of the economy that had been glorified in *Selected Passages,* other possibilities now glimmered: a limitation on all needs, poverty as the best and the preferred lot, a life lived according to the Gospels without concern for too many things, work for others and not for oneself.

However, various memoirs dealing with the final years of Gogol's life in Russia do not depict him as a gloomy hermit but, on the contrary, as a lively conversationalist, a man who made friends with children and was the ringleader in their games and pranks, a wit, a lover of nature (especially flowers), and an enthusiastic devotee of his native Ukrainian songs, ever ready to break into a dance at the first note. We also know of extensive plans, and not just literary ones—plans involving travel, including a long journey through Russia. These alternating spells of melancholia and elation can be explained in part by the peculiarities of Gogol's mental illness, but they are not automatically symptomatic of a tragic duality involving a "dancing" and a "weeping" Gogol, as Merezhkovsky, a lover of dualities, thought.[16] On the contrary, it was precisely in these final years that the possibility of achieving a genuine stability of mind became very real for Gogol. The wound that had been inflicted in 1847 by the disappointment other people felt in him and by the disappointment he felt in himself had already begun to heal; and—continuing in the realm of metaphor—it is more correct to see the events of 1847 as a surgical operation rather than as the infliction of a wound. The path he was following became more narrow and more difficult. What Vladimir Solovyov wrote in another context could easily apply here: "The fog has now lifted and my eye clearly sees/ how difficult is the mountain path and how far still/ how far away is everything I dreamed."[17] A state of elation was still a real possibility too, especially as he came closer to completing his work of many years, Part 2 of *Dead Souls.* What was no longer possible was the self-delusion of the recent past, when each success had looked like a final and decisive victory.

Thus, we have made an approximate reconstruction of the path being followed by Gogol the man at the beginning of the fateful year of 1852. It is only approximate, because all psychological constructs built on meager data are inevitably so. These were also the final years of his career as an artist, and we must now take a closer look at that.

CHAPTER XIII

THE FINAL COURSE

Part 1 of *Dead Souls* appeared at the beginning of the 1840s. In Russian literature, that was the time when the so-called Natural School was being formed, and in Russian literary criticism, the time when people were trying to articulate and substantiate a theory of "naturalism."[1] (This was the term used by contemporaries; essentially it is more accurate than "realism.") Shortly after *Dead Souls* had come out, Belinsky announced that Romanticism was dead, that it had been killed by "prose"—and prose for him was synonymous with naturalism. The following year he declared Russian literature to be in a state of crisis. "Crisis," a "noticeable sudden change," and finally, a "turning point"—these were the terms Belinsky used in evaluating the literature of his time; and he named Gogol as the one man responsible for the change. In his survey for 1847, he began by drawing a straight line from Kantemir to Gogol; but then he turned around and saw Gogol's appearance in literature as a phenomenon that was independent of any influences from the past, merely the *result* of that past.[2]

In everything that was written on the Natural School by its proponents and opponents, the name of Gogol was invariably invoked. The controversy about the School soon ceased to be just literary, and became social and political. For the journal *Notes of the Fatherland,* which advocated Westernism, the development toward naturalism was synonymous with social progress. *The Muscovite,* which was close to Slavophilism, levelled the same charges against naturalism that others had brought against Gogol: as being a slander against real life, and, most important, a slander against the Russian people. For *The Muscovite,* Gogol was not only an authority but a banner as well; and yet they did not attempt to dissociate him from the Natural School.[3]

In its beginning phases, the school was defined by the names of Vladimir Dahl and Vladimir Sollogub: the former had allied himself firmly with naturalism, the latter was merely gravitating in that direction. At different times, Belinsky ranked each of these writers in first place after Gogol (Gogol himself had been the earliest to recognize them).[4] But by 1844, a more limited group, which included already practicing writers as well as beginners, had come together around Nekrasov's literary miscellany, which appeared under the symptomatic title of *The Physiology of Petersburg (Fiziologiia Peterburga).* The contributors were Nekrasov, Belinsky, Grigorovich, Dahl, Panaev and Grebenka. In its prose, poetry and illustrative material, this miscellany set itself the task, as was clear from the title alone, of being a "faithful mirror" of the real life of St. Petersburg. The style was perhaps derived from Gogol, without the comic and rhetorical hyperbolism. The concern for content above all had a deleterious effect on the artistic qualities. Belinsky deemed Grigorovich capable of writing only "physiological sketches," not stories; he expressed displeasure over the "daguerreotype" feeling of Butkov's "Summits of Petersburg" ("Peterburgskie vershiny"); earlier he had criticized Sollogub for "limiting himself to faithfulness to reality."[5]

The ideology of the Natural School did not embody a fully and clearly developed theory, nor did it look to an actual model except for the work of Gogol himself (who had not been thoroughly understood). We can regard the formation of the Natural School as completed only in 1846, the year when Dostoevsky first appeared in print with "Poor Folk"("Bednye liudi"). (Later of course it broke down and ceased to be an integral whole.) And it was solidly established by the virtually simultaneous debuts in print of Alexander Herzen (with the novel *Who Is To Blame? [Kto vinovat?]*, 1846), Ivan Turgenev (with the peasant story "Khor and Kalinych" ["Khor' i Kalinych," 1847]), Ivan Goncharov (with the novel *An Ordinary Story [Obyknovennaia istoriia*, 1847]), and Alexander Ostrovsky (with a fragment, in 1847, of what eventually became the comedy *The Bankrupt [Bankrot]*).

But Herzen temporarily moved away from fiction; Goncharov wrote nothing for a long time thereafter; Turgenev showed stronger signs than the others of the Romantic tradition out of which he had developed; and Ostrovsky's initial attempt in 1847 did not attract attention for the moment. Only the young Dostoevsky could rival Gogol in success and significance; nonetheless he was greeted, by friends and foes alike, as a pupil of Gogol. Belinsky, an ardent admirer of "Poor Folk," wrote: "No matter how magnificently and splendidly Dostoevsky's talent may develop from now on, Gogol will always remain the Columbus of that immeasurable and inexhaustible area of creative activity which Mr. Dostoevsky must pursue."[6] Only at the beginning of the 1850s did it become possible to say what is said by one of the heroes of Boris Almazov's playlet "Dream on the Occasion of a Certain Comedy" ("Son po sluchaiiu odnoi komedii"): "It seems to me that its author [Ostrovsky] is the embodiment of that ideal of an artist of which I have long been dreaming. In my eyes, Gogol does not measure up to this ideal. I have long been dreaming of an artist who would give us a completely objective picture of man, utterly sincere and mathematically faithful to reality. And now such a poet has appeared." In the 1840s, there was no question in the minds of writers and readers at large that Gogol and the young naturalists were as one.

Belinsky could hardly have suspected how apt was his metaphor that made Gogol the Columbus of naturalism. In fact Gogol, like Columbus, did discover a land he had not counted on finding. His goal—and it was a very conscious one—was to depict "the contemptible and the insignificant," but he was content to draw more from subjective than objective experience and show primarily "the nightmares that have been oppressing my own soul."[7] And just before his greatest creation, *Dead Souls,* was published, he reworked it once more. It was constructed out of realistic materials, but he romanticized it, very deliberately and intensively, subordinating realism to pathos and turning a novel into a "poem." He perceived that his disciples and followers had surpassed him in naturalistic "faithfulness to reality," and he regarded them, not himself, as being right. "Our literature has recently taken a sharp turn," he said to Arnoldi in 1849, "and has hit upon the true road."[8] Soon after the appearance of *Dead Souls,* he himself began to move in the direction of this "true road" (naturalism), more and more resolutely with every passing year.

Besides the example and influence of the pupils on the teacher, there were other reasons why Gogol moved away from realism toward naturalism: personal reasons. The repulsion he felt for exister-freak types during his hyperindividualistic period had impelled him to create exaggerated characters and a style to match. But gradually he had put individualism behind him. There was good reason why he did not satisfy Almazov's ideal of the writer, in which objectivity was combined with a "mathematical faithfulness to reality." Only after Gogol felt himself capable of creating objectively (or, as he put it imagistically, capable of not sticking his own nose out, of not showing "an undisguised self")[9] was he able and in fact obliged to strive for a "mathematical faithfulness to reality."

The first signs of this turning-point can be dated from 1841-1842, when Gogol returned to Russia for the second time since his departure in 1836. He now filled his notebooks with far more material than ever before drawn from the trivia of ordinary life, even transcribing individual words and expressions. The task of "romanticizing" *Dead Souls* was now set aside in favor of another: "stuffing" certain episodes in the book with this new type of material. There might be a simpler explanation for this new tack: the homecoming traveler's feeling that he was out of touch with Russian life, and his desire to fill in the gaps. But it is important that we can observe nothing similar during his *first* return visit to Russia in 1839-1840, even though on that occasion he had more leisure and greater peace of mind than on this second trip. At the beginning of 1842, the "stuffing" was only tentative and was immediately swept away in a fresh surge of "romanticizing." But from the time Gogol again left Russia to go abroad, in June of that same year, he consciously and consistently strove to incorporate materials from ordinary life into *Dead Souls*; and it is during this period that the better part of the material was recorded in the notebooks that are dated approximately 1841-1842. Gogol began collecting this material in haste, and he explained his purpose somewhat later in the following fashion: "This is no plaything—to such an extent that if I do not accumulate a sufficient number of these playthings, my own nose might stick out in *Dead Souls,* instead of people" (letter to Arkady Osipovich Rosset, April 15, 1847). This same idea appears in various forms in many letters, from the middle of 1842 onward.[10]

Gogol was learning to be a naturalist, and this learning process was following three paths. The first he had already travelled while writing *Evenings on a Farm Near Dikanka*, when he first had to depict the "Slavic Ausonia" (the Ukraine), of which he knew very little, while sitting in his apartment in St. Petersburg. He wrote to his relatives and friends, asking them to send him materials bearing on ordinary life. Among them were his mother, who had been his very first correspondent; from her he received the descriptions of huts and peasants (see his letter of April 23, 1846), and he gave her the responsibility of questioning salesmen as to how they traded and how they lived, adding: "I need all these details very much, and only later will you learn what use all this will be to all of you" (letter of February 16, 1847). A. O. Smirnova, whose husband had been appointed governor of Kaluga Province, was to be his source of information on "the personalities of everyone in Kaluga," on "all the gossip...all the instructions...all the absues...the peasants...everything that concerns their lot...all the most important matters that face Nikolay Mikhailovich [her husband] in Kaluga" (letter of January 27, 1846). He asked Danilevsky and his wife to "sketch out quick little portraits of people," to draw up a list of types "under such headings as: a Kievan social lion; a provincial *femme incomprise*; an official with European ways; an official who is an Old Believer, etc." (letter of March 18, 1847). And in this same letter he expressed the hope that "they [his new works] will reflect that faithfulness [to reality] and simplicity which I did not possess, despite the liveliness of the personalities and characters." One of his earliest requests went to N. Sheremeteva: "Inform me of all...lofty deeds of the soul, whoever might have performed them" (letter of November, 1842). Evidently Gogol needed not only material on ordinary life, but also psychological material, or, as he put it in 1846, not only the "concrete" but also the "spiritual statistics of Russia" (letter to N. M. Yazykov, April 21).

"Statistics" is a significant term. It comes up again and again in the letters of those years, and defines the second path taken by Gogol in his study of reality: published scholarly sources. In July of 1842, he asked S. T. Aksakov to send him V. P. Androsov's *Statistics of Russia (Statistika Rossii)*, "and any other first-rate statistical work on Russia generally, if one exists," even "the record of all proceedings in the Senate for the past year." A few months later he ordered maps of Russia. This obviously had nothing to do with his project for a geography of Russia (that came later), but was connected with his work on *Dead Souls*. In a letter to Pletnyov (written between December 1 and December 14, 1844), he as usual does not deny that he has "a certain knowledge of human nature," and admits that "in all of Russia I've rubbed shoulders with quite a few people," and that "I have almost always been inaccurate when I have dealt with precise descriptions of locales and customs." The book-study of locales and customs went on without interruption; in 1847, he wrote to Shevyryov: "I am reading nothing but all kinds of statistical documents on Russia, as well as my own inner book" (February 11).

The third path was a study of the works of the Natural School, of which Gogol unexpectedly turned out to be the head. His purposes were all the more evident here, because his friends—Yazykov and others—had spoken disdainfully of the naturalist writers. As he wrote Yazykov on April 21, 1846, annoyed at not having received books: "I would very much like to read the stories by our present-day writers. They always have a stimulating effect on me, despite the great burden of my sickly condition. That is where the concrete and spiritual statistics of Russia show through, and I have great need of them." On learning that Nekrasov's *Petersburg Miscellany (Peterburgskii sbornik)* had appeared, he immediately asked that it be sent to him, and he was displeased that A. M. Vielgorskaya had torn out only "Poor Folk" instead of forwarding the entire volume (see the letter to her of May 14, 1846). He also requested Butkov's "Summits of Petersburg" (see the letter to Arkady Osipovich Rosset, April 24, 1847).

In a long letter to Pletnyov written at the end of 1846,[11] Gogol outlined an entire program for *The Contemporary,* without knowing that the journal had passed into the hands of the Naturalists—Nekrasov and Belinsky. In the front ranks he places Sollogub, as a "faithful painter," and Dahl, whom he defends in a very significant way: "this writer [referred to by his pseudonym of Lugansky], more than the others, has been pleasing to my particular kind of taste...each line of his teaches and instructs me, bringing me closer to a knowledge of the ordinary Russian way of life and the life of our people....His works are living and faithful statistics of Russia." Gogol mentions N. F. Pavlov and P. A. Kulish after Sollogub and Dahl, and also gives a brief characterization of the entire Natural School, as consisting of "several young writers" who "have shown a particular desire to observe real life." He reproaches them for formal deficiencies in composition and style ("the structure of the stories themselves seemed especially unskilful and clumsy to me; in one story I noted excess and verbosity, and an absence of simplicity in the style"); but he believed in their future.

In general, Gogol at first reacted to the writers of the Natural School in the same way that Chartkov, in "The Portrait," had been intending to speak of the picture by the young artist who had studied in Italy ("yes, of course, to be sure, one can't deny that the artist has talent; however, there is something..." etc.), and he kept up the disdainful tone longer. In a letter to A. M. Vielgorskaya (May 14, 1846), he essentially repeated—consciously or unconsciously—Belinsky's ideas about Dostoevsky's "Poor Folk," but without the same enthusiasm: "Talent is evident in the author of 'Poor Folk'; the choice of subjects speaks in favor of his qualities of mind; but it is also evident that he is young. There is still much wordiness and little focus; the result could have been much more lively and forceful if everything had been compressed." However, he does make the qualification that he has only leafed through it and not yet subjected it to a thorough perusal. He intends to read it, as he does everything new in contemporary Russian literature, "a little at a time, like a delicacy." He later spoke of Ostrovsky's *The Bankrupt* in a similar tone.[12] There was only one writer of the time whom Gogol acknowledged immediately and without reservation: Turgenev. In a letter to Annenkov (incidentally, the same one in which he expressed his hope of meeting Herzen), he writes: "As far as I can judge from what I have read, he has a *wonderful* talent and gives promise of great activity in the future" (September 7, 1847). Toward the end of his life, if we are to give credence to Arnoldi's memoirs, he acknowledged not only Goncharov, but also Grigorovich: "He read everything and followed everything. He spoke of the works of Turgenev, Grigorovich and Goncharov with great praise: 'These are all phenomena that are reassuring for the future,' he said. 'Our literature has recently taken a sharp turn and has hit upon the true road. Only our poets are weak, and there is no bringing back the days of Pushkin, Baratynsky and Yazykov.' "[13]

Gogol's turn toward naturalism became more abrupt from 1845 on, when he burned Part 2 of *Dead Souls* for its failure to indicate the "paths leading to the beautiful." If this psychological motive is translated into the language of literary theory, we can say that he burned the book because it did not contain enough naturalism. From that time on, he set himself the specific task of "not arbitrarily inventing things out of my own head, not being sidetracked into idealism, but sticking to...the most essential truth," creating characters "out of our material, out of our soil, so that everyone will feel that this has been taken from his own body."[14] In 1845, Belinsky said, in reference to Sollogub's *The Tarantass*: "Russian literature, to its credit, has long since revealed its aspiration to be a mirror of reality."[15] Much earlier, Gogol had used the image of the mirror in the epigraph to *The Inspector General* ("Don't blame the mirror if your own mug is crooked"); but in his commentaries to *The Inspector General* (specifically, in "Leaving the Theater"), he emphasized the imaginary nature of the setting, the obvious inaccuracies and anachronisms, and the "terrible, almost caricature-like intensity" of the play as a whole. And of Part 1 of *Dead Souls* he wrote: "*Dead Souls*...has cut many people to the quick with its mockery and truth and caricatures." In Part 2 there were no longer supposed to be any caricatures: it was necessary "for everyone to call the work a faithful mirror and not a caricature."[16]

Finally, the publication of *Selected Passages* and the reactions to it gave Gogol the decisive push he required. A book which was supposed to create a utopia out of contemporary life and transform characters who had only recently been "freaks" into real-life "epic heroes" of the workaday world, revealed to all (and to Gogol in particular) that all his constructs were based on a fantasy-Russia, not a real one. Subsequently, Gogol even attempted to explain the publication of his book as the expression of a desire to obtain accurate information about Russia, a desire that readers should refute him with facts. Of course, this was not the only motive, but he did cherish the idea:

during those same years he wrote a preface to the second edition of *Dead Souls* in which he asked his readers to point out mistakes and blunders, and send him comments, stories of various happenings, and even thoughts on what might befall his heroes later. "I cannot publish the final volumes of my work," he wrote in this preface, "until I somehow get to know Russian life from every angle, at least to the extent that I need to know it for my work."

"It Is Necessary to Travel through Russia": this was the title of one of the articles in *Selected Passages*, and it now became personally relevant for Gogol. He decided to return to Russia in order to see everything, "touch" everything for himself. He set himself the task of studying Russia in every possible way. Arnoldi happened to travel with Gogol in 1849, and he remembered the thoroughness with which Gogol questioned everyone they met. On encountering a provincial mayor who, it turned out, had read *The Inspector General,* Gogol "fastened on [him] like a leech and questioned him tirelessly about everything that had struck his interest."[17] Gogol was unable to make a long journey through Russia, or at least he did not do so; but he did undertake extensive preparations for such a journey, assiduously studying the geography of the country. Six large notebooks with his own synopses of such studies have been published. Of course, they record mostly details of ordinary life and characteristic local expressions. Gogol intended to use this material in *Dead Souls* and also in an "essential, speaking geography...a living, not a dead depiction of Russia," which would be written "in a powerful, living style."[18]

Once he struck out on this new path, he was obliged to alter the structure of his "poem" completely.[19] It was not simply a matter of introducing "positive" heroes, although the need to do so could be explained by the greater degree of naturalism that was required by the new conception. Everything now had to be changed—the overall plan, the material, and the artistic devices. The comic intrigue remained the same: it was still based on the same "old principle" of a sudden "obstacle," to which Gogol had taken such a fancy at the beginning of the 1830s. Now this idea is stated explicitly by Chichikov: "Every time you even begin to reach for the fruits and, so to speak, touch them, you suddenly run into a storm, a reef, and the ship is smashed to splinters." But the devices of composition change in their particulars too. In Part 1, Chichikov makes his rounds of the landowners in a systematic and seemingly patterned manner; but in Part 2, it is a purely chance conjuncture of circumstances that takes him from one landowner to another in a natural way. He is no longer just the thread on which the episodes and characters are strung, but becomes an active figure in his own right. The picaresque escapades which in Part 1 were mentioned only in the account of his past (except, of course, for the central one, which runs throughout the work) now figure directly in the action itself: he intends to deceive Kostanzhoglo, to sell all of Khlobuev's estate (except for the dead souls and the runaway peasants), which he has bought with a semblance of good intentions, and slip away without paying what he owes. It would seem that this is exactly what he does in those chapters that have been lost.[20] He also gets involved in the business of forging a will, and he plans to escape from jail too: the tradition of the adventure-novel, which Gogol avoided in Part 1, was now brought in to serve the purposes of greater and more realistic variety. The Chichikov of Part 1 is static, locked within his thematic traits; the Chichikov of Part 2 is to be shown as psychologically more complex, as being capable of experiencing vacillation and inner conflict. The psychological element was to be strengthened throughout, and *Dead Souls* was to become a psychological novel.

The groundwork had already been laid toward the second half of the 1840s by Lermontov (*A Hero of Our Times* [*Geroi nashego vremeni*]) and his successors: Herzen (*Who Is To Blame?*) and Goncharov (*An Ordinary Story*). Alongside the static, visceral type of "freakish landowner" in Part 1 there now appeared, for the first time in *Dead Souls*, people with minds, "intellectual" types. In fact, in all of Gogol's earlier work we find only two such types: Piskaryov ("Nevsky Prospect") and Chartkov ("The Portrait"). The first is an adherent to an esthetic faith, the second an apostate from it. For the first time since *Evenings on a Farm Near Dikanka* and "Taras Bulba," love episodes appear, but now on an entirely different level, as an expression of this whole new psychological tenor. Tentetnikov and Ulinka experience love, a falling out, a reconciliation, mutual happiness, and marriage. The relationship between Platonov and the "emancipated" Chagranova is more complex as far as the psychology of love is concerned. This we know from people who heard Gogol read the chapters that have been lost. Their accounts enable us to judge that the social backdrop of Part 2 was to be broader than in Part 1: Tentetnikov was to be arrested for belonging to a secret political society and exiled to Siberia; Ulinka was to follow him, thereby calling to mind what the wives of the Decembrists had done.

It is certainly not just the introduction of "positive" types that accounts for the failure of Part 2. At issue here is Gogol's attempt to create a realistic (as we would say today) and psychological novel on a broadly and variedly conceived scale. Belinsky had pointed to the figure of Taras Bulba by way of condemning Gogol's one-sidedness;[21] clearly, the old devices of hyperbole could be used for more than just insignificant characters. But in Part 2, it is not only the "ideal" figures who seem pallid, but also those who are anything but ideal—Tentetnikov, Platonov, Glebov, in fact all those for whom Gogol essays a psychological approach. Certainly he did not set himself the task of creating "idealized" characters; on the contrary, he burned everything he had done on Part 2 up to 1845 precisely because it was idealized. It was simply that he could not help but slide back into a schematic and idealized treatment of character, lacking, as he did, any experience in depicting psychological complexity. One of his correspondents, K. I. Markov, warned him against "heroes of virtue," and, as a convinced naturalist, gave him the following advice: "Hide your hands; the audience can see you moving your puppets around." Gogol did not fundamentally disagree, and replied: "Actually,

I did not have a *hero of virtues* in mind. On the contrary, nearly all the personages can be called heroes of defects. The point is simply that these characters are *more significant* than the earlier ones, and that the author's intention has been to delve more deeply into the higher meaning of life (which we have made trivial and banal), by exposing the Russian to greater view, instead of seeing him *from only one particular angle.*"[22] (By way of contrast, see Gogol's letter to Pushkin dated October 10 [o.s.], 1835, in which he speaks of his desire to "show all of Russia at least from one side.")

In Gogol's sense of the term, we can call the heroes of Part 2 "heroes of defects"—with the exception, at any rate, of Kostanzhoglo, Murazov and the governor-general. These three are depicted in the hues of Gogol's third idyll, and exemplify, respectively, the ideal household manager, the ideal (and pious!) man of wealth, and the ideal civil servant, all of whom had been schematically outlined in *Selected Passages.* In fleshing them out in Part 2 of *Dead Souls,* he could not avoid having to choose between two possibilities: either depicting an unblushingly unreal inhabitant of that fantasy-world that was his Russia, or substituting an "exister" of the old kind (slightly prettied up, but in effect made colorless) for the newer "idealized" exister that had evolved. Murazov and the governor-general are fantasy-characters, Murazov in particular ("he's got more than forty million roubles...soon half of Russia will be in his hands..."). Kostanzhoglo's enterprises border on fantasy ("for six years running, for instance, people dumped fish scales on my river bank; well, what was I supposed to do with them? I began boiling them down for glue, and I've raked in forty thousand from this enterprise alone"). There is also an element of fantasy in the description of Kostanzhoglo's outward appearance after his inspired account of his wealth ("he glowed all over like a tsar on the day of his solemn coronation, and it seemed as if rays were streaming from his face"). But no matter how much Kostanzhoglo may try to turn the expansion of his household into art for art's sake ("and it's not because the money increases—money is only money—but because all this is the work of your own hands"), he cannot conceal the self-satisfaction he feels as a proprietor and acquirer ("everything multiplies and multiplies, bearing fruit and income"). Essentially he is no different from Chichikov: there is good reason why Chichikov, while still his old self, long before showing any signs of regeneration, listens spellbound to Kostanzhoglo's words "as to the singing of a bird of heaven."

It is impossible to come to any final conclusions as to whether Part 2 of *Dead Souls* would have been successful or not. Chernyshevsky warned against drawing such conclusions, pointing out that we have only a rough draft of Part 2, which was subject to reworking.[23] We must also remember that the most characteristic instances of Gogol's new conception of the novel, the most "psychological" chapters, have not survived: the reconciliation of Tentetnikov and Betrishchev, Ulinka's prayer over her mother's grave, "two wonderful lyrical pages" depicting the happiness that got Tentetnikov all choked up, the love-affair between Platonov and Chagranova, the bored "heroes of our time" ("this happiness was only momentary, and a month after their first declaration of love they noticed that it had been only a flash, a caprice, that there was no real love here, that they were even incapable of it, and then came a cooling-off on both sides, and then again came boredom, profound boredom"); and finally, the experiences of Tentetnikov and Ulinka just before they go into exile.[24] The people who heard Gogol read these chapters—Arnoldi, Smirnova, Shevyryov—spoke of them enthusiastically. After the reading, Arnoldi said to Gogol:"In these chapters you come much closer to reality than in the first volume: here one feels life everywhere, as it is, without any exaggeration, and the description of the garden is the height of perfection."[25] The critic N. D. Mizko found that the heroes of Part 2 "represent a step forward...as objects of an experienced power of observation." Even Dmitry Pisemsky, who was sharply critical of Part 2, had an impression of Betrishchev, Tentetnikov, Petukh, Petukh's sons, and in particular Khlobuev as "fully living people" (although he did note an element of caricature in Petukh).[26] It is impossible to say whether Gogol would have developed into a naturalistic writer, and futile to speculate; the only thing clear is that these new artistic devices cost him agonizing effort.

Other devices are also employed for the portrayal of individual characters. The device of thematic traits still echoes, like a reminiscence, in the depiction of the two heroes who are the most exaggerated (and are therefore closest to the characters in Part 1): Petukh and Koshkaryov. Petukh is a watermelon. This is somewhat toned down in the revised version: he is just *like* a watermelon or a small barrel; yet the comparison with a watermelon does remain. In the first version, Koshkaryov is still a complete caricature: "a face that is somewhat prim, shaped like a triangle; the sidewhiskers on his cheeks were shaved into a fine line; his hair, the way it was styled, his nose, lips, chin —all gave the impression of having been kept under a press until then."[27] It is noteworthy that Gogol cuts this description, which still carries suggestions of earlier devices, out of the revised version, and puts *nothing* in its place: there is no description of Koshkaryov's outward appearance, just as there is none of Tentetkinov's, Khlobuev's, Murazov's or the prince's.[28]

The physical appearance of Betrishchev and Platonov is portrayed by means of a new and rather significant device: a comparison with familiar stereotypes. Betrishchev is "a picturesque general of 1812." Platonov is conventionally handsome and of a *picturesque* stature: he is "Achilles and Paris rolled into one." Naturalistic devices for depicting exteriors are tried out only in the case of Kostanzhoglo: "Chichikov was struck by the swarthiness of his face, the coarseness of his black hair, which had turned prematurely gray in spots, the lively expression of his eyes, and the rather jaundiced stamp of his ardent southern origin" (the first version speaks of an admixture of something jaundiced and embittered).

Ulinka is drawn with special care; but it is evident that this portrait simply eludes Gogol. Sometimes he wanders off into prosaisms, as when he talks

172

about the "unusual harmoniousness of all the parts of her body," sometimes he seeks help in clichéd expressions (like his description of Betrishchev and Platonov), as, for example: "such a pure, noble facial outline could not be found anywhere except perhaps on small ancient cameos." Then, finally, he indulges in exaggerated idealization: she was of a *"dazzling* stature." In the revised version, the idealization is considerably toned down. Instead of "a dazzling stature," Gogol simply says that "she seemed to tower over everyone else in stature." The sentence "she seemed to have appeared for the purpose of illuminating the room" is cut out altogether. Instead of "grasping with her marvellous little hand," Gogol simply says "grasping with her hand." Instead of "this little figure glowing with life," there is simply "this little figure." Undoubtedly this reworking of the figure of Ulinka reflected some advice given by A. O. Smirnova in a letter of August 1 (o.s.), 1849: "Take Ulinka just a bit off her pedestal, and give Kostanzhoglo's wife some work to do: she is terribly pathetic."[29] Gogol did make use of the second item here. Instead of the idle, "somnolent" woman of the first version, he presented the entirely new image of an energetic, cheerful and talkative woman who has work of her own: preparing medicines for the peasants and raising her daughter, whom she does not want to entrust to a governess. Smirnova's letter, and the fact that Gogol took the advice it offered, constitute a new and, it seems to me, decisive piece of evidence for determining just when Gogol was working on the later version of Part 2: the first was completed by 1850, the second was being worked on in 1850 and 1851.[30]

A comparison of the two surviving versions shows that Gogol continued to move in the direction of naturalism with undiminished vigor during the final years of his life. The nature-scenes, even their details, are done with greater polish and care. Some of the botanical terms that he was painstakingly collecting and recording in his notebooks are introduced, as are whole new scenes (such as the arrival of spring, in Chapter I), and new details of ordinary life (such as the description of Perfilievna in that same chapter). On the other hand, scenes that smack too strongly of caricature are toned down or cut out altogether. The scene where Tentetnikov is met by the peasants was a caricature and was dropped (the women fight; a flabby old woman who looks like a dried pear screams "dear young master," and "beards" drive her away "with spade, shovel and wedge"). Gogol tones down the scene where "some twenty fishermen" haul Petukh out of a pond along with the fish they have caught. He cuts from Chapter III the conversations between Selifan and Petrushka, with the narrator's gibes at Petrushka's "ugly mug." In working on Part 1, Gogol had persistently interpolated "pathetic" passages into various parts of the text. In Chapter II, for instance, there is a passage about "a sullied man who is perishing" and "a brother's soul that is perishing." These are omitted from the final version; and this process is characteristic of Part 2 as a whole.

In addition, the social backdrop in the final version is broadened, and the social satire sharpened and directed both to the right and the left. At first, the "man in the case"[31]—the pedantic pedagogue Fyodor Ivanych, who has replaced the ideal headmaster Alexander Petrovich in the school attended by Tentetnikov—was pictured as basically kind-hearted and diligent, merely incompetent. But in the final version, no attempt is made to justify him. Nor is any attempt made to justify the bureaucrats—Tentetnikov's uncle and his superior. Tentetnikov's reflections on bureaucracy as being "a fantastic...directing of the provinces" involving "the scribbling of dead papers" are introduced. But the same sharp tone also comes out in Gogol's attitudes toward forward-looking revolutionary tendencies. New details are introduced into the scornful portrayal of a secret society. Here readers have seen allusions to the Petrashevsky Circle, and, in the figure of "the esthete who did not finish school," a belated attack on Belinsky. New also are Kostanzhoglo's attacks on "political economists" and on factories, which echo the appeals for a patriarchal way of life that Gogol had been making not too long before in *Selected Passages.* On the other hand, the attacks on schools are toned down; Kostanzhoglo's discourse on their harmfulness (and on the harmfulness of almshouses) is omitted; Platonov's objections are gone too; all that remain are a few words on the "Don Quixotes" of philanthropy and enlightenment. (We can also see, from the draft version of the letter to Belinsky and from "An Author's Confession," that Gogol had been fearful of earning the reputation of being a defender of ignorance, and that he had abandoned his paradoxical position.)

Finally, the *psychological* element is also strengthened in the last version. Originally, the possibility of Chichikov's regeneration, under Murazov's influence, had flickered and promptly disappeared. Now, however, this possibility is developed into a complex psychological portrait. Originally, Chichikov promptly gives verbal assent to Murazov's exhortations to begin a new life, and only vague, ephemeral feelings match his words. In the new version, he at first agrees automatically, and then promptly catches himself: "No, it's too late...too late!..No, I have been brought up wrong....I have a coarse nature...I don't have the same desire to work for the good as I do to acquire property." Murazov's renewed exhortations have their effect: Chichikov's entire being is shakened and softened, and "it seemed that he felt a stirring of the half-awakened forces in his soul." It no longer occurs to him to keep all the profits from his swindling; he is close to undergoing a really basic change; but a new temptation—to justify himself in completely dishonest ways—again returns him to the Chichikov of old, and he embarks on new fraudulent ventures. Moralistic and artistic purposes coincided in the way Gogol developed Chichikov's vacillations. In Khlobuev's life, the change for the time being is only outward, but there is some hope for inner change, also under the influence of that conventional moralist Murazov. This change is depicted essentially the same way in both versions, expect that the close resemblance to particular ideas and phrases in *Selected Passages* is now played down.

While abandoning explicit moralizing in the last years of his life, Gogol did not abandon the idea of expressing moralistic conclusions in the continuation of *Dead Souls*. These conclusions, however, were not final. The figure of Kostanzhoglo was created entirely in the spirit of *Selected Passages*; but he is followed by the quite different figure of Khlobuev, for whom Gogol foresees a great and almost ascetic deed. And we do not know whether Gogol would have remained content with his idea of turning Chichikov into an ideal "Russian landowner" of the kind seen in *Selected Passages,* or whether he would have depicted his regeneration differently. Such uncertainties in themselves tended to complicate Gogol's work; and the conjunction of ideological factors with artistic ones, and with the requirements of a naturalistic "faithfulness," made his task exceptionally complex. He would have faced even greater difficulties in Part 3: there Plyushkin was to undergo regeneration, and the book was to end with "Chichikov's first deeply-felt desire for a truly stable life."

A. N. Veselovsky suggested a parallel between the three projected parts of *Dead Souls* and the three parts of Dante's *Divine Comedy*.[32] It is difficult to say to what extent this actually corresponded with Gogol's intentions. Apparently Part 3 was to become a "purgatory" only for Khlobuev, Plyushkin and Chichikov. As for his other heroes, Gogol merely remarked enigmatically that they would rise again "if they wish to."[33] If Chichikov's regeneration was conceived of as the denouement of the entire "poem," then Gogol hardly had anything like Dante's "paradise" in mind. It is difficult even to imagine how "paradise" could be depicted in the terms of the realistic psychological novel that Gogol's "poem" was turning into. Similarly, a depiction of "inferno" was possible only in terms of the old hyperbolism, which he had abandoned.

CHAPTER XIV

Gogol began to regain a stability of mind toward the end of his life. The psychiatric analysis which N. N. Bazhenov made in a long article determined that this occurred toward the end of 1851, after an unbroken run of illness throughout 1849 and 1850.[1] The work that had been hanging over his head— Part 2 of *Dead Souls*—was finally nearing completion. All that remained, apparently, was to make a fair copy and put in final corrections, as was his habit. At the same time, he was preparing a new edition of his works for the press, beginning with *Evenings on a Farm Near Dikanka* which, after some hesitation, he agreed to include. As late as January 25, 1852, O. M. Bodyansky found him hard at work, and was invited to come to the Aksakovs to listen to Ukrainian songs, as transcribed from Gogol's own renditions.[2]

The next day A. S. Khomyakov's wife died. She was the sister of the poet Yazykov, who had been close to Gogol and had died six years earlier. According to eyewitnesses, her death hit Gogol exceptionally hard. Thoughts of death and the premonition of his own end began to haunt him. "At the funeral," as Khomyakov recalled after Gogol had died, "he said: 'Everything is over for me.' From that time on, he manifested a kind of nervous disorder, which took the form of religious mania. He fasted to the point where he began to starve, while reproaching himself for gluttony. Inozemtsev, one of his doctors, did not understand what was wrong with him, and treated him in such a way as to reduce him to utter exhaustion."[3] The meaning of the words "from that time one" is not entirely clear. For several days after the death of Khomyakov's wife, Gogol went on working; he visited the Aksakovs; he talked to S. T. Aksakov's daughter Vera about his work (he still had the proofs of *The Inspector General* to correct) and about her father's work. Yet thoughts of death and his own fear of death all weighed upon him and came out in these conversations too. A few lines that he jotted down just before his death, as well as his last will and testament, show that the demonic images which had so impressed themselves upon his imagination as a young man had now taken on a more concrete and more terrible significance for him. (Whenever he had used such images in his letters during the past ten years, it had always been with a touch of humor.)

On February 2, he wrote his last letters to Zhukovsky and to his mother. In them he says nothing about the death of Khomyakov's wife, as if fearing to touch the wound.[4] They testify to the fact that he was going on with his work and that he had great hopes for it. February 4 was a day of radical change: it marked the onset of the frenzied asceticism which sapped his remaining strength. This is what Khomyakov was referring to in the passage cited above, and others have described it in greater detail.[5] Gogol was not simply observing the rituals of the Church, but deliberately wearing himself down. His friends tried to stop him by appealing to the authority of Metropolitan Filaret, who ordered Gogol, in the name of the Church, to submit to the doctors. But Gogol would not obey even Filaret. As Pletnyov wrote Zhukovsky: "He [Gogol] would take only a few drops of water with red wine, and he continued to kneel before the many icons that had been placed before him, and to pray." To all exhortations he replied quietly and succinctly: "Leave me alone, I am all right."[6]

It is difficult to say what role was played in this radical change by the arrival of Father Matvey Konstantinovsky and by the talks he had with Gogol. Only one sentence that someone chanced to overhear has come to our knowledge. Merezhkovsky's conjectures (he even tried to determine the nature of the visions Gogol had just before his death) remain only conjectures.[7] Matvey's personality has not yet been fully studied. If in fact he was the new Savonarola he is depicted as being, we must also remember that Gogol, up to his last year of life, had no doubts about the significance of his own work, and that his stubborn belief in himself did not affect his good relations with Matvey. The priest could not have been the only one to have exerted an influence on Gogol (whatever the nature of his particular influence might have been). Others were involved; Gogol's own experiences played their part as well. Matvey may not actually have been the cause of Gogol's sudden turn toward extreme asceticism (the decisive push came from the death of Khomyakov's wife), but it is entirely possible that he encouraged it. However, we will remain within the realm of conjecture until new evidence comes to hand.

While preparing himself for death, Gogol naturally must have given serious thought on more than one occasion to the value of the literary legacy he was leaving. Heretofore he had often cast an eye over his earlier work and had renounced much of it, especially what he had written in his youth. He reluctantly agreed that *Evenings on a Farm Near Dikanka* should be republished in the new edition of his collected works. Shortly before his death, he tore several of his manuscripts into tiny pieces; some of them had to do with *Evenings* and *Arabesques*, and some with unpublished drafts of historical and other works dating from the same period.[8] On February 10, 1852, he gave A. P. Tolstoy (in whose house he was living) instructions as to what was to be done with his works after his death: some were to be published, and some (perhaps "Meditations on the Divine Liturgy"?) were to be left to the discretion of Metropolitan Filaret.[9] On the night of February 11-12, he decided to burn part of his manuscripts. The accounts of this (contradictory as to detail) are based on the testimony of Gogol's servant Semyon. Entering the room, Gogol told Semyon to "give him the portfolio from the wardrobe. When the portfolio had been brought, Gogol took out a sheaf of notebooks tied with a ribbon, placed it in the stove, and lit it with a candle that he himself was holding. The servant guessed what he was about to do, fell on his knees before him, and said: 'Master! What are you doing? Stop!'—'It's none of your concern,' he replied. 'Pray!' The boy began to pray and to implore Gogol. Meanwhile, the fire had gone out after scorching the corners of the notebooks. Gogol noticed this, removed the sheaf of papers from the stove, undid the ribbon, and, arranging the pages in such as way that they would catch more easily, again set them afire, and sat in a chair before the fire, waiting until everything had burned to ashes. Then, crossing himself, he went back into the room he had come from. He kissed his servant, lay down on the couch, and began to weep."[10]

This is the account given in the most reliable of the three versions, as related to M. P. Pogodin. From it one can see that Gogol was in anguish as he took leave of his literary labors. But we can also see that he did not know exactly what was contained in this sheaf of papers that was tied with a ribbon.[11] According to Pogodin, the next day Gogol said to A. P. Tolstoy: "Just imagine how powerful the evil spirit is! I wanted to burn some papers I had intended to burn long ago, but instead I burned the chapters of *Dead Souls* which I wanted to leave my friends to remember me by after my death."[12]

This is the only thing we have from Gogol himself regarding the burning of Part 2 of *Dead Souls*. But people have developed the habit of refusing to believe anything Gogol said. Practically every utterance of his has been declared an exercise in deliberate mystification that is unworthy of attention. The biographers needed a nice legend about Gogol—a Gogol who, just before his death, renounced the beloved work on which he had been laboring for many years.[13] And the legend was created. The only thing remaining was to create the appropriate psychology. Here we find a divergence of opinion. According to some, Gogol was dissatisfied, as an artist, with what he had written. According to others, his burning of *Dead Souls* represented a "sacrifice" he made just before dying.

But all these conjectures rest on a presupposition which for a long time seemed truly unshakable: that the drafts of Part 2 of *Dead Souls* which have come down to us survived the first burning (as Trushkovsky supposed), or even the first two burnings (as Tikhonravov supposed)—that is, they date from the first half of the 1840s—and that it was the *fair* copy which was actually burned. Tikhonravov did not explain precisely how the *first few* chapters survived the first burning (needless to say, there was only *one* deliberate burning), or in any event, those chapters that were written (whether more were actually written, no one can say). The first burning (if we are not to consider *that* an exercise in mystification as well!) was the conscious act of an artist. It is difficult to suppose that Gogol, in the course of seven years of work on Part 2, did not know what he had burned and what he had not. But there are other arguments (advanced in the preceding chapter) in favor of regarding Gogol's work on the surviving chapters of Part 2 as the work precisely of the *final* years of his life. There is no reliable evidence that any other manuscript of *Dead Souls* existed (in fair copy) other than the one that has come down to us. The only fact we have is the following: the survival of the first four and one of the last (if not the very last) chapters of Gogol's final work. The middle chapters are missing, the very ones about which we know something from the people who heard Gogol read them aloud. It is clear that *these* were the ones that were burned, and in fact Gogol makes mention of this: "I burned the chapters of *Dead Souls* which (i.e., evidently meaning the work as a whole, and not just "the chapters") I wanted to leave my friends to remember me by after my death." What kind of "sacrifice" is this—several chapters from the middle of the manuscript?[14]

Of course, we cannot regard the riddle of the burning of *Dead Souls* as being definitively solved. We do not know—and we probably never shall know —exactly what Gogol *wished* to burn instead of the chapters he did burn. We can construct hypotheses; we can carry caution to the point of regarding Gogol's own statements as those of a person no longer responsible for what he is saying and refusing to believe them. But hypotheses must remain hypotheses; they cannot be passed off as facts.[15] And all hypotheses ought to be based on the statement made by Gogol himself until it is refuted by facts. Except for the details in the account given by Gogol's servant—details which A. I. Kirpichnikov, a supporter of the idea of Gogol's "sacrifice," considered untrustworthy[16]—there is nothing to contradict Gogol's statement. This statement is supported by what actually befell the manuscripts: the *destruction* of the early versions and the *preservation* of a considerable portion of the later ones. Therefore, it is most plausible to assume that Gogol did not wish to burn *Dead Souls* and did so by accident. Insofar as the burning of his beloved work, even partially, was accidental, the discovery of the fateful mistake must have had an even greater effect on him. In the memoirs of Dr. Tarasenkov, who was one of his physicians, the words in which Gogol tells of the burning of the manuscript are virtually identical with those in Pogodin's version, and are followed by a report of the conversation with A. P. Tolstoy. Tolstoy said: " 'That's a good sign—you burned everything before too, and then you wrote even better. So you are not going to die this time either. Can you remember everything?' 'Yes,' Gogol replied, placing his hand on his forehead, 'I can, I can, it's all in my head,' and he grew seemingly calmer and stopped weeping."[17]

Was Gogol trying to set Tolstoy's mind at rest—or his own? Of course he could not help but know that he would soon die and that the burned chapters of *Dead Souls* would not be recreated. Already exhausted by hunger, he was now being even more exhausted by grief over what had just happened, and was moving inexorably toward death. "Clear signs of nervous fever" were apparently combined with starvation and typhus.[18] The doctors who were called into consultation could not agree on a diagnosis of the illness; and Dr. Tarasenkov made no attempt to look into "the many conditions which seemed deliberately to conjoin to lead to his death." One thing was clear, however: on February 16, when the doctors were called in, they were already helpless. The consultation of February 20 was useless; it is painful to read how the doctors tormented him on the eve of his death in hopes of saving him, although he was patently incurable.

On the morning of February 21, 1852, nine days after he had burned the manuscript, and toward the end of his forty-third year of life, Gogol died.

* * * * * *

NOTES TO TRANSLATOR'S FOREWORD

1. Most of the information for this biographical sketch is taken from G. Fridlender, "Ot redaktora," foreword to V. V. Gippius, OT PUSHKINA DO BLOKA, Moscow-Leningrad, 1966, pp. 3-6. This is a collection of Gippius's essays, and also contains a bibliography of his works (pp. 341-46).

2. The collection is not really "complete," although it is so designated in the title (POLNOE SOBRANIE SOCHINENII). Among the works omitted is "Meditations on the Divine Liturgy."

3. According to Fridlender, p. 5.

4. See his article entitled "Problematika i kompozitsiia 'Revizora,'" which appeared in an important two-volume collection of new source materials and scholarly essays on Gogol, published in 1936 and edited by Gippius (N. V. GOGOL'. MATERIALY I ISSLEDOVANIIA, Moscow-Leningrad). It is available in English, under the title "THE INSPECTOR GENERAL: Structure and Problems," in R. A. Maguire, GOGOL FROM THE TWENTIETH CENTURY: ELEVEN ESSAYS, Princeton, 1974, pp. 215-265. For a brief account of the development of the "official" Soviet attitude toward Gogol, and for an account of Formalist views, see my GOGOL..., esp. pp. 35-38, 45-48.

5. In TRUDY OTDELA NOVOI RUSSKOI LITERATURY, Izd. AN SSSR, Moscow-Leningrad, 1948, pp. 9-38.

6. "Tvorcheskii put' Gogolia," OT PUSHKINA DO BLOKA, Moscow-Leningrad, 1966, pp. 46-200.

NOTES TO AUTHOR'S PREFACE

1. [Presumably Gippius has in mind: N. A. Kotlyarevsky, N. V. GOGOL' (1829-1842). OCHERK IZ ISTORII RUSSKOI POVESTI I DRAMY, St. Petersburg, 1903; I. D. Mandelshtam, O KHARAKTERE GOGOLEVSKOGO STILIA. GLAVA IZ ISTORII RUSSKOGO LITERATURNOGO IAZYKA, Helsingfors, 1902; V. F. Pereverzev, TVORCHESTVO GOGOLIA, Moscow, 1914; V. V. Zenkovsky, "N. V. Gogol' v ego religioznykh iskaniiakh," KHRISTIANSKAIA MYSL', Nos. 1-3, 5, 7-8, 10, 12, 1916 (these articles formed the basis for Zenkovsky's book N. V. GOGOL', Paris, 1961, which Gippius could not of course have known).]

2. [See the Translator's Foreword.]

3. [For students of literature, Modzalevsky and Eikhenbaum are the most important of the scholars mentioned here. Boris Leonidovich Modzalevsky (1874-1928) was one of the founders of the Pushkin House of the Institute of Russian Literature of the Academy of Sciences in St. Petersburg. He was a prominent specialist in Pushkin, and an indefatigable collector and publisher of documents by and about Russian writers. Boris Mikhailovich Eikhenbaum (1886-1959) won fame as a Formalist critic, particularly with the essay "How Gogol's 'Overcoat' Is Made" ("Kak sdelana 'Shinel'" Gogolia," 1918), although he soon broadened his approach to take historical, social and biographical factors into account in literary studies. His best work is devoted to Lermontov and Tolstoy. (The essay on Gogol has been translated into English in R. A. Maguire, GOGOL FROM THE TWENTIETH CENTURY: ELEVEN ESSAYS, Princeton, 1974.)]

1. M. A. Trakhimovsky, "Mar'ia Ivanovna Gogol'," RUSSKAIA STARINA, No. 7, 1888, p. 30. [Gippius mistakenly identifies the author as "Trokhimovich." "Three thousand acres" in the next sentence of the paragraph is the English equivalent of "more than a thousand *desiatinas,*" one *desiatina* equalling 2.7 acres.]

2. [This is a composite quote. "Full cup" is from Trakhimovsky, as cited in Note 1; the rest is from Gogol's story "Old-Fashioned Landowners."]

3. [The first quote is from Pushkin's poem "Epistle to the Censor" ("Poslanie k tsenzoru," 1822); the Russian reads: "Dnei Aleksandrovykh prekrasnoe nachalo." The second (noted by Gippius) is from Ya. M. Markovich, ZAPISKI O MALOROSSII, EE PISATELIAKH I PROIZVEDENIIAKH, 1798.]

4. [The first quote is from Gogol's "Old-Fashioned Landowners," the second from THE INSPECTOR GENERAL.]

5. [Dmitry Prokofievich Troshchinsky (1754-1829) was a State Secretary under Emperor Paul, and under Alexander I a member of the State Council, chief director of postal services, and Minister of Crown Lands. He retired in 1806, but returned to service as Minister of Justice between 1814 and 1817. "Buffoon-hecklers" in this paragraph renders *shutodrazniteli.* Troshchinsky kept buffoons (*shuty*) to entertain himself and his guests. When their resources were exhausted, the "buffoon-hecklers" were summoned, "that is, people who did not shrink from cruel and stupid mockery of the unfortunate, downtrodden idiots or the half-insane clowns..." (V. I. Shenrok, MATERIALY DLIA BIOGRAFII GOGOLIA, I, Moscow, 1892, pp. 68-69).]

6. [Gogol-Yanovsky was the family's full name, although it was not genealogically correct. Gogol (the writer) dropped the "Yanovsky." The question of Gogol's ancestry is very complex. For a convenient discussion, in English, see Leon Stilman, "Nikolaj Gogol and Ostap Hohol," ORBIS SCRIPTUS. DMITRIJ TSCHIŽEWSKIJ ZUM 70 GEBURTSTAG, Munich, Wilhelm Fink Verlag, 1966, pp. 811-825.]

7. Shenrok, MATERIALY, I, p. 62. ["Church calendar" renders *chet'i-minei,* literally "reading menaia." These consisted of various spiritual readings, especially from the lives of the saints, arranged by months (hence *menaia,* the Greek for "months"). There are four menaia in the Russian Orthodox Church.]

8. V. V. Zenkovsky, "N. V. Gogol' v ego religioznykh iskaniiakh": see Note 1 of "Author's Preface" for full reference. [The "belief in a prophetic dream" at the beginning of the sentence evidently refers to Maria Ivanovna's report of a dream her husband had as a very young man, in which the Blessed Virgin appeared to him and pointed to an infant sitting at her feet, who would, she said, be his wife. Later, on visiting neighbors, he saw a seven-month-old child in the arms of a wet nurse, with features identical to those of the child in the dream. At the time he said nothing about the coincidence, but he knew that he had seen his future wife. Thirteen years later, he had the same dream, in a somewhat different form. (Told by Gogol's mother to S. T. Aksakov, and published in SOVREMENNIK, IV, 1913, p. 252, as in V. V. Veresaev, GOGOL' V ZHIZNI, Moscow-Leningrad, 1933, p. 23.]

9. [ISTORIIA MOEGO ZNAKOMSTVA S GOGOLEM (written largely in 1854, first complete edition 1890).]

10. Shenrok, MATERIALY, I, p. 202. [Quote from Gogol's mother as in RUSSKAIA STARINA, No. 6, 1886.]

11. I. G. Pashchenko, "Cherty iz zhizni Gogolia," BEREG, No. 268, 1880. [The reference above is to I. P. Zhitetsky, "Gogol'—propovednik i pisatel'," ZHURNAL MINISTERSTVA NARODNOGO PROSVESHCHENIIA, 1909.]

12. [By "interludes" Gippius undoubtedly means the so-called *intermedii*. Of these Y. M. Sokolov writes: "Already in Poland, the Jesuit school drama which had elaborated biblical and legendary Church subjects according to all the rules of the scholastic Latin poetics...permitted the so-called *intermedii*. The *intermedii* are comic scenes from everyday life, which were already being performed, not in the Latin, but in the vernacular tongue, frequently not even in Polish, but in Ukrainian or White-Russian. In these *intermedii* of the Polish school drama, one cannot help perceiving elements of the popular theater" (RUSSIAN FOLKLORE, trans. Catherine Ruth Smith, N. Y., 1950, p. 500). "Nativity puppet play" renders *vertep*. Another term sometimes used is "crèche play." See Sokolov's definition: "The crèche performances consist of two sharply differentiated elements—the religious-biblical, and the realistic-comic. This division was emphasized and maintained by the very outward arrangement of the crèche stage—a box, divided into two parts: the upper, where plays were presented which were connected with the legend of the birth of Christ in the manger at Bethlehem, and the lower, intended for the comic plays based on everyday life. Those who participated in the latter, in the Ukraine, were the traditional personages—peasants, soldiers, gypsies, Jews, and Poles, and also the Dnieper Cossack..." (RUSSIAN FOLKLORE, pp. 500-501). The characters were represented by puppets.]

13. Both soldiers sing and unsuccessfully translate the same song. On the source of the plot, see N. P. Dashkevich, in KIEVSKAIA STARINA (No. 12, 1893), and N. I. Korobka, "Detstvo i iunost' Gogolia," ZHURNAL MINISTERSTVA NARODNOGO PROSVESHCHENIIA, Feb., 1902, pp. 251-257. THE SIMPLETON was published in OSNOVA, No. 2, 1862. [As for the title of the Kotlyarevsky play, the word *moskal'* in Ukrainian can mean either "soldier" or "Russian."]

14. According to P. A. Kulish, "Neskol'ko chert dlia biografii Nikolaia Vasil'evicha Gogolia" (OTECHESTVENNYE ZAPISKI, Vol. 81, Section VIII, 1852), on one occasion Gogol brought DOG OR SHEEP back to Nezhin with him after the holidays; but it is not specifically stated that the play was put on. According to Pashchenko [a schoolmate of Gogol's; see Note 11], the pupils performed "some Little Russian play, written at that time by Gogol, which made the audience nearly explode with laughter." Shenrok (MATERIALY, I, p. 241) considers, on insufficient grounds, that "the author [Pashchenko] probably means a comedy written by Gogol's father." [Panteleymon Alexandrovich Kulish (1819-1897), a Ukrainian writer who began in the Romantic vein but switched to "naturalism" and ethnography, was best known for his LITTLE RUSSIAN STORIES (MALOROSSIISKIE RASSKAZY, 1841). He edited an edition of Gogol's works (SOCHINENIIA I PIS'MA, 6 vols., St. Petersburg, 1857), and made two attempts at a biography of Gogol (OPYT BIOGRAFII GOGOLIA, 1854; ZAPISKI O ZHIZNI GOGOLIA, 1856).

["Little Russian" and "Ukrainian" were used more or less interchangeably throughout much of the nineteenth century, with official preference going to "Little Russian."]

15. See Gogol's letter to his parents, of October 1 (o.s.), 1824.

16. Subsequently, in the 1860s, Kulzhinsky became a Ukrainophobe, and ridiculed the "spoiled" "Little Russian dialect." Cf. V. V. Danilov, "K kharakteristike I. G. Kulzhinskogo," UKRAINA, Kiev, 1908, and his article in the miscellany devoted to Gogol published in 1909 by Novorossiisk University ("Vliianie bytovoi i literaturnoi sredy na 'Vechera na khutore bliz Dikan'ki,'" SBORNIK, izd. Imperatorskim Novorosiiskim Universitetom, po sluchaiu stoletiia so dnia rozhdeniia N. V. Gogolia, Odessa, 1909). [The dates of Ivan Grigorievich Kulzhinsky are 1803-1884. Cf. his memoirs, "Vospominaniia uchitelia," MOSKVITIANIN, VI, 1854, which include a mention of Gogol.]

17. V. V. Danilov, polemicizing with Professor M. N. Speransky (Vliianie...,"

p. 103), explains Gogol's reaction by the fact that he had "made no conscious assimilation of the theory and ideas of nationality." Did this not instead reflect Gogol's esthetic fastidiousness, which was reinforced by the generally mocking attitude the pupils took toward the young teacher?

18. Kulish [see Note 14] speaks of a journal written by Gogol himself; Lyubich-Romanovich mentions journals by Kukolnik and Bazili; but it was only in the latter that Gogol's compositions appeared.

[Konstantin Mikhailovich Bazili (1809-1884), a Greek by birth, later became a diplomat and historian, who wrote much about the East. He left memoirs of Gogol. Nikolay Yakovlevich Prokopovich (1810-1857), later a teacher of Russian literature and a minor poet, was a frequent correspondent of Gogol's. Yevgeny Pavlovich Grebenka (1812-1842) wrote both in Russian and Ukrainian, but mainly on Ukrainian themes regardless of language. The Lyubich-Romanovich in question is Vasily Ignatievich (1805-1888), a civil servant in the Ministry of Justice and the Ministry of Foreign Affairs, a poet and translator, and the author of memoirs of Gogol.]

19. V. V. Kallash considered that the radical change occurred "in the direction of sentimentally romantic dreaminess" ("N. V. Gogol' i ego pis'ma," RUSSKAIA MYSL', No. 2, 1902, pp. 102-120). Professor P. V. Vladimirov saw it as a change toward naturalness and in part, toward satire (IZ UCHENICHESKIKH LET GOGOLIA, Kiev, 1890). [These exact words do not occur in Kallash's article, but they do express his sentiments. Here, as in many other instances, Gippius is undoubtedly quoting inaccurately from memory.]

20. ["Estates" renders *sosloviia*, which are not the same as "classes." The estate-system, codified under Catherine the Great, recognized four basic divisions: gentry, clergy, peasantry, and town-dwellers (subdivided into merchants and into lower middle-folk, or *meshchane*).

[By "poems" Gippius presumably means "A New Abode" (1826) and one "ascribed" to Gogol, entitled (in the scholarly editions) "An Acrostic." See POLNOE SOBRANIE SOCHINENII, IX, 1952, pp. 613-614.]

21. [Alexander Semyonovich Danilevsky (1809-1888), a professional civil servant, was one of Gogol's closest life-long friends, despite some stormy interludes, and is the source of much valuable biographical information.]

22. [These are the only two surviving lines of the poem entitled "Russia Under the Yoke of the Tartars." The Russian is: "Razdvinuv tuchi srebrorunny,/ Iavilas' trepetno luna."]

23. N. A. Kotlyarevsky, N. V. GOGOL' (OCHERK IZ ISTORII RUSSKOI POVESTI I DRAMY), 4th ed., Petrograd, 1915; S. A. Vengerov, PISATEL'-GRAZHDANIN. GOGOL' (SOBRANIE SOCHINENII, II), St. Petersburg, 1913.

24. [As in Shenrok, MATERIALY, I, p. 180.]

25. The date given by Gogol (1827) was confirmed by N. S. Tikhonravov, but was later called under suspicion as being a mystification on Gogol's part. I. V. Sharovolsky gives 1829 as the date of HANZ ("Iunosheskaia idilliia Gogolia," PAMIATI GOGOLIA, Kiev, 1902. [The spelling of Hanz—"Gants" in exact transliteration—is incorrect for "Hans," but is the one used by Gogol himself. Throughout, the references to Tikhonravov are specifically to his annotated edition of Gogol's works: SOCHINENIIA N. V. GOGOLIA, 7 vols. Moscow-St. Petersburg, 1889-1896 (Vols. VI and VII edited by V. I. Shenrok). In the last sentence of this paragraph, Gippius calls HANZ Gogol's "first long poem" (*poema*) because DEAD SOULS, though written in prose, was also styled a "long poem" by Gogol.]

26.[P. Teryaev, "Luiza, sel'skoe stikhotvorenie v 3 idilliiakh. Soch. Ivana Fossa," St. Petersburg, 1820.]

27. [The Russian is in rhymed iambic tetrameter, as are the other fragments

quoted in this chapter; but I have been more interested in suggesting how bad the poetry is than in honoring the rhyme and meter of the original.]

28. ["Iamb" is the title of the manuscript (which does not survive) of the poem written in 1828 and first published the following year under the title "The Mob" ("Chern' "). Shortly before his death, Pushkin changed the title to "The Poet and the Crowd" ("Poet i tolpa"), and it has been known as that ever since. "Sonnet" ("Sonet") is the poem whose first line reads: "Stern Dante did not scorn the sonnet" ("Surovyi Dant ne prezival soneta," 1830). By Horace, Gippius surely means Ode 30 of Book III, "Exegi monumentum," of which Derzhavin's "The Monument" ("Pamiatnik," 1798) is an imitation.]

29. G. I. Chudakov, "Otnoshenie tvorchestva N. V. Gogolia k zapadno-evropeiskim literaturam," KIEVSKIE UNIVERSITETSKIE IZVESTIIA, VII, 1907; III, VIII, X, 1908.

30. [Pushkin, "Conversation of a Bookseller with the Poet" ("Razgovor knigo-prodavtsa s poetom," 1824).]

31. ["Existers" renders *sushchestvovateli*, a word that Gogol himself apparently coined to refer to individuals, so common in his works, who are dedicated to a mindless, visceral way of life.]

32. [Letter to his mother, May 22 (o.s.), 1829.] Shenrok (MATERIALY, I, pp. 183-184) attempts to explain this piece of news as a mystification, on the grounds that Danilevsky had no explanation for it. But we must remember that it was not Danilevsky but rather Vysotsky in whom Gogol confided regarding his plan for the trip. We may go along with Shenrok and Tikhonravov in seeing the failure of HANZ as the major impetus for the trip, but we cannot say that in this particular letter Gogol was "gradually preparing his mother for the idea of a trip abroad." HANZ had not yet been published.

33. The date given by N. P. Mundt—1830 or 1831—is from memory and is approximate. [Gippius has in mind "Popytka Gogolia," SANKT-PETERBURGSKIE VEDO-MOSTI (THE ST. PETERSBURG REGISTER), No. 235, October 24, 1861. Nikolay Petrovich Mundt (1803-1872) was a secretary to Prince Gagarin, the Director of Imperial Theaters.] From what Gogol said to Prince Gagarin—that he "did not intend to work in the civil service"—Shenrok concludes that his audition dates from the beginning of 1830 (MATERIALY, I, p. 231). But Gogol began working in the civil service at the end of 1829.

34. The 1829 poem "Italy," which is included in all editions of Gogol's works, is considerably superior to HANZ in technique. Gogol's authorship is established according to a statement made by P. A. Kulish. However, besides "Italy," Kulish also attributed to Gogol the authorship of the article "Poltava," which was actually written by P. P. Svin-in (cf. Kulish, "Neskol'ko chert dlia biografii Nikolaia Vasil'evicha Gogolia," OTE-CHESTVENNYE ZAPISKI, Vol. 81, Section VIII, 1852, p. 200).

35. [The Russian versions of the various points of style mentioned in this paragraph are: (1) "the sportive dragon-fly..."—*rezvun'ia strekoza treshcha vilas'...rozy ognevye;* (2) parenthetical words: *vot, uzhe, ved';* (3) Church Slavonicisms: *pro sebia mladu sirenu; kakoi-to mutnye vody;* (4) the verb that "does not fit the meter": *ne pre-davaisia* is shortened to *ne predavais';* (5) misplaced stresses: *razórenny, zakálennyi;* (6) mixtures of Ukrainian and Russian: *povidali, dva zubchatye mechi;* (7) Ukrainian words: *posunulas', sdaleka;* (8) instances of ineptitude and bad taste: *nazad on nogi obrashchaet i v domik tot on pospevaet; zemlia koletsia i—bukh teni razom v bezdnu—Uf!* Gippius adds, in the text: "and there are not a few such lines."]

36. [Orest Mikhailovich Somov (1793-1833) was a prominent journalist and critic, the author of stories based on Ukrainian folklore, and one of the important theorists of Russian romanticism.]

37. As do A. I. Kirpichnikov, "Somneniia i protivorechiia v biografii Gogolia,"

IZVESTIIA 2 OTD. AKADEMII NAUK, No. 2, 4, 1900; No. 1, 1902; and V. V. Kallash, "N. V. Gogol' i ego pis'ma," RUSSKAIA MYSL', No. 2, 3, 1902.

38. Apparently only one attempt at interpreting these words has been made: see I. P. Zhitetsky's original but questionable opinion that by "foreign language" Gogol—a Ukrainian—meant Russian ("Gogol'—propovednik i pisatel'," ZHURNAL MINISTERSTVA NARODNOGO PROSVESHCHENIIA, 1909). [The quote is from Gogol's letter to his mother, July 29 (o.s.), 1829.]

39. [The source for Gippius's statement regarding Bulgarin's patronage is Kirpichnikov. The Third Section (*Tret'e Otdelenie*) "of His Imperial Highness's Chancellery" was established by Nicholas I in 1826 to perform various police functions; it was abolished in 1880 and its duties were taken over by other organs of the bureaucracy. Whether Gogol actually worked there is a matter of some dispute. Later Soviet scholars have been very touchy on this point. See, for example, POLNOE SOBRANIE SOCHINENII, X. 1940, p.422, where such service is called a "legend" based on certain statements that Bulgarin made after Gogol's death with an eye to "discrediting him in the minds of democratic readers." Gippius himself later changed his mind, stating that: "Bulgarin probably did offer to set Gogol up in the Third Section, but Gogol had no desire to heed his advice..." (N. V. GOGOL'. MATERIALY I ISSLEDOVANIIA, I, Moscow 1936, p. 294, as quoted in POLNOE SOBRANIE SOCHINENII, X, 1940, p. 422). Certain scholars tend to regard Bulgarin's version as more or less accurate. In any event, Gogol did hold at least two very minor jobs in the civic service for short periods of time, in the Department of State Economy and Public Buildings, and in the Department of Crown Properties.]

NOTES TO CHAPTER II

1. [Ivan Mikhailovich Snegiryov (1793-1868) was an archeologist and ethnographer, Professor of Latin at Moscow University, and the author of several works on folk poetry. In his capacity as a government censor, he was the first reader of DEAD SOULS in manuscript; for Gogol's account of that, see the letter to P. A. Pletnyov, January 7, 1842. Mikhail Alexandrovich Maximovich (1804-1873) was Professor of Botany at Moscow University, then Professor of Russian Literature and Rector at Kiev University. He was also an important collector of Ukrainian folksongs, and the author of works on Ukrainian history, culture and language.]

2. [Gippius attributes the term to N. I. Nadezhdin. "Ausonia" ("Avzoniia") is one of the ancient names for Italy: cf. Virgil, AENEID, 3, V, 171.]

3. [For Somov, see Note No. 36, Chapter I. Somov had planned to write a novel entitled THE HAIDAMAK, and he published excerpts at various times (beginning in 1827), but never completed it. Originally, "haidamak" meant "brigand," but eventually came almost exclusively to refer to bands of men from various social classes and nationalities who for much of the eighteenth century operated from the Ukraine (particularly the left bank of the Dnieper) mainly against Poles and Jews. They met constant opposition from established authority, but measures against them were not effective until well into the reign of Catherine the Great.

[The other two names in this paragraph not included in Mirsky's HISTORY OF RUSSIAN LITERATURE are: (1) Yegor Vasilievich Aladin (1796-1860), a life-long civil servant and a prominent literary figure. He worked for the journal NOTES OF THE FATHERLAND (OTECHESTVENNYE ZAPISKI), and was publisher of several literary miscellanies, the most important being THE NEVSKY MISCELLANY (NEVSKII AL'-MANAKH, 1828-1833). He wrote numerous works of prose fiction, collections of which were published in 1832 and 1833. (2) Valerian Nikolaevich Olin (ca. 1788-1840s) was an author, editor, and translator who, although prolific, was not much respected even in his own time and has been virtually forgotten. One testimony to his obscurity is that the RUSSIAN BIOGRAPHICAL DICTIONARY (RUSSKII BIOGRAFICHESKII SLO-VAR') lists his dates of birth and death as above.

[In the Russian title of "The Poppyseed-Cake Woman from Lefortovo," "Lafertovskaia" is a popular corruption, no doubt suggested by *fert*, which is the old designation for the letter "f" and also means "fop."]

4. " 'What sort of title is this,' you will say or think, my dear readers" (POD-SNEZHNIK, 1829); "What sort of oddity is this, 'Evenings on a Farm Near Dikanka?' What sort of evenings are these?" (Gogol, foreword to EVENINGS). The title of the story "St. John's Eve" is closer to the title of the story published in translation in THE SLAV (SLAVIANIN, 1828), "New Year's Eve" ("Vecher nakanune novogo goda"), which is also devoted to "legends" and "superstitions"; and the title of the book as a whole is reminiscent of the title of Pogorelsky's THE DOUBLE, OR MY EVENINGS IN LITTLE RUSSIA (DVOINIK, ILI MOI VECHERA V MALOROSSII, 1828).

[The Titov mentioned earlier in the paragraph is Vladimir Pavlovich Titov (1807-1891), who was connected with the "Lovers of Wisdom" Circle (*Liubomudry*), and contributed fiction and literary theory to THE MOSCOW HERALD and THE CONTEMPORARY (SOVREMENNIK).]

4. [The expression "tag-ends of my state of mind at that time" occurs in a letter to A. O. Smirnova, December 24, 1844; it renders *khvostiki dushevnogo sostoianiia moego togdashnego*. Gippius may be trying to make the expression suggest something it does not mean in the original context. Smirnova has been speculating as to whether Gogol has more of a Russian or Ukrainian "soul" (or "mind": the word *dusha* can serve for both). Gogol says he does not really know, but that in any case, she should not draw "any conclusions about me personally" from "my writings," for: "They were all written long ago, when I was a stupid young man....To be sure, they do contain, here and there, the tag-ends of my state of mind at that time, but no one would notice or perceive them unless I myself should point them out."]

6. [Petro Petrovich Gulak-Artemovsky (1790-1865), a Ukrainian poet, was the author of the fable "Master and Dog" ("Pan ta sobaka"), published in UKRAINSKII VESTNIK, No. 12, 1818, which was the source of the epigraph to Chapter XII.]

7. V. N. Peretts, KUKOL'NYI TEATR NA RUSI, St. Petersburg, 1895.

8. V. A. Rozov, "Traditsionnye tipy malorusskogo teatra XVII-XVIII vv. Iunosheskie povesti N. V. Gogolia," PAMIATI N. V. GOGOLIA. SBORNIK RECHEI I STATEI, Kiev, 1911.

9. Peretts. [For nativity play, see Note 12, Chapter I.]

10. That Gogol was familiar with the Ukrainian nativity play can be seen from a striking passage in "The Tale of How Ivan Ivanovich Quarrelled with Ivan Nikiforovich": "The rays of the sun...playing on the point of the sword turned it into something unusual, like the nativity puppet theater carried from village to village by wandering vagrants. Particularly when a crowd of tightly-packed people looks at King Herod in his golden crown or at Anton leading the goat," etc.

11. "The character and the action are not true to life, even at a fair" (Andry Tsarynny, SYN OTECHESTVA, No. 137, 1832).

12. [The names are all "meaningful": Golopupenko: naked navel; Sverbyguz: itch-arse; Goloputsek: naked nestling, tadpole, infant; Patsyuk: rat.]

13. E.g., N. A. Kotlyarevsky, N. V. GOGOL' (OCHERK IZ ISTORII RUSSKOI POVESTI I DRAMY), 4th ed., Petrograd, 1915; V. F. Pereverzev, TVORCHESTVO GOGOLIA, Moscow, 1914.

14. P. A. Kulish's statement that Gogol depicted the Ukraine like an aristocrat (*barin*) who saw only a comic side to the peasant is more applicable to Somov, who

depicted "peasantly" love in the colors appropriate to a puppet show (cf. "The Were-wolf"). [Kulish, "Gogol', kak avtor povestei iz ukrainskoi zhizni," OSNOVA, No. 2, 1861, p. 79.]

15. Russian translations appeared in THE SLAV in 1827 and in GALATEA in 1830. The first translation was not known to Tikhonravov or to later scholars; hence the needless complexity (in Tikhonravov and elsewhere) of the treatment of the question of the dependence of Gogol's story on Tieck's.

16. "Quarantines have turned these twenty-four versts [between Petersburg and Tsarskoe Selo, where Zhukovsky was staying] into a road running from Petersburg to Kamchatka [the peninsula off the coast of Siberia]. Do you know what I have learned just recently? That... But you won't believe me, you'll call me superstitious. That the one to blame for all this is none other than the enemy of the honest cross of the Lord's churches and of everything protected by His holy banner. The devil has donned a green uniform with insignia-buttons, has hung a sharp-pointed sword at his side, and has become a quarantine-inspector. But Pushkin, like a holy angel, was not afraid of this horned official, sped past him like a spirit, and in the twinkling of an eye turned up in Petersburg...." (Letter of September 10 [o.s.], 1831.)

17. For details, see my study "Kuznets Kuz'ma-Dem'ian v narodnoi poezii i mifologii," which has been prepared for press. [No article with anything resembling this title is listed in the bibliography of Gippius's works that appears in the collection OT PUSHKINA DO BLOKA, Moscow-Leningrad, 1966. Presumably Gippius has in mind an article that later appeared in Ukrainian, entitled "Koval' Kuz'ma-Dem'ian u fol'klori," ETNOGRAFICHNYI VISNYK, No. 8, 1929.]

18. Cf. the misfortune that befalls those who have attempted to destroy the sorceress in Pogorelsky's "The Poppyseed-Cake Woman from Lefortovo" and later in Gogol's "The Portrait."

19. Cf. the denouement of Olin's "An Old Pal's Bed."

20. G. I. Chudakov evidently made use of very limited comparative material ("Otnoshenie motivov narodnoi slovesnosti v proizvedeniiakh N. V. Gogolia," KIEVSKIE UNIVERSITETSKIE IZVESTIIA, XII, 1906, pp. 1-37). For instance, Chubinsky is not used at all, not to speak of Great Russian folk tales: in principle, Chudakov considers it necessary to study these sources, but he goes no farther than Afanasiev and Sadovnikov. Ukrainian material is used more fully by K. Nevirova, "Motyvy ukrains'koi demonol'ogii v 'Vecherakh' ta 'Myrgorodi' Gogolia," ZAPYSKY UKRAINS'KOGO NAUKOVO-GO TOVARYSTVA V KYIVI, V, 1909, pp. 27-60. [Alexander Nikolaevich Afanasiev (1826-1871) was the most distinguished of the Russian ethnographers; Pavel Platonovich Chubinsky (1839-1884) was a Ukrainian ethnographer; Dmitry Nikolaevich Sadovnikov (1847-1883) was a prolific writer of verses, but was especially well known for his articles on the history and ethnography of the Volga region.]

21. The study of prose rhythm has begun relatively recently. In Russian, cf. the article by E. Kagarov, "O ritme russkoi prozaicheskoi rechi," NAUKA NA UKRAINE, No. 4 [1923?]. Let me note that the recognition of the *rhythmic* value of Gogol's prose obliges us to be especially cautious in dealing with Gogol's text. (Cf. the article by N. I. Korobka, "Sud'ba Gogolevskogo teksta," in the first volume of the complete works as edited by him: POLNOE SOBRANIE SOCHINENII N. V. GOGOLIA, I, St. Petersburg, 1915.)

22. [The example given by Gippius is: "tol'ko odnu lemishku s molokom i el staryi otets..." ("the old father ate only porridge with milk...").]

23. Gogol's syntax has not yet been studied. Random observations can be found in I. E. Mandelshtam's book, O KHARAKTERE GOGOLEVSKOGO STILIA. GLAVA IZ ISTORII RUSSKOGO LITERATURNOGO IAZYKA, Helsingfors, 1902. Inversions of various kinds stand out as being favorite devices.

24. [Pushkin, review of second edition of EVENINGS ON A FARM NEAR DI-
KANKA, SOVREMENNIK, No. 1, 1836; Polevoy, review of EVENINGS, MOSKOVSKII
TELEGRAF, No. 17 (September), 1831, as in V. A. Zelinsky, RUSSKAIA KRITICHES-
KAIA LITERATURA O PROIZVEDENIIAKH N. V. GOGOLIA, I, Moscow, 1910,
p. 27; Tsarynny, "Mysli malorossiianina po prochtenii povestei pasichnika Rudogo Pan'-
ka, izdannykh im v knizhke pod zaglaviem VECHERA NA KHUTORE BLIZ DIKAN'-
KI, i retsenzii na onye," SYN OTECHESTVA, XXV, No. 1-4, 1832, as in Zelinsky,
I, p. 42n; Nadezhdin, review of EVENINGS, TELESKOP, Part V, Section 6, 1831, as in
Zelinsky, I, p. 29. The first quote from Kulish is in OPYT BIOGRAFII N. V. GOGOLIA,
SO VKLIUCHENIEM DO SOROKA EGO PISEM, St. Petersburg, 1854, p. 5; the second,
from his later opinion of EVENINGS, runs throughout his article "Gogol', kak avtor
povestei iz ukrainskoi zhizni," OSNOVA, No. 2, 1861, pp. 67-90.]
25. [Grigory Fyodorovich Kvitka-Osnovyanenko (1778-1843), a Ukrainian writer
best known as the author of the play A VISITOR FROM THE CAPITAL (PRIEZZHII
IZ STOLITSY, 1827, publ. 1840), whose plot is close to that of THE INSPECTOR GEN-
ERAL. The stories in question are included in MALOROSSIISKIE POVESTI, RASSKA-
ZYVAEMYE GRYTSKOM OSNOV'IANENKOM, published in 1834 and 1837. The Grigorovich that Gippius has in mind is Dmitry Vasilievich (see Mirsky).]

NOTES TO CHAPTER III

1. ["Esthetic self-awareness" renders *esteticheskoe samosoznanie*, a favorite term
of Gippius's. Neither the Russian nor the English is very clear here, as is often the case
with German-derived philosophical terms; but a literal translation, for all its clumsiness,
seems preferable to a paraphrase, by way of "establishing" the term. What I take Gippius
to mean is Gogol's growing awareness of esthetic values, qualities and criteria within
himself, and his increasing tendency to measure everything accordingly. I have rendered
the term, and Gippius's variations on it, somewhat differently in different contexts
throughout.]
2. V. V. Kallash, "Zametki o Gogole (Gogol' o petrashevtsakh)," GOLOS MI-
NUVSHEGO, No. 9, 1913, pp. 234-35; subsequently, B. Ye. Lukyanovsky, "Pushkin i
Gogol' v ikh lichnykh otnosheniiakh. Vopros o druzhbe," BESEDY. SBORNIK OB-
SHCHESTVA ISTORII LITERATURY V MOSKVE, I, Moscow, 1915; and, more con-
vincingly than the latter, A. S. Dolinin, "Pushkin i Gogol'. K voprosu ob ikh lichnykh
otnosheniiakh," PUSHKINSKII SBORNIK PAMIATI PROF. S. A. VENGEROVA.
PUSHKINIST, IV, Moscow-Petrograd, 1922, pp. 181-197.
3. [Letter to A. F. Voeikov, first published in LITERATURNYE PRIBAVLENI-
IA K RUSSKOMU INVALIDU, No. 79, 1831, in the form of a letter to the editor.]
4. [The Russian versions are: "molniia ognennykh zvukov...pylaiushchie planety
prevratilis' v slova i bukvy...dukhovnoe more...potop blagodarnykh slov...zvon srebrian-
ogo neba."]
5. Cf. Alexander Glebov's poem "Woman" ("Zhenshchina," in SYN OTECHE-
STVA, No. 1, 1829): "Like a spectre dark but beautiful,/ A being from another world,/
The object of dreams and thoughts unclear,/ Like a denizen of heaven, a divinity,/ Appeared woman.../ The proud tsar fell into the dust/ At the feet of the weak creature of
nature."
6. S. K. Shambinago (TRILOGIIA ROMANTIZMA [N. V. GOGOL'], Moscow,
1911) tries to make a direct link between the Platonism of "Woman" and EVENINGS
(which is possible), as well as "Taras Bulba" (interpreting Andry's words "my native
land is you" as an expression of this Platonism), and even the play MARRIAGE. But this
attempt must be deemed unsuccessful.
7. [The German title is HERZENSERGIESSUNGEN EINES KUNSTLIEBEND-

EN KLOSTERBRUDERS, the Russian title SERDECHNYE IZLIIANIIA LIUBIA-SHCHEGO ISKUSSTVO MONAKHA. Alexander Ivanovich Galich (1783-1848) was one of the first Russian Schellingites. He was sent abroad in 1808 by the government to prepare for the chair of philosophy at the not yet established university in St. Petersburg. He became a well-known teacher of philosophy in Russia. One of his pupils, at the Lyceum in Tsarskoe Selo, was Pushkin.]

8. The literal correspondence of these words of Nadezhdin's with verses from Vladimir Solovyov's "Three Meetings" ("Tri svidaniia") is remarkable: "Not believing in the deceptive world,/ I grasped the imperishable purple/ Beneath the rude crust of matter...."

9. "Razmyshleniia i razbory," LITERATURNAIA GAZETA, 1830. This same journal also published an article by Feti on the *physical* effects of music. An intermediate position was taken by a contributor to THE LITERARY GAZETTE, Trilunny-Struisky, who saw in art not harmony but a *struggle* between the finite and the infinite, and who drew analogies between esthetic feelings and physical sensations. Characteristic of the position of THE LITERARY GAZETTE is what Pushkin said about Delvig: "Delvig did not like mystical poetry. He used to say: the closer to heaven, the colder" ("Table-Talk," XV). Cf. also Pushkin's letter to Delvig, as published by B. L. Modzalevsky in LITERATURNYE PORTFELI, I, 1923. [This volume has not been available to me; perhaps Gippius has in mind Pushkin's letter of March 2 (o.s.), 1827, especially his remarks therein on "German metaphysics."]

10. It is interesting to note that in describing the cathedral church in Lübeck, Gogol uses the same words as Titov: "The entire structure terminates, in each corner, in a long, angular stone spire of unusual thickness that disappears into the sky..." (letter to his mother, August 25, 1829). In Titov, a Gothic church ends in "an angular spire that disappears into the sky."

11. [This is the title of a famous painting by K. P. Bryullov (1799-1852) which hangs in the Russian Museum in Leningrad.]

12. I shall cite the most interesting parallel from the sketches for THE HETMAN: "He saw the *resilient* young breasts raise their cupola-like (breasts) summits, languourously hazy, and (immediately) lower them, after which they resiliently quivered beneath their covering." The *cloudy* white surface of cupolas recalls the "two transparent *clouds* of breasts" of "Woman" and the "cloudy breasts" of "Viy." [Emphases are by Gippius.]

13. [The term "judgment of fools" (*sud gluptsov*) is taken, with one slight change, from Pushkin's sonnet "To the Poet" ("Poetu," 1830), whose first stanza reads: "Oh, poet! Do not cherish the love of the people,/ The momentary éclat of enthusiastic praise will pass;/ You will hear the judgment of the fool and the laughter of the indifferent crowd;/ But remain firm, calm and morose." Many were commencing to say that Pushkin had written himself out.]

14. ["Graf L. Tolstoi i ego sochineniia," VREMIA, No. 1, 1862. The Druzhinin in question is Alexander Vasilievich.]

15. I. F. Annensky, "O formakh fantasticheskogo u Gogolia," RUSSKAIA SHKO-LA, No. 10, 1890.

16. K. Nevirova, "Motyvy ukrains'koi demonol'ogii v 'Vecherakh' ta 'Myrgorodi' Gogolia," ZAPYSKY UKRAINS'KOGO NAUKOVOGO TOVARYSTVA V KYIVI, V, 1909.

17. Cf. P. N. Sakulin, IZ ISTORII RUSSKOGO IDEALIZMA. KN. V. F. ODOEV-SKII, I, Part 2, Moscow, 1913, pp. 22-27; and V. V. Gippius, "Uzkii put' . Kn. V. F. Odoesvkii i romantizm," RUSSKAIA MYSL', XII, 1914, pp. 1-26.

18. The same puppet-theater touches can be seen in V. F. Odoevsky's "A Tale of How Dangerous It Is for Young Ladies to Walk in a Crowd Along the Nevsky Prospect" ("Skazka o tom, kak opasno devushkam khodit' tolpoiu po Nevskomu Propektu"):

"The pretty little heads turned, the little feet pattered...." Odoevsky actually turns his heroine into a doll. Cf. E. T. A. Hoffmann's story "The Sandman" [in Russian translation as "Pesochnyi chelovek" and "Domovoi-pesochnik"], which was imitated by Pogorelsky in "The Baneful Consequences of Unbridled Imagination" ("Pagubnye posledstviia neobuzdannogo voobrazheniia"). The heroes of Hoffmann and Pogorelsky fall in love with a doll, as does the hero of Odoevsky's tale. Piskaryov falls in love with a prostitute, in Gogol's "Nevsky Prospect," and suffers the same loss of a sense of reality as do those other heroes.

19. [Belinsky, "O russkoi povesti i povestiakh g. Gogolia ('Arabeski' i 'Mirgorod')," 1835.]

20. [Review of second edition of EVENINGS ON A FARM NEAR DIKANKA, SOVREMENNIK, No. 1, 1836.]

21. Maturin's MELMOTH THE WANDERER appeared in Russian translation in 1833 (excerpts had been published in SYN OTECHESTVA in 1831). [The Russian title is MEL'MOT SKITALETS.] Its similarity with Gogol's story was first noted by I. A. Shlyapkin, " 'Portret' Gogolia i 'Mel'mot-Skitalets' Matiurena," LITERATURNYI VESTNIK, No. 1, 1902, pp. 66-68. [Gippius ends this note with a remark that is of interest only to readers who know some Russian: "The transliteration of the name 'Maturin' that has been accepted until now—'Matiuren'—does not correspond with the generally accepted way of transliterating English names into Russian." Gippius renders it as "Mech'-iurin."]

22. G. I. Chudakov incorrectly summarized the plot of Spinello's story. The artist did not of course select the girl he was in love with "as the original" when he was painting Lucifer, but rather, *unwittingly* transferred her traits to him. Neither did he "throw himself off a cliff"; rather, he fell off accidentally. Besides Washington Irving's "The Adventure of the Mysterious Picture" [Russian title: "Tainstvennyi portret"], which is noted by Chudakov, one can also cite "The Haunted House" (Russian translation in MOSKOVSKII TELEGRAF, No. 3, 1827 [under the title "Zakoldovannyi dom"]). Cf. G. I. Chudakov, "Otnoshenie tvorchestva N. V. Gogolia k zapadno-evropeiskim literaturam," KIEVSKIE UNIVERSITETSKIE IZVESTIIA, VII, 1907; III, VIII, X, 1908. [I am unable to identify Spinello. Chudakov (III, 1908, Part 2, p. 94) refers to him only as "the unknown foreign author" of a tale published in VESTNIK EVROPY, Nos. 13-16, 1830.]

23. "The Queen of Spades" and "The Devil's Elixirs" are examples of influence by way of contrast. Hoffmann's hero wins *after* he has seen the inspiring features of his beloved Aurora in a Queen of *Hearts.*

24. Pushkin's "Mozart and Salieri" appeared in 1832, Odoesvky's "The Improvisator" in 1833. The Salieri-like traits of the Improvisator have been noted in Professor Sakulin's book [see Note No. 17].

25. An expression of N. P. Ogaryov (letter to A. I. Herzen, end of August, 1860, as in RUSSKIE PROPILEI, ed. M. O. Gershenzon, IV, Moscow, 1917.

26. [Paterikons—*pateriki*—were collections consisting of short tales relating the feats of ascetics in well-known monasteries, and sometimes offering edifying words uttered by such ascetics. One of the most famous originated in the Kiev Caves Monastery; the oldest edition dates from the fifteenth century.]

NOTES TO CHAPTER IV

1. ["Bisavryuk, or St. John's Eve" is the title of the first version of "St. John's Eve" (published in OTECHESTVENNYE ZAPISKI, February-March, 1830). The chapter of THE HETMAN in question has been given the title "A Chapter from a Historical

Novel," written in 1830 but actually published in 1831 (in SEVERNYE TSVETY). "A Few Thoughts on the Teaching of Geography to Children," mentioned below, was the first version of what eventually became "Thoughts on Geography," which was published in ARABESQUES.]

2. [Gippius does not provide any specifics of bibliography here. For Vengerov, he probably has in mind PISATEL'-GRAZHDANIN. GOGOL' (SOBRANIE SOCHIN-ENII, II), St. Petersburg, 1913; for Kirpichnikov, perhaps the section on Gogol in OCHERKI PO ISTORII NOVOI RUSSKOI LITERATURY, St. Petersburg, 1896, or "Somneniia i protivorechiia v biografii Gogolia," IZVESTIIA 2 OTD. AKADEMII NAUK, Nos. 2, 4, 1900; No. 1, 1902; for Vitberg, "Gogol' kak istorik," ISTORI-CHESKII VESTNIK, No. 1, 1892.]

3. Vengerov; Kotlyarevsky, N. V. GOGOL' (OCHERK IZ ISTORII RUSSKOI POVESTI I DRAMY), 4th ed., Petrograd, 1915.

4. [For Gogol's desire to go to Kiev with Maximovich, see the letter of July 2 (o.s.), 1833. But the quotes are contained in a letter, also to Maximovich, written after December 20 (o.s.), 1833.]

5. [Besides the letters cited in the text, see the following: to M. P. Pogodin, January 11 (o.s.), 1834 and February 1 (o.s.), 1833; to M. A. Maximovich, November 9 (o.s.), 1833 (for the quote about "our poor, unequalled Ukraine"), February 12 (o.s.), 1834, and January 22 (o.s.), 1835.]

6. [Lectures in question are "On the Middle Ages" and "On the Teaching of World History."]

7. As Gogol says in the same article, Napoleon was destroyed by "expanses that were unfamiliar to him, by the ferocity of the climate, and by the Russian armed forces, which were trained in Suvorov's tactics." Here we find a hero summoned up from the past, along with the weather. Tentetnikov, in Part 2 of DEAD SOULS, speaks of the War of 1812 in an entirely different manner. He is not interested in the history of "individual battles and individual personalities," but in "the people as a whole."

8. Cf. Zacharias (Friedrich Ludwig) Werner's tragedy ATTILA, KÖNIG DER HUNNEN (1808), excerpts in the translation by A. S. Shishkov, TELESKOP, No. 6, 1831. Here we find the traditional story of Attila's love of luxury and his nickname "God's scourge."

9. [All these examples are found in the excerpts for which the following title has been devised by editors: "From University Lectures on the History of the Middle Ages," most of which were prepared between 1831 and 1835. Gippius is slightly inaccurate in referring to wars "in the reign of Clothard II"; according to Gogol, they began some forty-six years earlier and continued for four decades. (As in POLNOE SOBRANIE SOCHINENII, IX, 1952.)]

10. Gogol endeavored to explain the failure of Al-Mamun as a strong individual (in the article entitled "Al-Mamun") by his failure to understand his people and by his beliefs, which arose "out of the fiery Arabian climate, out of the fiery nature of the Arab." This is an example of far-fetched attraction to the idea of "visible nature," but at least Gogol did not develop these suggestions.

11. Cf. the transactions of the Moscow Society of the History of Literature (BESEDY, 1915), for an account of a report by S. Ye. Bogomolov.

12. Translations of articles about Schloezer and Miller appeared in MOSKOV-SKII VESTNIK in 1827. ["Ioann Miller, soch. Gerena," Vol. 2, Sections VII and VIII; "Avgust Liubvig (sic) Shletser, soch. Gerena," Vol. 4, Section XV.]

13. Kulish expended much energy noting the anachronisms in "St. John's Eve." It is clear in any event that this story is not historical, and that the words "How very many years ago! More than a hundred," which come toward the beginning, are a variation on the usual folktale formula.

14. N. A. Kotlyarevsky, N. V. GOGOL'..., Ch. VIII.

15. [The italics are Gippius's. Wenden was the site of an ancient castle and later a town, near Riga. It is now called Cēsis.]

16. First published by Yu. G. Oksman in NIVA, No. 1, 1917. "The Bloody Bandore-Player" (i.e., "The Captive" and its continuation) was scheduled for publication in 1834 in THE LIBRARY FOR READING (BIBLIOTEKA DLIA CHTENIIA), but was forbidden by the censorship because of the "disgusting...picture of sufferings and human degradation, which is painted wholly in the spirit of the modern French school." [The textological history here is very complicated. For present purposes it is enough to say that all the titles mentioned in this paragraph are now considered part of THE HETMAN. For details see Gogol, POLNOE SOBRANIE SOCHINENII, III, 1938, pp. 711-716. Bogdan Khmelnitsky (ca. 1595-1657) was a hetman of the Zaporozhian Cossacks, who led a mass uprising against the Poles in 1649, which ultimately brought about the absorption of the Ukraine by Russia.]

17. [The examples Gippius gives are *mashinal'no* ("mechanically") and *agoniia* ("agony"), both legitimate Russian words (though of foreign origin), but presumably inappropriate in the context.]

18. Cf. Orest Somov's "Wandering Fire" ("Brodiashchii ogon'," AL'TSIONA, 1832) for a model of rhythmic prose which is like that of Gogol's "A Terrible Vengeance" and "Taras Bulba." [The Belinsky reference in the sentence is to the article "O russkoi povesti i povestiakh g. Gogolia...," 1835.]

19. Taras Bulba exclaims "I hear!" in response to his son Ostap's cry as he is being put to death. Belinsky compared this to the ejaculations in the classical tragedies, and introduced parallels from Corneille and Ozerov ("O russkoi povesti...").

20. [Review of MIRGOROD, in MOSKOVSKII NABLIUDATEL', Book 2, March, 1835.]

21. [Letter to M. A. Maximovich, November 9 (o.s.), 1833.]

22.["Gogol', kak avtor povestei iz ukrainskoi zhizni," OSNOVA, No. 2, 1861, p. 71.]

NOTES TO CHAPTER V

1. ["Petersburg Tales" is not a title: it is conventionlly used by scholars to refer to the stories by Gogol that have a Petersburg setting: "The Portrait," "The Nose," "Diary of a Madman," "Nevskii Prospect," "The Overcoat."]

2. [Gippius incorrectly calls the girl "Oniska."]

3. Cf. Gogol's letter to A. S. Danilevsky of March 30 (o.s.), 1832, in which he says that Shponka "after his marriage will be made into something worthy of Pushkin's poetry." From this scholars have concluded that Gogol intended to write a continuation of "Shponka," and, what is more, *after* the publication of EVENINGS (where he had already told his readers of the notebook that was torn up to provide paper on which to bake meat pies.) Of course, Gogol could have been speaking of his hero as one does of a living person; there is no reason to take "will be made" *(sdelaetsia)* literally.

4. Of course, I use the term "caricature" merely as a way of designating one of the artist's devices, and without any suggestion of censure or value-judgment. This was the sense in which friendly critics and Gogol himself spoke of his caricatures (see Chapter X of this study).

5. An even stronger caricature of a glutton—more so than Petukh in Part 2 of DEAD SOULS— is Orest Somov's Pan Prosechinsky in THE HAIDAMAK. [The "impersonal manner" in the next sentence refers to the fact that "semblance" is a neuter noun in Russian *(podobie)* and therefore takes neuter verbs in the past tense: *kopalos', korpelo, pisalo.*]

6. ["Comedy, General Materials," from Gogol's notebook, late 1832-early 1833.

(It can be found in POLNOE SOBRANIE SOCHINENII, IX, 1952, pp. 18-19.)]

7. Review of MIRGOROD, in MOSKOVSKII NABLIUDATEL', March, 1835, Book 2, as in V. A. Zelinsky, RUSSKAIA KRITICHESKAIA LITERATURA O PROIZ-VEDENIIAKH N. V. GOGOLIA, I, Moscow, 1910, p. 64.

8. ["O russkoi povesti i povestiakh g. Gogolia ('Arabeski' i 'Mirgorod')," TELE-SKOP, Vol. 26, No. 8, 1835.]

9. Gogol gave the date 1831 for both the article on architecture and the story about the two Ivans. Tikhonravov disputes this, and dates the writing of both from the second half of 1833.

10. [Both quotes from Gogol are found in his letter to G. I. Vysotsky, June 26 (o.s.), 1827. Pereverzev's term (rendered as "loafers") is *nebokoptiteli*, and is found throughout his book TVORCHESTVO GOGOLIA, Moscow, 1914. The quote from Belinsky occurs in "O russkoi povesti i povestiakh g. Gogolia...."]

11. V. F. Pereverzev supposes that Gogol's melancholia, dreaminess and inclination to fantasy were an expression of the same psychology that characterized the small-landowner milieu. This is not adequately supported in his book either by social or historical data, or by data from the history of literature. [The reference earlier in the paragraph is to D. S. Merezhkovsky, GOGOL' I CHERT (in English as "Gogol and the Devil" in R. A. Maguire, GOGOL FROM THE TWENTIETH CENTURY: ELEVEN ESSAYS, Princeton, 1974, pp. 55-102) and to N. A. Kotlyarevsky, N. V. GOGOL' (OCHERK IZ ISTORII RUSSKOI POVESTI I DRAMY), 4th ed., Petrograd, 1915. The statement about an "unquenchable desire" in the next sentence is from a letter to P. P. Kosyarovsky, October 3 (o.s.), 1827.]

12. ["O russkoi povesti i povestiakh g. Gogolia...."]

13. I borrow this expression from the article by Iv. Ivanov, "Gogol', chelovek i pisatel'," Kiev, 1909. This little-known article places appropriately strong emphasis on the *attraction* Gogol felt for the "old-fashioned" tradition, but is careless in the way it brings the entire course of his life into conformity with this tendency. A diametrically opposed (and equally one-sided) view can be seen in S. A. Vengerov, PISATEL'-GRA-ZHDANIN. GOGOL' (SOBRANIE SOCHINENII, II), St. Petersburg, 1913. Both elements in Gogol have been noted by Ye. V. Petukhov, GOGOL' I ZHUKOVSKII, Yuriev, 1903.

14. The first to call attention to this was L. Leder, NICOLAS GOGOL, Paris, 1914.

15. [Vilgelm Ivanovich Karlgof (1796-1841) was primarily a civil servant (spending many years as assistant to the administrator of the Odessa school district), but also published translations of articles on military matters and on literature, and wrote some original fiction (e.g., POVESTI I RASSKAZY, St. Petersburg, 1832).]

NOTES TO CHAPTER VI

1. [Gogol's remark about "kissing the University goodbye" is contained in a letter to M. P. Pogodin, December 6 (o.s.), 1835; the other quotes in the rest of the paragraph are from S. T. Aksakov, ISTORIIA MOEGO ZNAKOMSTVA S GOGOLEM (with reference to the year 1832), Moscow, 1960, pp. 11-12.]

2. The most plausible suppositions are those of N. I. Korobka, in Volume V of the collected works of Gogol, edited by him (POLNOE SOBRANIE SOCHINENII N. V. GOGOLIA, 5 vols., St. Petersburg, 1915).

3. [The history of these texts is extremely complicated. Suffice it to say here that the uncompleted VLADIMIR manuscript was the basis of the four "scenes" enumerated. Sobachkin figures in the last of them, "A Fragment." It is supposed that he is a

version of the character Zakatishchev, who appears in the original VLADIMIR manuscript but not in any of the "scenes." As the Academy of Sciences edition of Gogol's works points out, the two characters have a number of traits in common (POLNOE SOBRANIE SOCHINENII, V, 1949, p. 480). The point of Misha's passion for Ryleev, in the next sentence, is that the latter, besides being a poet, was also one of the leaders of the Decembrist uprising (1825) and was hanged for it.]

4. Excerpts from the diary of a dog carry on a tradition found in Tieck (Hinze, in PUSS IN BOOTS, speaks of publishing a journal; the dog in the play PRINCE ZERBINO becomes a writer), and in E. T. A. Hoffmann (KATER MURR). The novellas of Cervantes served as the literary prototype.

5. Gogol's original idea was entitled "Diary of a Mad Musician" ("Zapiski sumasshedshego muzykanta"); scholars have seen connections with the musicians in V. F. Odoevsky's stories, and with the basic idea for his MADHOUSE.

6. [Anatoly Nikolaevich Verstovsky (1799-1862) was a translator and an editor of various miscellanies, and wrote much of the music for the vaudevilles of Alexander Ivanovich Pisarev (1803-1828). About the three foreign stories mentioned earlier in the paragraph: Hoffmann's "The Sandman" ("Der Sandmann") was originally published in 1816, and the Russian title of the translation was "Pesochnyi chelovek"; Balzac's "Sarrasine" was originally published in 1830, and was radically abridged in Russian translation and given the title of "Strast' khudozhnika, ili chelovek ne chelovek" ("The Passion of an Artist, or, A Man's Not a Man"); the anonymous English story (with the Russian title "Gosudarstvennyi chelovek") appeared originally as Chapter IX ("The Statesman") of PASSAGES FROM THE DIARY OF A LATE PHYSICIAN in BLACKWOOD'S EDINBURGH MAGAZINE, Vol. XXIX, No. CLXXX, May, 1831, pp. 802-829.]

7. "...this flame would turn me into ashes in an instant...it is my salvation that I have a firm will, which twice has turned me away from the desire to glance into the abyss" (letter to A. S. Danilevsky, December 20 [o.s.], 1832).

8. Letter to M. P. Pogodin, February 20 [o.s.], 1833.

9. A considerable number of such stories are mentioned by V. V. Vinogradov in his article "Siuzhet i kompozitsiia povesti Gogolia 'Nos'" (NACHALA, No. 1, 1921). We can also cite N.I. Khmelnitsky, "My Little Ball" ("Moi miachik"), A. I. Pisarev's 'The Magic Nose" ("Volshebnyi nos") and certain others. A rather unusual interpretation of the story was made by I. F. Annensky in "Problemy Gogolevskogo iumora" (KNIGA OTRAZHENII, St. Petersburg, 1906).

10. An expression of M. A. Kuzmin. [Gippius means the famous Symbolist poet, whose dates are 1875-1936.]

[The name "Destouches" in the next sentence is a guess on my part. Gippius has "Getum," but there seems to be no such writer. Misprints are common in this book, and it requires only two rather plausible ones to convert "Destouches" (in transliteration, "Detush") into "Getum." Certainly Destouches fits the context, if he refers—as I am virtually certain he does—to Philippe Néricault Destouches (1680-1754), the French writer of comedies, who, in the words of THE OXFORD COMPANION TO THE THEATER (Third Edition, 1967, p. 238), "was an imitator of Molière, but spoilt his plays by emphasizing the moral, which Molière had allowed to emerge naturally in the course of the action....His stay in England had helped to heighten his taste for gothic romance, and accounts for the mingling of sentiment and tragedy with comedy in his later plays, though many of them, particularly towards the end of his career, were spoilt by sententiousness."]

11. [Pyotr Andreevich Karatygin (1805-1879) wrote nearly seventy plays, many of which were highly popular in his own time. Dmitry Timofeevich Lensky (1806-1860) was an actor and a highly successful writer of vaudevilles, some translated directly from the French, some recast in Russian form. Fyodor Alexeevich Koni (1809-1879) was a

well-known writer of vaudevilles.]

12. Galich's views of comedy are somewhat confused. Apparently he makes a distinction only between the "wilful" comedy of the ancients and the "decorous" new comedy, or, as he put it, the "romantic" comedy, which "depicts the ideal nature of the comic more than individual caricatures."

13. In the article "The Petersburg Stage in the 1835-36 Season," Gogol takes a cooler attitude toward Molière, criticizing him because "the action of the play is too decorous and is constructed in disregard of the age and times in which he lived." The charge of decorousness evidently stems from Gogol's impression of certain Molière plays of the MISANTHROPE type. But in this case it also gives evidence of his attempt to fill the traditional form of comedy with a new content that would be Russian and contemporary. [The titles of these articles on the theater can be confusing. Originally Gogol wrote two articles, "Petersburg and Moscow" and "The Petersburg Stage in the 1835-36 Season." He then combined them and published the result under the title "Petersburg Notes of 1836."]

14. O. I. Senkovsky, review in BIBLIOTEKA DLIA CHTENIIA, Vol. 16, 1836.

15. Cf. D. T. Lensky's translated vaudeville BLAMELESS IN BLAME, OR, A JUDICIAL SENTENCE (NEVINNYI V VINE ILI SUDEISKII PRIGOVOR, 1829), in which the owner of a wine cellar is accused of making imitation wine, and extricates himself by getting the judge and two inspectors-general drunk. [The *vine* in the title could also be translated as "wine."]

16. The similarity between these two plots was noted by O. I. Senkovsky in A LIBRARY FOR READING (BIBLIOTEKA DLIA CHTENIIA, Vol 16, 1836): "It [this anecdote] was even related on one occasion by Mr. Veltman [Weltmann] in A LIBRARY FOR READING." Until very recently, no one considered it necessary to verify this statement. We find a reference to Weltmann (but none to Senkovsky) in Ieremiya Aizenshtok, "K voprosu o literaturnykh vliianiiakh (G. F. Kvitka i N. V. Gogol')," IZVESTIIA 2 OTD. AKADEMII NAUK, XXIV, Book 1, Petrograd, 1922.

17. "I don't know, Your Excellency...I had no advance knowledge of your arrival...I do have an apartment ready for Your Excellency...I've been fulfilling my duty assiduously and unflaggingly for six years...."

18. *Op. cit.*

19. Cf. N. V. Volkov, K ISTORII RUSSKOI KOMEDII. ZAVISIMOST' "REVIZORA" GOGOLIA OT KOMEDII KVITKI "PRIIEZZHII IZ STOLITSY," St. Petersburg, 1899; the objection by A. I. Lyashchenko, " 'Revizor' Gogolia i komediia Kvitki 'Priezzhii iz stolitsy'," PAMIATI L. N. MAIKOVA, St. Petersburg, 1902, pp. 523-40, and the above-mentioned article by Aizenshtok.

20. Cf. the statement by Tomin, UFIMSKIE GUBERNSKIE VEDOMOSTI, 1894, regarding a 1796 verse-comedy by Zhukov based on Siberian life, entitled THE INSPECTOR GENERAL, the manuscript of which Tomin bought in the 1860s or 1870s. This has not yet been verified. There are reasons to suspect mystification, if not in the statement itself, then in the date given by the author.

21. [Both quotes are from "Excerpt from a Letter Written by the Author to a Certain Man of Letters Shortly After the First Performance of THE INSPECTOR GENERAL."]

22. There are similar misunderstandings in Zagoskin's NOBLES' THEATER (BLAGORODNYI TEATR, 1827), and in many other plays. For an interesting parallel with THE INSPECTOR GENERAL, see a scene in Pisarev's vaudeville FIVE YEARS IN TWO HOURS, OR, HOW EXPENSIVE DUCKS ARE (PIAT' LET V DVA CHASA, ILI DOROGI UTKI, 1829), where a pie-maker, frightened by a story about a robber, takes a fisherman selling a duck for the robber, and the fisherman unwittingly provides grounds for such suspicions.

23. Cf. Yashutkin's remarks: "Come on, serve it right now! I'm terribly hungry.... Just you go and tell that ass this is the last time....But you try to persuade him, you

swear to him." The effect created by the appearance of the meal is similar. In general, difficulties experienced in an inn by a hero who has squandered his money constitute a traditional motif. Cf. Zagoskin's A ROMANCE ON THE HIGH ROAD (ROMAN NA BOL'SHOI DOROGE, 1819) and Lensky's AN ATTORNEY UNDER THE TABLE (STRIAPCHII POD STOLOM, 1834).

24. The entire second act of Molière's DON JUAN provided a prime model for the wooing of two women simultaneously. Cf. also the vaudevilles of Lensky, Koni and others.

25. Cf. A. I. Klushin's comedy LAUGHTER AND WOE (SMEKH I GORE, 1793) for a double exposé of the hero by two rival women (the older enters when he is on his knees in front of the younger, and vice-versa). A. A. Fomin noted the similarity between the second of these two scenes and Griboedov's WOE FROM WIT, without remarking on its similarity to THE INSPECTOR GENERAL, although he did call attention to the "mute scene" in the latter ("Staroe v novom," RUSSKAIA MYSL', No. 2, 1893).

26. Cf. P. Stolpyansky, "Zametki na poliakh Gogolia," EZHEGODNIK IMPER-ATORSKIKH TEATROV, No. 6, 1910, for a parallel with Paul de Kock.

27. [The first quote from Gogol is found in his notebook (end of 1832 or beginning of 1833) under the heading "Comedy. General Materials": cf. POLNOE SOBRA-NIE SOCHINENII, IX, 1952, pp. 18-19. The other quote from Gogol is in "Advance Notice for Those Who Would Like to Play THE INSPECTOR GENERAL As It Should Be." Belinsky's remarks are found in his review of Griboedov's WOE FROM WIT (second edition), in OTECHESTVENNYE ZAPISKI, VIII, No. 1, 1840. Belinsky's "Hegelian period" coincided with his entry into literature in the mid-1830s. In keeping with Hegel's idea that "all that is, is rational," Belinsky justified the existing political and social structures. After the early 1840s, however, he abandoned this brand of Hegelianism and turned increasingly radical. The most famous version of the fairy tale mentioned earlier in the paragraph is Pushkin's "Tale of the Fisherman and the Fish" ("Skazka o rybake i rybe," 1833), which was based on the Brothers Grimm.]

28. Cf. Molière, LE MISANTHROPE; Krylov, THE PIE (PIROG); Zagoskin, A GOOD FELLOW (DOBRYI MALYI); and certain others. Mute scenes are found in Klushin and Kvitka, though not at the end.

29. Cf. his review in SOVREMENNIK, No. 2, 1836.

30. "Leaving the Theater" has been closely linked with Molière's LA CRITIQUE DE L'ECOLE DES FEMMES, 1663. Attempts to present the public's opinions of a play were also made by Tieck (PUSS IN BOOTS, 1797) and Sheridan (THE CRITIC; OR, A TRAGEDY REHEARSED, 1779).

31. Bulgarin's review of the play is in SEVERNAIA PCHELA, Nos. 97 and 98, 1836. Vengerov's opinion is in PISATEL'-GRAZHDANIN. GOGOL' (SOBRANIE SO-CHINENII, II), St. Petersburg, 1913.

32. While subjecting THE INSPECTOR GENERAL to a final polishing, Gogol threw out certain earlier allusions to a love intrigue. Thus, in all the earlier versions, mention was made of "that awful Avdotia," who was in love with Zemlyanika's coachman (the traditional love between two servants), and the sergeant's widow was flogged for having frightened a suitor away from Maria Antonovna, the mayor's daughter. [For Senkovsky's advice, see his review in BIBLIOTEKA DLIA CHTENIIA, Vol.16, 1836.]

33. [Ivan Ivanovich Sosnitsky (1794-1872) played the role of the mayor in the first performance of THE INSPECTOR GENERAL.]

34. V. V. Danilov was the first to call attention to this comedy (RUSSKII FILO-LOGICHESKII VESTNIK, No. 4, 1912). [Here, as in a few other places, I am expanding Gippius somewhat: otherwise, his remarks on Khmelnitsky's play are incomprehensible to anyone who has not read it.]

35. The busybody-type had already appeared in Ya. B. Knyazhnin's play THE

ECCENTRICS (CHUDAKI, 1794), in the character of Trusim, "a friend of one and all" and "a man who loves to be of service to all without their asking." He brings suitors into his house, and this makes for scenes far more elaborate structurally than analogous scenes in Gogol's MARRIAGE. The parallel to Gogol's Podkolyosin in Knyazhnin's comedy is the "wavering," "very romantic" and therefore timid Priyat. However, the role assigned to Kochkaryov in MARRIAGE (pushing Podkolyosin to get married) is not played by Knyazhnin's Trusim at the crucial moment, but by the traditional servant-type Prolaz.

36. ["Intellection" renders *soobrazhenie,* which Gogol sometimes uses by way of contrast with "imagination" *(voobrazhenie).* Cf. esp. "An Author's Confession," where he gives an account of the process of "intellection."]

NOTES TO CHAPTER VII

1. [A slightly misquoted version of a statement found in "The Petersburg Stage in the 1835-36 Season."]

2. [See Note No. 13, Chapter III.]

3. [Bulgarin's review appeared in SEVERNAIA PCHELA, Nos. 97 and 98, 1836; Senkovsky's in BIBLIOTEKA DLIA CHTENIIA, Vol. 16, 1836; Vyazemsky's in SOVREMENNIK, No 2, 1836; Androsov's in MOSKOVSKII NABLIUDATEL', No. 1, 1836. Vasily Petrovich Androsov (1803-1841) had a varied career. He wrote on philosophy; was assistant to the director of the Agricultural School; a member of the editorial board and then publisher of THE MOSCOW OBSERVER; and publisher of THE JOURNAL FOR SHEEP-BREEDERS (ZHURNAL DLIA OVTSEVODOV). One of his great interests was in collecting statistical data and applying them to policy-making matters.]

4. [Letter to P. A. Pletnyov, December 4, 1846, published separately as an article entitled "On THE CONTEMPORARY."]

5. One favorable remark about Belinsky was omitted, evidently for reasons of journalistic tactics. [See the draft version of the article "Trends in Journal Literature in 1834 and 1835," as in POLNOE SOBRANIE SOCHINENII, VIII, 1952, p. 533.] Also omitted was a review of S. P. Shevyryov's lectures, in which Gogol called Shevyryov the best "of all our writers who so far have been primarily concerned with criticism." Nor was a review devoted to an unnamed book and interesting for its evaluation of German Romanticism, included. For the relationship between Pushkin and Gogol as journalists, see V. V. Kallash, "Zametki o. Gogole," GOLOS MINUVSHEGO, No. 9, 1913. The review for which Pushkin apologized to Pogodin was of his HISTORICAL APHORISMS (ISTORICHESKIE AFORIZMY). [Cf. the characterization in POLNOE SOBRANIE SOCHINENII, VIII, 1952, p. 770: the rough draft of the review contains "a number of caustic comments, which were removed or greatly toned down in the published version. This was probably done at the insistence of Pushkin, who intended to bring M. Pogodin into the journal as a collaborator" and naturally did not wish to offend him. In a letter to Pogodin (April 14 [o.s.], 1836), Pushkin observed that "the article on your aphorisms was not written by me....Don't be angry at me if you are dissatisfied with it."]

6. Cf. the note that Pushkin appended to Gogol's story "The Nose" (published in THE CONTEMPORARY, No. 3, 1836), in which he said that Gogol "for a long time would not agree to the publication of this joke." The facts contradict this statement; and it takes on the quality of a tacit apology to the reading public.

7. On March 30, 1837, Gogol wrote Pogodin about Pushkin's death, using expressions that coincided with those in Lermontov's poem on the same subject ("The Death of the Poet" ["Smert' poeta," 1827]): "Why should I come back to Russia? Haven't I seen the dear assemblage of our enlightened ignoramuses? Or perhaps I don't know what sort of people all councilors are, from titular ones all the way up to the

actual privy kind? [The reference is to civil-service ranks.] You write that everyone, even cold people, has been deeply moved by this loss. And what were these people prepared to do to him while he was still alive? Was I not witness to the bitter, bitter moments that Pushkin had occasion to experience? Despite the fact that the monarch himself (blessed be his name for that!) honored his talent? Oh, whenever I remember our judges, our maecenases, our learned wise men, our noble aristocracy...my heart shudders at the mere thought."

[The words "beautiful dream" earlier in the paragraph occur in Gogol's letter to Zhukovsky, October 30, 1837; the other quotes are from the above-mentioned letter to Zhukovsky.]

8.[The first quote in this paragraph is from a letter to A. S. Danilevsky, April 15, 1837; the others, in order, are from letters to V. A. Zhukovsky, October 30, 1837; N. Ya. Prokopovich, June 3, 1847; Zhukovsky, October 30, 1837; M. P. Balabina, April, 1838; Zhukovsky, October 30, 1837; A. S. Danilevsky, February 2, 1838].

9. [As does D. S. Merezhkovsky, GOGOL' I CHERT, St. Petersburg, 1906.]

10. ["Ob"iasnenie na ob"iasneniia po povodu poemy Gogolia 'Mertvye dushi,' " OTECHESTVENNYE ZAPISKI, XXV, No. 11, 1842.]

11. In a letter to S. P. Shevyryov, dated September 1, 1843, Gogol tried to play down the autobiographical aspect of "Rome," saying that he could not be "of the same opinion as the hero" with regard to presently existing nationalities (the French). But this was written when Gogol's enthusiasm for Italy had flagged.

12. The coincidence with Pushkin's poem "The Beautiful Lady" ("Krasavitsa," 1832) is not accidental. Later Gogol quoted the lines "devoutly reverential/ before the sacred object of beauty" in a review of the miscellany THE DAWN (UTRENNIAIA ZARIA) published in THE MUSCOVITE (MOSKVITIANIN) in 1842, in which he speaks of the portraits of seven northern beauties. Suggestions of the same image are found in the article "Woman in Society" in SELECTED PASSAGES FROM CORRESPOND- ENCE WITH FRIENDS, and in the rough draft of "Meditations on the Divine Liturgy."

13. This pedantic substitution in the hero's name of just one letter for another, with the name preserved intact as a phonetic whole, cannot be considered accidental. Evidently Gogol wanted to reader to avoid instinctively making any 'demonic" associa- tions. ["Chertkov," in the first version, is made from the word chert, "devil." What Gippius presumably means by "new correspondences" in the preceding sentence is that Gogol's ideology had not yet developed sufficiently in the direction of moralism and re- ligion (see Chapter VIII) to give relevance and meaning to a new "demonic" principle (of a less "mythic" and more specifically Christian kind).]

14. In Tieck's novel THE WANDERINGS OF FRANZ STERNBALD, the hero, a painter, *unintentionally* begins endowing the faces of saints with the sensuous features of his beloved Emma. In Hoffmann's "The Devil's Elixirs," the artist *consciously* wishes to depict Venus instead of St. Rosalia, but does not succeed in doing so. Only after he has tasted of the devil's elixir does he think it is Venus, not the saint, who looks out at him from the canvas. He asks Venus in a prayer to breathe life into his painting, and he thinks he sees it start to move. G. I. Chudakov does not mention these parallels in his article "Otnoshenie tvorchestva N. V. Gogolia k zapadno-evropeiskim literaturam," KIEVSKIE UNIVERSITETSKIE IZVESTIIA, VII, 1907; III, VIII, X, 1908.

NOTES TO CHAPTER VIII

1. [Gippius probably has in mind Fyodor Ivanovich Iordan, ZAPISKI, Moscow, 1918. Iordan (1800-1883) was an engraver who was trained in Russia but lived in Rome. Later he became Professor and Rector of the Academy of Arts in St. Petersburg.]

2. "Somneniia i protivorechiia v biografii Gogolia," IZVESTIIA 2 OTD. AKA-DEMII NAUK, Nos. 2 and 4, 1900; No. 1, 1902.

3. [Boldino was a small estate in the area of Nizhny-Novgorod owned by Push-kin's father. The poet went there in the early autumn of 1830, planning to remain only a month. But he was detained for three months by a quarantine established because of a cholera epidemic. It was a period of great productivity, which yielded lyric poems, polishing work on EUGENE ONEGIN, the TALES OF BELKIN, "The Little House in Kolomna," and the four "little tragedies." It has come to be known as the "Boldino autumn."

["Society scene" refers to "Scenes from Society Life," which was the original title of what eventually became "A Fragment."]

4. [Letter to N. M. Yazykov, September 22, 1841; letter to A. S. Danilevsky, August 7, 1841; letter to A. A. Ivanov, December 25, 1841.

[Alexander Andreevich Ivanov (1806-1858) was a Russian painter who lived most of his life in Rome. He was greatly admired by Gogol (who devoted an article in SELECTED PASSAGES FROM CORRESPONDENCE WITH FRIENDS to him) as a model of a true artist, i.e., one who sacrificed everything to his art and specialized in religious themes. His best-known work is "The Appearance of the Messiah to the People," on which he labored for more than twenty years.]

5. Cf. A. G. Tseitlin, POVEST' O BEDNOM CHINOVNIKE DOSTOEVSKOGO (K ISTORII ODNOGO SIUZHETA), Moscow, 1923. [Gippius misquotes the author's name as "Tseitman."]

6. Cf. V. V. Kallash, "Melkie zametki o Gogole," LITERATURNYI VESTNIK, No. 1, 1902, concerning the relationship between Gogol and Vasily Apollonovich Usha-kov (1789-1838) [a minor writer who dedicated his book THE VETERAN'S LEISURE HOURS (DOSUGI INVALIDA, 1832) to Gogol].

7. [The Russian title of Bulgarin's story is "Plach pod"iachego Pankratiia Fom-icha Tychkova pod svodom zakonov." It contains an untranslatable pun: svod means both "code of laws" and "vault" or "arch." The Russian title of the second Bulgarin story is "Gosudarstvennyi grib ili zhizn', t. e. proziabanie i podvigi priiatelia moego Fomy Fomicha Openkina." [" 'Jeered and gibed' at people who were unable to bite back" in the preceding sentence is a quote and a paraphrase from Gogol's "The Overcoat."]

8. V. V. Rozanov makes a major error by regarding Akaky Akakievich, in "The Overcoat," as an amplification of the type in "The Tale of a Clerk Who Stole Overcoats" ("Kak proizoshel tip Akakiia Akakievicha," LEGENDA O VELIKOM INKVIZITORE F. M. DOSTOEVSKOGO, S PRILOZHENIEM DVUKH ETIUDOV O GOGOLE, 3rd ed., St. Petersburg, 1906). [Grigoriev's words, in the next sentence, are found in his article "Gogol' i ego 'Perepiska s druz'iami'," MOSKOVSKII GORODSKOI LISTOK, Nos. 56, 62-64, 1847, as in SOBRANIE SOCHINENII, ed. V. F. Savodnik, II, Moscow, 1916, p. 9. The Russian is posledniaia gran' obmeleniia.]

9. Op. cit.

10. B. M. Eikhenbaum, "Kak sdelana 'Shinel'" Gogolia," POETIKA, Opoiaz, 1919.

11. "The element of fantasy in this story is made up of those fears and specters that appear in man's fantasy as the result of a disturbed conscience" (V. N. Mochulsky, MALOROSSIISKIE I PETERBURGSKIE POVESTI GOGOLIA, Odessa, 1902).

12. Cf. I. F. Annensky, "O formakh fantasticheskogo u Gogolia," RUSSKAIA SHKOLA, No. 10, 1890.

13. It is possible (though it has not been proved) that this is precisely what F. V. Chizhov had in mind when he reported that Gogol burned a play after Zhukovsky had fallen asleep while Gogol was reading it aloud. Cf. I. M. Kamanin, "Neskol'ko slov

ob istoricheskoi drame N. V. Gogolia," PAMIATI N. V. GOGOLIA. SBORNIK RECHEI I STATEI, Izd. imp. Un-m sv. Vladimira, Kiev, 1911. The title "The Shaved-Off Mustache" ("Vybrityi us") has often been used by writers about Gogol in reference to this play; this, however, is derived from Gogol's own words in a conversation with the actor Shchepkin, and cannot be regarded as accurate. [Fyodor Vasilievich Chizhov (1811-1877) taught mathematics at St. Petersburg University while Gogol was teaching history there. He was a Slavophile, took a keen interest in art and literature, and remained a good friend of Gogol's. He wrote his memoirs at the beginning of the 1850s. A selection can conveniently be found under the title "Vstrechi s Gogolem" in GOGOL' V VOSPOMI-NANIIAKH SOVREMENNIKOV, Moscow, 1952, pp. 225-229.]

14. Cf. Alexander Blok, "The Scythians" ("Skify," 1918): "Yes, *to love as* our blood loves—none of you has loved that way for a very long time" ("Da, *tak liubit'*, kak liubit nasha krov'—nikto iz vas davno ne liubit"). (Stresses supplied.)

15. An expression of Alexander Yevlakhov, TAINA GENIIA GOGOLIA, Warsaw, 1910.

NOTES TO CHAPTER IX

1. Gogol's mother assumed that he was the author of P. P. Svinin's YAGUB SKUPALOV, but Gogol assured her that Svinin himself had written the work: "The action of this novel takes place in the depths of Russia, where I haven't yet set foot. If I had written something in this vein, then I would probably have taken Little Russia, which I know, rather than countries and people whose manners, customs and occupations I don't know" (letter of December 19 [o.s.], 1830). [According to the Academy of Sciences edition of Gogol's works, there is no such novel in Svinin's *oeuvre*. It appeared anonymously, but the real author was Alexander Karlovich Boshnyak(1787-1831): cf. POLNOE SOBRANIE SOCHINENII, X, 1940, pp. 429-430.] As to how small were the chances Gogol had of expanding his factual knowledge of the Russian provinces, cf. S. A. Vengerov, "Gogol' sovershenno ne znal real'noi russkoi zhizni," RECH', No. 56-57, 1913, reworked for his book PISATEL'-GRAZHDANIN. GOGOL' (SOBRANIE SOCHINENII, II), St. Petersburg, 1913. [All the quotes from Gogol in this paragraph are found in "An Author's Confession."]

2. Before Vengerov, this had been pointed out by A. N. Veselovsky ("Mertvye Dushi. Glava iz etiuda o Gogole," VESTNIK EVROPY, March, 1891, pp. 69-74), and also by V. V. Rozanov ("Gogol'," MIR ISKUSSTVA, 1902), and by I. P. Zhitetsky ("Gogol'—propovednik i pisatel'," ZHURNAL MINISTERSTVA NARODNOGO PROSVESHCHENIIA, 1909). [Gippius has in mind Alexey Nikolaevich Veselovsky (1843-1918), a professor of Russian literature at Moscow University. He is not to be confused with his more famous brother Alexander Nikolaevich (1838-1906), Russia's greatest specialist in comparative literature, although the two shared many scholarly interests.]

2. [The quote about "the provinces" in the preceding sentence is from a letter to M. P. Pogodin, May 15 (o.s.), 1836. Pushkin' s words are as reported in "An Author's Confession." For "intellection," see Note No. 36 of Chapter VI.]

4. Cf. V. A. Gilyarovsky, "V Gogolevshchine," RUSSKAIA MYSL', No 1, 1902. Ye. A. Bobrov was the first to point to the episode in Dal's (Dahl's) work ("Dva voprosa iz tvorchestva Gogolia," IZVESTIIA 2 OTD. AKADEMII NAUK, I, 1910).

5. From a statement by Dmitry Ivanovich Gippius (1812-1893); cf. RUSSKII BIOGRAFICHESKII SLOVAR', V, Moscow, 1916, pp. 227-228. A portrait of the person presumed to be Chichikov has been preserved. Because of the death of Dmitry Ivanovich and all his close relatives, it is impossible to establish the details. The author of the present book was still a child the year Dmitry Ivanovich died.

6. Developed in the above-mentioned article by A. N. Veselovsky (see Note No. 2). Cf. also the article by M. N. Markovsky, "Istoriia vozniknoveniia i sozdaniia 'Mertvykh Dush,' " PAMIATI GOGOLIA, Kiev, 1902.

[The passage in question comes in "An Author's Confession." Gogol reports that Pushkin urged him to undertake a large-scale work because of his "capacity to get to the heart of man and present him all at once, as a totality, through just a few characteristics," citing the example of Cervantes, who "did write several very remarkable and good stories" but who "would never have occupied the place he now occupies among writers if he had not undertaken DON QUIXOTE...." The Izmaylov mentioned in the next sentence in the text is Vladimir Vasilievich Izmaylov (1773-1830), a follower of Karamzin in the Sentimental manner.]

7. [The article in ARABESQUES is "Schloezer, Miller and Herder"; the one in THE CONTEMPORARY (No. 1, 1836) is "Trends in Journal Literature in 1834 and 1835."]

8. [The title of the article is "Textbook of Literature for Russian Youth." It is undated, but according to the Academy of Sciences edition of Gogol's works (VIII, 1952), the most likely date for the completion of the manuscript such as we have it is between 1844 and the beginning of 1845.]

9. Toward the beginning of the 1840s, the name of Fielding had already been overshadowed by that of Dickens, as far as Russian readers were concerned. Polevoy excluded Dickens and Gogol "from the realm of the beautiful," but ranked Dickens higher. There is no information concerning Gogol's knowledge of Dickens's works before 1841; we know, however, that he was reading him in 1841 (cf. V. I. Shenrok, MATERIALY DLIA BIOGRAFII GOGOLIA, III, Moscow, 1895, p. 343). In the "list of authors definitely known to Gogol" that is appended to his book, G. I. Chudakov does not make any mention of Fielding, although he does include a number of names based on Smirnova's apocryphal memoirs and on other no less shaky evidence. (Cf. "Otnoshenie tvorchestva N. V. Gogolia k zapadno-evropeiskim literaturam," KIEVSKIE UNIVERSITETSKIE IZVESTIIA, VII, 1907; III, VIII, X, 1908).

[Here Gippius presumably means Alexandra Osipovna Smirnova. Her "Notes" ("Zapiski") were actually written by her daughter, Olga Nikolaevna, who attributed them to her. (See Note No. 1 to Chapter XI.) Although no systematic attempt is being made to update Gippius's bibliography—that would involve rewriting some of his book—mention can be made here of a useful recent work on Gogol's relationship with Western literature: A. A. Yelistratova, GOGOL' I PROBLEMY ZAPADNOEVROPEISKOGO ROMANA, Moscow, 1972.]

10. [Third letter of DEAD SOULS in SELECTED PASSAGES FROM CORRESPONDENCE WITH FRIENDS.]

11. [Shevyryov's review in MOSKVITIANIN, No. 7, 1842. Aksakov's phrase is found in his ISTORIIA MOEGO ZNAKOMSTVA S GOGOLEM.]

12; [Belinsky's remarks are found in "O russkoi povesti i povestiakh g. Gogolia ('Arabeski' i 'Mirgorod')," TELESKOP, Vol. 26, No. 8, 1935, and Aksakov's in the pamphlet NESKOL'KO SLOV O POEME GOGOLIA "POKHOZHDENIIA CHICHIKOVA ILI MERTVYE DUSHI," Moscow, 1842. Belinsky's objections to Aksakov are contained in an unsigned article in OTECHESTVENNYE ZAPISKI, No. 8, 1842.]

13. [IZ ZAPISOK PO TEORII SLOVESNOSTI, Kharkov, 1905, p. 294.]

14. [Review of DEAD SOULS, MOSKVITIANIN, No. 8, 1842.]

15. Second letter on DEAD SOULS, in SELECTED PASSAGES FROM CORRESPONDENCE WITH FRIENDS.

16. ["Poor Liza" ("Bednaia Liza") is the title of the most famous Sentimentalist short story in Russian literature. It was written by N. M. Karamzin in 1792. The review by Sorokin is found in Nos. 163, 164, and 165 of SANKT-PETERBURGSKIE VEDO-

MOSTI for 1842.]

17. "Estetika Mertvykh Dush i ee nasledie," APOLLON, No. 8, 1911.

18. [Misha (the diminutive of Mikhail[o]) is the typical pet name for a bear in Russian. Sobakevich is derived from *sobaka,* "dog."]

19. A summary of the information available on the prototypes of Plyushkin can be found in Ier. Aizenshtok, "K voprosu o literaturnykh vliianiiakh (G. F. Kvitka i N. V. Gogol')," IZVESTIIA 2 OTD. AKADEMII NAUK, XXIV, Book 1, Petrograd, 1922. [The works referred to later in the paragraph are: S. P. Shevyryov, review of DEAD SOULS, MOSKVITIANIN, Nos. 7 and 8, 1842; V. F. Pereverzev, TVORCHESTVO GO-GOLIA, Moscow, 1914; D. S. Merezhkovsky, GOGOL' I CHERT, Moscow, 1906.]

20. ["Pokhozhdeniia Chichikova ili Mertvye Dushi," OTECHESTVENNYE ZA-PISKI, No. 7, 1842.]

21. It is interesting that the time of year is defined more exactly in the first version Gogol wrote while living abroad: "The day was still rather hot, despite the fact that summer was on the wane, and he [Chichikov] had to take out his handkerchief and wipe his brow, on which large drops of sweat had appeared." Here too the "peasants were wearing shirts and were carrying their boots and sheepskins on poles." The beginning of Chapters II and VII have not survived; we do not known whether there were bearskin coats in this version as well. In reworking Chapter VII (after the book had already been published), Gogol gave the following explanation for the bearskin coat: "He had thrown on a bearskin coat not because it was cold outside, but in order to inspire fear in the office small fry."

22. M. I. Sukhomlinov, "Poiavlenie v pechati sochinenii Gogolia," ISSLEDO-VANIIA I STATI, II, St. Petersburg, 1879. [The quotation from Belinsky earlier in the paragraph comes from "Pokhozhdeniia Chichikova...," OTECHESTVENNYE ZAPISKI, No. 7, 1842. The quotes from Gogol in this paragraph come from his letter to P. A. Pletnyov, January 7 (o.s.), 1842.]

23. [Polevoy's review is in RUSSKII VESTNIK, Nos. 5-6, 1842.]

24. Cf. Fonvizin, "A General Court Grammar" ("Vseobshchaia pridvornaia gram-matika," 1788); Derzhavin's poem "The Bigwig" ("Vel'mozha," 1798); and Krylov's journal SPIRITS' MAIL (POCHTA DUKHOV, 1789), Part III, Letter 26. [The reference to the folk motif in the next sentence is to a song entitled "Kopeikin so Stepanom na Volge" ("Kopeikin with Stepan on the Volga"); it existed in several written variants, with which Gogol was familiar.]

25. Belinsky, in OTECHESTVENNYE ZAPISKI, No. 7, 1842; Shevyryov, in MO-SKVITIANIN, No. 7-8, 1842; Grech, in SEVERNAIA PCHELA, No. 137, 1842; K. P. Masalsky, in SYN OTECHESTVA, No. 6, 1842; Senkovsky, in BIBLIOTEKA DLIA CHTENIIA, Vol. 53, 1842; Polevoy, in RUSSKII VESTNIK, No. 5-6, 1842.

26. [All the quotes in this paragraph are from "(Notes) to the First Part (of DEAD SOULS)."]

NOTES TO CHAPTER X

1. [The "nightmares" statement comes in the third of the "Four Letters on DEAD SOULS," in SELECTED PASSAGES.]

2. ["What, Then, Constitutes the Essence of Russian Poetry and What Is Its Special Nature," in SELECTED PASSAGES.]

3. We find the term "caricature" being used in two ways by Gogol as well: without the slightest suggestion of disapproval, as in the examples cited in the text, and with a suggestion of disapproval, as in the article "Advance Notice for Those Who Would Like to Play THE INSPECTOR GENERAL As It Should Be": "Most of all one must

take care not to lapse into caricature." Evidently two different meanings are intended to be conveyed by the same word, and with reference to the same play. The sense of "Advance Notice" is of course clear: the already exaggerated figures in THE INSPECTOR GENERAL must necessarily suffer if there is further exaggeration, and become "bad caricatures."

4. "Iazykov-Gogol'," SANKT-PETERBURGSKIE VEDOMOSTI, Nos. 90 and 91, 1847. [The "letter to Pletnyov" in the preceding sentence was intended as an article for THE CONTEMPORARY and sent to Pletnyov along with a letter dated December 4, 1846. It is published as an article, under the title, "O Sovremennike," in POLNOE SOBRANIE SOCHINENII, VIII, 1952.]

5. Valuable observations on Gogol's use of hyperbole can be found in A. A. Potebnya, IZ ZAPISOK PO TEORII SLOVESNOSTI, Kharkov, 1905, p. 355 ff. I. E. Mandelshtam, in a special work devoted to Gogol's style, touches only lightly on his use of hyperbole (O KHARAKTERE GOGOLEVSKOGO STILIA..., Helsingfors, 1902). [V. V. Rozanov, "Pushkin i Gogol'," "Kak proizoshel tip Akakiia Akakievicha," LEGENDA O VELIKOM INKVIZITORE F. M. DOSTOEVSKOGO..., 3rd ed., St. Petersburg, 1906; V. Ya. Bryusov, "Ispepelennyi," VESY, No. 4, 1909: in English as "Burnt to Ashes" in R. A. Maguire, GOGOL FROM THE TWENTIETH CENTURY: ELEVEN ESSAYS, Princeton, 1974, pp. 105-132.]

6. [For a compact discussion of the "Natural School," see D. S. Mirsky, A HISTORY OF RUSSIAN LITERATURE, Chapter V.]

7. The expression "fervor" (*zador*) was not immediately arrived at by Gogol. At first he tried "his hobby-horse" (*svoi konek*) and "his yen" (*svoe vlechenie*). Cf. Pushkin's EUGENE ONEGIN (Chapter IV, Verse 36, of the first edition): "Each man has his inclination (*okhota*),/ His favorite concern,/ Some take aim at ducks with a gun,/ Some rant in rhymes, like me;/ Some squash insolent flies with a swatter,/ Some rule the crowd in their designs,/ Some amuse themselves with war,/ Some luxuriate in sad feelings,/ Some occupy themselves with wine,/ And good is mingled with evil."

8. [GOGOL' I CHERT, Moscow, 1906.]

9. [This quote comes in Act II, Scene 5. Khlestakov is in the inn, bemoaning his lack of money and thinking how nice it would be to hire a fine carriage and play the gentleman. The "pretty little daughter" appears by association with the milieu he is creating in his fantasy.]

10. "Sensually intoxicated" is a phrase of S. K. Shambinago, TRILOGIIA ROMANTIZMA (N. V. GOGOL'), Moscow, 1911.

11. In the very first versions, Khlestakov says, for example, that he has a "small decoration." By 1836, this expression has been cut. Originally, Chichikov was "head of a ministry"; then this was replaced by a department.

12. [LEGENDA O VELIKOM INKVIZITORE F. M. DOSTOEVSKOGO, 3rd. ed., St. Petersburg, 1906, p. 15ff.]

13. In any case, the expression "laughter through tears" is not Gogol's. Gogol spoke of the tears of someone who laughs more than anyone else in the world ("Leaving the Theater"), of looking at the world through laughter (which is visible) and tears (which are invisible), of sorrow that is heard through laughter ("An Author's Confession"). Among Gogol's contemporaries, Belinsky spoke of laughter diluted with bile, and Shevyryov of sorrow in laughter. The expression "laughter through tears" is Pushkin's (review of second edition of EVENINGS ON A FARM NEAR DIKANKA, in SOVREMENNIK, No. 1, 1836). It is said of "Old-Fashioned Landowners," but the emphasis is evidently on the word "laugh." For a reassessment of the expression "laughter through tears," cf. N. K. Bokadorov, "Komediia Gogolia," PAMIATI GOGOLIA, Kiev, 1902. Other reassessments (by V. Shmidt and S. K. Shambinago) are one-sided.

1. [Count Alexander Petrovich Tolstoy (1801-1873) occupied several high-ranking civil service posts, as governor of Tver, military governor of Odessa, and Minister of Church Affairs. He was one of Gogol's closest friends. Alexandra Osipovna Smirnova (1810-1882) was a lady-in-waiting to two Russian empresses, the wife of the governor of Kaluga Province, a friend of many Russian writers, and a spiritual disciple of Gogol's. Nadezhda Nikolaevna Sheremeteva (1775-1850) was the aunt of the famous poet Fyodor Tyutchev, and a highly religious woman, who corresponded with Gogol and with his mother. The Vielgorsky family was rich and well-connected, and especially interested in the arts. It was headed by Count Mikhail Yurevich (1788-1856). The most important of the children, for Gogol's life, were: Iosif, a sensitive and talented young man who died of consumption in Gogol's arms in Rome; Sofia, the wife of the writer V. A. Sollogub (Sollohub); and Anna, to whom Gogol may have proposed marriage.]

2. "N. V. Gogol' v ego religioznykh iskaniiakh," KHRISTIANSKAIA MYSL', Nos. 1-3, 5, 7-8, 10, 12, 1916.

3. [Cf. Note No. 19 to Chapter XIII. "The beautiful" in the preceding paragraph renders *prekrasnoe,* which can also mean "the excellent."]

4. Writing in THE ST. PETERSBURG REGISTER in 1847, P. A. Vyazemsky compared SELECTED PASSAGES with Silvio Pellico's ON THE OBLIGATIONS OF MAN. On this topic, and on possible contemporary Italian influences on Gogol see S. K. Shambinago, TRILOGIIA ROMANTIZMA (N. V. GOGOL'), Moscow, 1911. Of course, the question is not exhausted by these parallels alone.

5. [ISTORIIA MOEGO ZNAKOMSTVA S GOGOLEM.]

6. [The words about the mayor are in "Leaving the Theater"; the advice to the Aksakov brothers is in a letter to their father, S. T. Aksakov, dated December 22, 1844.]

7. [The phrase "an honest bribe-taker" is found in a letter to A. O. Smirnova, February 22, 1847. The first quote in the paragraph, on "freaks," comes from "What Is the Wife of a Provincial Governor" (SELECTED PASSAGES); the other, on the "cheat," comes from "To One Who Occupies an Important Place" (SELECTED PASSAGES).]

8. According to Alexey Veselovsky, Plyushkin was supposed to develop into a man uninterested in money, who would distribute his property to the poor ("Mertvye Dushi. Glava iz etiuda o Gogole," VESTNIK EVROPY, No. 3, 1891). The conjecture is plausible, inasmuch as Gogol, toward the end of his life, was moving away from the ideology of SELECTED PASSAGES toward an ideology of asceticism. However, we do not know what Gogol's real intentions were.

9. [The full title of the article is: "What, Then, Constitutes the Essence of Russian Poetry, and What Is Its Special Nature."]

10. On this matter, cf. A. A. Potebnya, IZ ZAPISOK PO TEORII SLOVES-NOSTI, Kharkov, 1905, pp. 374-375.

11. The article "What a Wife Can Be..." was intended as a guide to household management. It is not surprising that when Gogol got to know the Monk Sylvester's edition of the so-called DOMOSTROI (HOUSEHOLD MANAGEMENT), that sixteenth-century book of rules and regulations for successfully running a household, he became very enthusiastic about it and expressed his enthusiasm in a letter to A. M. Vielgorskaya (March 30·[o.s.], 1849). In this same letter one can also notice signs of a turn toward asceticism (cf., eg., the hesitation betrayed in his attitude toward Martha and Mary).

12. [The Novikov in question is the satirist Nikolay Ivanovich Novikov, editor of THE DRONE. The words in the quotation are spoken by Bezrassud (lit., "Reasonless"), in the issue cited.]

13. Thus Pushkin: "The calling of landowner is the same kind of service. To concern oneself with three thousand souls, whose entire welfare depends wholly upon us, is more important than to command a platoon or to copy diplomatic dispatches" (Letter

No. 8). Cf. Tentetnikov's reflections in Part 2 of DEAD SOULS. [Pushkin's A NOVEL IN LETTERS was probably written in 1829, but was published—with cuts—in 1857.]

14. In Russian literature before Gogol, one can point to M. M. Shcherbatov's JOURNEY INTO THE LAND OF OPHIR BY MR. S., SWEDISH NOBLEMAN (PUTE-SHESTVIE V ZEMLIU OFIRSKUIU G-NA S., SHVEDSKOGO DVORIANINA, 1786), the first Russian utopia. In addition, there are : F. V. Bulgarin's PLAUSIBLE FABLES, OR, WANDERINGS ABOUT THE WORLD IN THE TWENTY-NINTH CENTURY (PRAV-DOPODOBNYE NEBYLITSY ILI STRANSTVOVANIIA PO SVETU V 29-M VEKE, 1824); A. F. Veltman's [Weltmann's] novel THE YEAR 3448 (3448-OI GOD, 1833); the concluding chapter of V. A. Sollogub's [Sollohub's] THE TARANTASS (TARAN-TAS, 1845); and others. Only a fragment of V. F. Odoevsky's utopia THE YEAR 4338 (4338-YI GOD) was published in UTRENNIAIA ZARIA in 1840; concerning it, see P. N. Sakulin, IZ ISTORII RUSSKOGO IDEALIZMA. KN. V. F. ODOEVSKII, Vol. 1, Part 2, Moscow, 1913, p. 178ff. Besides this last parallel, Sakulin also makes the others cited above.

15. [In a letter to Gogol written on July 15, 1847. This is often referred to as the "Salzbrunn letter" because it was written from Salzbrunn, Silesia, where Belinsky was undergoing treatment for consumption.]

16. Cf. Zhukovsky's poem "A Singer in the Kremlin" ("Pevets v Kremle," 1814), especially the line: "Let the Heavenly Tsar come down into the council of earthly tsars" ("V sovet k tsariam—nebesnyi Tsar' ") and others like it.

17. Vs. M. Zummer, O VERE I KHRAME IVANOVA, Kiev, 1918. [The Ivanov in question is the famous painter: see Note No. 4 to Chapter VIII. The full Russian text of THOUGHTS ON READING THE BIBLE is printed in Vs. M. Zummer, ESKHATOLO-GIIA AL. IVANOVA. UCHENYE ZAPISKI NAUCHNO-ISSLEDOVATEL'SKOI KAFE-DRY ISTORII EVROPEISKOI KUL'TURY, vyp. 3, Kharkov, 1929. For a discussion of this work, and of Ivanov's relationship to Gogol, see M. V. Alpatov, ALEKSANDR ANDREEVICH IVANOV. ZHIZN' I TVORCHESTVO, Moscow, 1956, Vol. II, esp. Chapter XI.

[The quote from Gogol earlier in the paragraph about "general reconciliation" comes from a letter to Belinsky written about June 20, 1847. About Herzen's fleeing a "dead" Paris: Alexander Herzen went to Paris in 1847 and took a keen interest in the events and moods leading up to the Revolution of 1848. Disillusionment with the bourgeois mentality and with what he saw as misconceived revolutionary efforts quickly set in. He left the city, but returned after the February Revolution of 1848, ready to greet the new order of things. Again he became disillusioned, however, and he had to flee France in the summer of 1848 to avoid arrest.]

18. [For the correspondence with Annenkov, see the letters by Gogol dated August 12, August 31, September 7 and September 20, 1847. For Gogol's attempts to make friends with Herzen, see his letter to Annenkov, September 7, 1847. For the "upset reaction" to Belinsky, see his reply to Belinsky's letter of July 3, 1847, dated August 10, 1847 (the first version of this letter was written but not sent, at the end of July or the beginning of August, 1847). See also Note No. 7 to Chapter XII.]

19. [The letter to Zhukovsky is dated January 10, 1848. It was never used as an article.]

NOTES TO CHAPTER XII

1. [Gippius's citations from Gogol are not exact, but "preparation" is a constant theme in Gogol's letters to N. N. Sheremeteva in 1846 and 1847 (cf. e.g., November 8, 1846). The "external reasons" are detailed by Gogol in a letter to Sheremeteva dated March 20 (April 1), 1847: difficulties connected with the printing of SELECTED

PASSAGES, ill health, and the lack of a travelling companion.]

2. [Dmitry Nikolaevich Sverbeev (1799-1876) was one of Gogol's friends from the mid-1840s onward. The leader of a well-known Moscow intellectual circle, he is now remembered chiefly for his memoirs. His wife was Yekaterina Alexandrovna.]

3. [V. I. Shenrok, MATERIALY DLIA BIOGRAFII GOGOLIA, IV, Moscow, 1897, p. 519ff.]

4. [N. F. Pavlov wrote four letters to Gogol; Nos. 1, 2, and 4 were published in MOSKOVSKIE VEDOMOSTI in 1847 (March 6, March 29 and April 17); the third was not published at all. Belinsky thought that they were "a model of skilful writing" and that they had "defeated Gogol with his own weapons" (letter to V. P. Botkin, March 15 [o.s.], 1847).]

5. [Vyazemsky's article is entitled "Iazykov-Gogol'," and was published in SANKT-PETERBURGSKIE VEDOMOSTI, Nos. 90, 91, 1847; Gogol's reply is in a letter written on June 11, 1847. Filipp Filippovich Vigel (1786-1856) was a professional civil servant, who is remembered for his memoirs. Grigoriev's article is "Gogol' i ego 'Perepis-ka s druz'iami'," MOSKOVSKII GORODSKOI LISTOK, Nos. 56, 62-64, 1847. Bryan-chaninov (Ignaty, 1807-1867), was Archimandrite of Sergiev Monastery by the Strelna, and later Bishop of the Caucasus (for Gogol's reaction to his comments on SELECTED PASSAGES, see the letter to P. A. Pletnyov, May 9, 1847). Innokenty (Borisov, 1800-1857) was diocesan bishop in Kharkov and later Archbishop of Kherson and Tauris; cf. Gogol's letter to him dated about July 8, 1847. Matvey Alexandrovich Konstantin-ovsky (1792-1857) was a fanatically devout priest from Rzhev, who became a spiritual adviser to Gogol from the 1840s onward. Alexey Dmitrievich Galakhov (1807-1892) was a literary historian and a journalist; his article is in the form of a letter to Gogol, published in OTECHESTVENNYE ZAPISKI, No. 2, 1847.]

6. [Gippius probably has in mind Gogol's remarks on Pavlov in his letter to S. P. Shevyryov, May 25, 1847.]

7. The relationship between Gogol and Belinsky is the subject of special articles by S. A. Vengerov (PISATEL'-GRAZHDANIN. GOGOL' [SOBRANIE SOCHINENII, II], St. Petersburg, 1913); G. V. Alexandrovsky ("Gogol' i Belinskii," PAMIATI GOGO-LIA, Kiev, 1902); and S. Ashevsky ("Gogol' i Belinskii," OBRAZOVANIE, Nos. 2-4, 1902). [Gogol's first letter to Belinsky was written on June 20, 1847 (in response to Belinsky's article on SELECTED PASSAGES published in SOVREMENNIK, No. 2, 1847); it was sent through Prokopovich. Belinsky then replied with his "Salzbrunn let-ter" of July 15, 1847. Gogol wrote an anguished, virtually incoherent reply some time at the end of July or the beginning of August, 1847, which he did not send. He then wrote and sent his relatively mild rejoinder dated August 10, 1847.]

8. Gogol undoubtedly did treat the spread of literacy among the common people ironically. He tried to soft-pedal his views after receiving Belinsky's letter, but his atti-tude comes out in his treatment of the figure of Petrushka (DEAD SOULS), and earlier (1836) in a review written for THE CONTEMPORARY of the book A JOURNEY TO THE HOLY PLACES MADE IN THE SEVENTEENTH CENTURY (PUTESHESTVIE K SVIATYM MESTAM, SOVERSHENNOE V XVII V.): "This is one of those books which are read most often and most reverentially....Other books are read by Russian people for the sole purpose of...showing off to themselves and others that they can read easily what others read only haltingly, but without the slightest attention to the contents of the book. And therefore it is extremely difficult to select reading for our people." [The quote from Gogol in the text comes from his first, unsent letter to Belinsky in late July/early August, 1847. As for the "old" Gogol mentioned earlier in the paragraph, this refers to Gogol the writer of fiction and drama, who was greatly admired by Belin-sky, in contrast to the "new" Gogol of SELECTED PASSAGES.]

9. See the above-mentioned works by M. O. Gershenzon and S. A. Vengerov. [For Vengerov, Gippius has in mind PISATEL'-GRAZHDANIN.... For Gershenzon, the

earlier reference is in Note No. 25 to Chapter III. A more plausible source, however, is Gershenzon's notes to Turgenev's story "The Adventures of Second Lieutenant Bubnov" ("Pokhozhdeniia podporuchika Bubnova"), in which he mentions Gogol's influence on Turgenev: see RUSSKIE PROPILEI, III: I. S. TURGENEV, MATERIALY PO ISTORII RUSSKOI MYSLI I LITERATURY (ed. M. O. Gershenzon), Moscow, 1916, esp. pp. 298-299.]

10. Cf. G. V. Alexandrovsky, "Gogol' i Belinskii," PAMIATI GOGOLIA, Kiev, 1902, where he takes issue with A. I. Kirpichnikov, "Somneniia i protivorechiia v biografii Gogolia," IZVESTIIA 2 OTD. AKADEMII NAUK, Nos. 2 and 4, 1900; No. 1, 1902.

11 [The first part of the quote is from a letter to Father Matvey Konstantinovsky, April 28, 1848; the second from a letter to A. P. Tolstoy, April 13, 1848.]

12. [This seems to be a not entirely accurate quote from Gogol's letter to A. O. Smirnova, November 28 (o.s.), 1849.]

13. [Optina Pustyn was located in Kaluga Province, and by tradition went back to the fourteenth century. It was renowned for its antiquities and, especially in the nineteenth century, for its elders (*startsy*), some of whom played an important part in the spiritual life of certain prominent writers and thinkers such as Gogol, Dostoevsky, and Vladimir Solovyov.]

14. [The quotes in this paragraph have the following sources: (1) about his mother and the gentry: letters written in the middle of February, 1849; (2) "all these things shall be added...": letter to M. I., A. V., Ye. V. and O. V. Gogol (i.e., his mother and sisters), March 4 (o.s.), 1851; (3) about prosperity: letter to M. I., A.V. and Ye. V. Gogol, April 3 (o.s.), 1849; (4) to Smirnova: letter at the end of March, 1851; (5) to his sister Yelizaveta: letter of July 14 (o.s.), 1851. For a detailed discussion of the complex matter of the gentry-status of the Gogol family, see Leon Stilman, "Nikolaj Gogol and Ostap Hohol," ORBIS SCRIPTUS. DMITRIJ TSCHIŽEWSKIJ ZUM 70 GEBURTSTAG, Munich, Wilhelm Fink Verlag, 1966, esp. pp. 816-817.]

15. As in a letter to A. M. Vielgorskaya which, according to V. I. Shenrok, dates from 1850: "As if this is a trifling matter: they are the ones who feed us, while calling us the ones who feed them, and we have no time, even after twenty years, to cast so much as a glance at them." [The Academy of Sciences edition of Gogol's works dates this letter from spring, 1850: see POLNOE SOBRANIE SOCHINENII, XIV, 1952, p. 187. The S. M. Sollogub who is one of the addressees of the letter of October 20 cited earlier in the paragraph was the sister of Anna Mikhailovna Vielgorskaya—Sofia Mikhailovna—and the wife of the writer V. A. Sollogub (Sollohub).]

16. [GOGOL' I CHERT, Moscow, 1906.]

17. [These lines are from Solovyov's poem "In the Morning Mist with Uncertain Steps" ("V tumane utrennem nevernymi shagami"), published in RUSSKII VESTNIK, No. 11, 1884.]

NOTES TO CHAPTER XIII

1. [For a compact characterization of the Natural School, see D. S. Mirsky, A HISTORY OF RUSSIAN LITERATURE, Chapter V, "The First Naturalists."]

2. In an 1846 article on THE PETERSBURG MISCELLANY (PETERBURGSKII SBORNIK), Belinsky wrote: "Gogol had no predecessors in Russian literature, he had no models in foreign literatures (nor could he). There were not the slightest suggestions of his particular kind of poetry before it actually appeared" (OTECHESTVENNYE ZAPISKI, XLV, No. 3, 1846). [The other references to Belinsky in this paragraph are found, sequentially, in the following articles: "Russkaia literatura v 1842 godu" (OTECHESTVENNYE ZAPISKI, XXVI, No. 1, 1843); "Russkaia literatura v 1843 godu"

(OTECHESTVENNYE ZAPISKI, XXXII, No. 1, 1844); "Vzgliad na russkuiu literaturu 1847 goda," (SOVREMENNIK, VII, No. 1, 1848).]

    3. "It seems that the origin of naturalism can be explained much more simply: there is no need to invent a pedigree for it when it shows clear signs of the influences to which it is indebted for its existence. The material has been provided by Gogol, or rather, has been taken from him..." (MOSKVITIANIN, September, 1847).

    4. [With reference to Dal's (Dahl's) "physiological" stories "Sausage-Makers and Bearded Men" ("Kolbasniki i borodachi"), "The Yardman" ("Dvornik") and "The Batman" ("Denshchik"), which he called "models of works in this genre," Belinsky wrote: "After Gogol he is definitely the finest talent in Russian literature to date" ("Russkaia literatura v 1845 godu," OTECHESTVENNYE ZAPISKI, XLIV, No. 1, 1846). Earlier he had given Sollogub (Sollohub) this place of honor ("Russkaia literatura v 1842 godu," OTECHESTVENNYE ZAPISKI, XXVI, No. 1, 1843).]

    5. In his edition of Gogol's letters (PIS'MA GOGOLIA, St. Petersburg, 1902), V. I. Shenrok has "Gutkov" in both the text and the index. [Belinsky's words about Grigorovich and Butkov are found in "Vzgliad na russkuiu literaturu 1846 goda," SOVREMENNIK, I, No. 1, 1847; about Sollogub (Sollohub) in "Russkaia literatura v 1842 godu," OTECHESTVENNYE ZAPISKI, XXVI, No. 1, 1843.]

    6. [Review of PETERBURGSKII SBORNIK, 1846, in OTECHESTVENNYE ZAPISKI, XLV, No. 3, 1846. Boris Nikolaevich Almazov, quoted in the following sentence, lived between 1827 and 1876, and was best known as a writer of humorous and satirical verses. He was also a journalist, who worked on THE MUSCOVITE in the 1850s.]

    7. ["Contemptible and insignificant" occurs in "Leaving the Theater"; the statement about nightmares comes in the third of the "Four Letters on DEAD SOULS" in SELECTED PASSAGES.]

    8. As cited by Arnoldi, "Moe znakomstvo s Gogolem," RUSSKII VESTNIK, No. 1, 1862. [Lev Ivanovich Arnoldi (1822-1860) was the half-brother of A. O. Smirnova (see Note No. 1 to Chapter XI), and worked for her husband, who was the governor of Kaluga Province.]

    9. [For "sticking out the nose," see the quote in the paragraph below; for "undigested self," see the letter to S. P. Shevyryov, December 12, 1847.]

    10. The traditional definition of Gogol as a realist has usually been demonstrated by quotes taken out of the context of the chronology and evolution of his work and intended to show his attraction to naturalism. Cf., e.g., D. N. Ovsyaniko-Kulikovsky, GOGOL', 2nd ed., St. Petersburg, 1907, where such quotes serve to force all of Gogol's development into a straight line, as being the work of what Ovsyaniko-Kulikovsky calls an "experimenter" [i.e., one who gives his own psyche primacy and perceives and organizes the outside world accordingly, in contrast to the "observer," who tries to give a faithful reproduction of that world.]

    11. [Actually, this was intended as an article for THE CONTEMPORARY (No. 1, 1847), and was sent to Pletnyov along with a letter dated December 4, 1846. It was never published during Gogol's lifetime, and appeared in full form only in 1889. (It is classified as an "article" and published, under the title "On THE CONTEMPORARY," in the Academy of Sciences edition, Vol. IX, 1952.]

    12. [As reported in the memoirs of Nikolay Vasilievich Berg, "Vospominaniia o N. V. Gogole," RUSSKAIA STARINA, No. 1, 1872. Berg (1824-1884) was also a poet and translator.]

    13. Arnoldi, "Moe znakomstvo s Gogolem."

    14. [The first quote is from a letter to A. O. Smirnova, April 20, 1847; the second is from a letter also to Smirnova, February 22, 1847.]

    15. [Review of THE TARANTASS, in OTECHESTVENNYE ZAPISKI, XL, No. 6, 1845.]

16. [The quote on DEAD SOULS is from the first of "Four Letters to Various Persons on DEAD SOULS," in SELECTED PASSAGES; the quote following it is from a letter to Arkady Osipovich Rosset, April 15, 1847.]

17. ["Moe znakomstvo s Gogolem."]

18. The materials on geography were published by G. P. Georgievsky, GOGOLEV-SKIE TEKSTY, St. Petersburg, 1910 [and are also found in the Academy of Sciences edition of Gogol's works, Vol. IX, 1952, under the title "Materials on Geography, Ethnography and Agriculture."] At the same time, Gogol was collecting regional and other characteristic words and expressions; and from this came a plan for a dictionary of the Russian language (which he did not bring to fruition either). [Gogol's words come from a petition either to Count L. A. Perovsky or Prince P. A. Shirinsky-Shikhmatov or Count A. F. Orlov, written between July 10-18, 1850. Gippius flatly identifies the addressee as Count Orlov, but the more recent Academy of Sciences edition of Gogol's works lists three possible addressees, as just indicated (POLNOE SOBRANIE SOCHINENII, XIV, 1952, p. 444.]

19. The dating of the surviving chapters of Part 2 was provided by N. P. Trushkov-sky in the foreword to the posthumous edition of Gogol's works (SOCHINENIIA I PIS'MA, 6 vols., 1857), and was basically supported by A. S. Tikhonravov (SOCHINE-NIIA N. V. GOGOLIA, 10th ed., III, Moscow, 1889, p. 579ff.). Tikhonravov regarded the first four chapters as a survival of Gogol's manuscript burning of the first half of the 1840s, and he attributes only the last, unnumbered chapter to the period after 1846. Serious doubt was cast on Tikhonravov's supposition by V. V. Kallash ("Zametki o Gogole," GOLOS MINUVSHEGO, No. 9, 1913), who dated both surviving versions from the final years of Gogol's life, finding allusions to members of the Petrashevsky Circle and to T. N. Granovsky in the text. Without getting into an examination of *all* of Kallash's evidence, I will say something in defense of his dating in my text proper. This dating allows us to regard the second half of DEAD SOULS as an expression of the *final* phase of Gogol's evolution.

20 This provides a fully satisfactory explanation of something that perplexed Shenrok: "Chichikov's decision to mortgage the dead souls in order to...buy a real estate... as if this chapter had been written before the one in which Chichikov has already bought Khlobuev's estate" (MATERIALY DLIA BIOGRAFII GOGOLIA, IV, Moscow, 1897, p. 908).

21. [I do not find this in Belinsky. He was consistently full of praise for "Taras Bulba." It sounds more like M. A. Grabovsky, e.g. SOVREMENNIK, Vol. 41, 1846: cf. V. A. Zelinsky, RUSSKAIA KRITICHESKAIA LITERATURA O PROIZVEDENIIAKH N. V. GOGOLIA, III, 1907, esp. pp. 69-73).]

22. [For Markov's letter to Gogol, written some time in 1847, see Shenrok, MATERIALY, IV, pp. 552, 553. Gogol's reply is dated December 3, 1849 (actually it is in reply, two years late, to a *second* letter from Markov dated November 23, 1847, in which Gogol says that he did not answer Markov's first letter because he did not know the address.) Konstantin Ivanovich Markov, one of Gogol's more obscure correspondents, was a retired army lieutenant and a landowner of Kharkov Province. His dates of birth and death are not listed in the standard reference works.]

23. [Cf., e.g., his review of SOCHINENIIA I PIS'MA N. V. GOGOLIA, ed. P. A. Kulish (6 vols., St. Petersburg, 1857), as in SOVREMENNIK, No. 8, 1857.]

24. Cf. N. V. GOGOL' V VOSPOMINANIIAKH SOVREMENNIKOV I PEREPIS-KA, comp. V. V. Kallash, Moscow, 1909, p. 115ff. (memoirs of L. I. Arnoldi), 127ff. (memoirs of Prince D. A. Obolensky).

25. ["Moe znakomstvo s Gogolem."]

26. Mizko, as cited in Shenrok, MATERIALY, IV, p. 886. [Pisemsky's remarks are contained in the article "Sochineniia N. V. Gogolia, naidennye posle ego smerti: POKHOZHDENIIA CHICHIKOVA ILI MERTVYE DUSHI, TOM VTOROI,"

27. Cf. a fragment from Gogol's very early work "The Dread Hand": "It was a triangle, the apex of which was located in the nose: faces which express stupidity more than anything else."

28. However, these figures could have been characterized in the chapters that were destroyed by burning.

29. As in N. V. GOGOL' V VOSPOMINANIIAKH SOVREMENNIKOV, Moscow, 1909, p. 126.

30. Ivan Aksakov conjectured that Gogol would not have read the first few chapters if the rest had not already been completed. This is supported by Gogol's letter of January 21 (o.s.), 1850, to Pletnyov: "Almost all the chapters have been thought out and even sketched out...but only two or three have actually been written, that's all." In Gogol's language, as Tikhonravov explained, "sketched out" meant written in rough draft, and "written" meant polished. In the summer of 1851, N. V. Berg heard in Moscow that eleven chapters of Part 2 had been written. If the rumors were correct, this was the second version, in which Gogol availed himself of Smirnova's advice.

31. [The reference is, of course, to Chekhov's famous story "The Man in the Case" ("Chelovek v futliare," 1898).]

32. "Mertvye Dushi. Glava iz etiuda o Gogole," VESTNIK EVROPY, No. 3, 1891, pp. 69-74.

33. As reported in N. V. GOGOL' V VOSPOMINANIIAKH SOVREMENNIKOV, Moscow, 1909, p. 114. [The remark was made to Archimandrite Fyodorov and published in his "Tri pis'ma k N. V. Gogoliu" (written 1848, published 1861).]

NOTES TO CHAPTER XIV

1. N. N. Bazhenov, "Bolezn' i smert' Gogolia," RUSSKAIA MYSL', Nos. 1 & 2, 1902. Cf. also V. F. Chizh, "Bolezn' Gogolia," VOPROSY FILOSOFII I PSIKHOLOGII, 1903-1904.

2. [Cf. V. I. Shenrok, MATERIALY DLIA BIOGRAFII GOGOLIA, IV, Moscow, 1897, pp. 815-817. Osip Maximovich Bodyansky (1808-1877) was professor of the history and literature of Slavic dialects in Moscow University.]

3. A. S. Khomyakov, POLNOE SOBRANIE SOCHINENII (Moscow, 1900-1907), VII (PIS'MA, 1822-1857), p. 208; and N. P. Barsukov, ZHIZN' I TRUDY M. P. POGODINA, XI, St. Petersburg, 1897, pp. 530-31.

4. Cf. A. I. Kirpichnikov, "Somneniia i protivorechiia v biografii Gogolia," IZVESTIIA 2 OTD. AKADEMII NAUK, Nos. 2 & 4, 1900; No. 1, 1902.

5. Cf. Barsukov; Shenrok, MATERIALY, IV, pp. 840-865.

6. Barsukov, p. 545.

7. [GOGOL' I CHERT, Moscow, 1906.]

8. Part of these manuscripts were saved by M. P. Pogodin and are at present in the Pushkin House of the Academy of Sciences in Leningrad. The most important of them were published (in a very slipshod manner) by K. N. Mikhaylov ("Vnov' naidennye rukopisi Gogolia," ISTORICHESKII VESTNIK, II, 1902). [The Academy of Sciences edition of Gogol's works contains this manuscript material.]

9. Cf. M. P. Pogodin, as in Barsukov, XI, p. 533. The version of Dr. A. T. Tarasenkov (who was among those attending Gogol in his last illness) has become the commonly accepted one: "[Gogol said:] Let him [Filaret] place his hand on them: whatever may seem unnecessary to him, let him cross it out unmercifully" (as in Shenrok, MATERIALY, IV, p. 854). In essence, this does not contradict Pogodin's version; it merely says nothing about the works that were designated for publication and not given over to Filaret. The memoirs of N. V. Berg make the same point, but also put forth the

unfounded assertion that it was precisely (and only) Part 2 of DEAD SOULS on which Filaret was supposed to pass judgment.

10. M. P. Pogodin, MOSKVITIANIN, No. 5, Book 1, Section VII, March, 1852, p. 49. [As in V. V. Veresaev, GOGOL' V ZHIZNI, Moscow-Leningrad, 1933, p. 498. I have expanded Gippius's quote somewhat.]

11. Only S. P. Shevyryov gives a different version, in a letter to M. N. Sinelnikova: "Meanwhile he was sorting out his papers: some he put away into a portfolio, others he consigned to burning" (RUSSKAIA STARINA, No. 5, 1902).

12. Tarasenkov's version differs as follows: instead of "he burned the chapters of DEAD SOULS," it has "he burned everything"; and it says that immediately after the burning (i.e., late at night) Gogol "had the Count [Tolstoy] summoned," and made this statement to him. Given such a sequence of events (he had just burned the papers and immediately spoke of the work of the evil spirit), Gogol's words really do look like mystification. In Pogodin's article in MOSKVITIANIN (see Note No. 10), and in Barsukov's book (*op. cit.*), there is a statement—quoted from the account given by Gogol's servant Semyon—allegedly made by Gogol after the burning of the papers: "Some things had to be burned, but for the other things [that were also burned] people should pray to God for me; but if God grants it, I will regain my health and put everything right."

13. Shortly after Gogol's death, people began to show concern about preserving the legend. See the letter written by A. P. Tolstoy to M. P. Pogodin after reading his article on Gogol's final days (published in MOSKVITIANIN; see Note No. 10). This same letter also confirms the fact that Gogol did make a statement about the burning episode. Tolstoy does not dispute the accuracy of the words themselves, but is displeased that they have been made public: "I think that the last lines, which concern the active part taken by the Evil One in the burning of the papers, can and should be left out. That was said to me alone, without any witnesses. I would have been capable of not telling anyone about it, and perhaps the deceased himself would not have wished to tell it to everyone.... Here is one further observation: the last lines spoil the moving effect of the whole story of the burning of the papers" (Barsukov, XI, p. 534).

14. Berg calls attention to this: "The heroic deed (if it was a heroic deed) was far from fully done, however: subsequently, sketches by Gogol, that had been brought to a certain completeness, were found in the wardrobe....Had he forgotten about these notebooks, or had he left them there intentionally?" (RUSSKAIA STARINA, V, 1872).

15. The only hint of a solution can be seen in a story told by Father Matvey Konstantinovsky as related by Archpriest F. I. Obraztsov (TVERSKIE EPARKHIAL'NYE VEDOMOSTI, No. 5, 1902, pp. 137-141). Although contradictory as to details, this story contains one very significant reference to Father Matvey's advice not to publish those chapters of Part 2 in which a priest is depicted ("he was a real person, who would be recognized by everyone, and traits of character have been added which...I do not have—and what is more, with Catholic touches—and the result is a priest who is not wholly Orthodox"). He advised Gogol to destroy those chapters. He took a milder but also disapproving attitude toward the way the governor-general was depicted, and predicted that people would make fun of it. The priest (Gogol also spoke of him to A.O. Smirnova) was a character "in one or two notebooks" (cf. P. A. Kulish, ZAPISKI O ZHIZNI N. V. GOGOLIA, II, St. Petersburg, 1856; and N. V. GOGOL' V VOSPOMINANIIAKH SOVREMENNIKOV, Moscow, 1909). The following hypothesis can be made: Gogol decided to leave his friends, posthumously, the chapters of DEAD SOULS (according to S. P. Shevyryov, "his intention was to distribute *one chapter* to each of his friends"). On Father Matvey's advice, he agreed to destroy *certain* chapters (along with other papers "long since intended for that"), but in actuality, what was burned were certain of the chapters to which Father Matvey had taken no exception. Gogol could well have taken the loss of these chapters (which were particularly successful, according to all reports) especially hard. Father Matvey denied that the compositions could have been burned because they

were "sinful," and said to Terenty Filippov: "Gogol burned some things, but he did not burn all the notebooks he had at hand." [Terenty Ivanovich Filippov (1825-1899) was a civil servant and sometime writer, who in his youth had worked on THE MUSCOVITE.]

16. "Somneniia i protivorechiia v biografii Gogolia," IZVESTIIA 2 OTD. AKADEMII NAUK, Nos. 2 and 4, 1900; No. 1, 1902.

17. As in Shenrok, MATERIALY, IV, p. 854.

18. [Gippius uses the term "starvation typhus" (*golodnyi tif*). Certainly Gogol was starving himself to death, and there does seem to have been an outbreak of typhus in Moscow at that time. However, it is impossible to say just what caused Gogol's death, as Dr. Tarasenkov admitted (see Shenrok, MATERIALY, IV, pp. 864-865).]

An Acrostic: Akrostikh.
Advance Note for Those Who Would Like to Play *The Inspector General* As It Should
Be: Preduvedomlenie dlia tekh, kotorye pozhelali by sygrat' kak sleduet "Revizora."
Alfred: Al'fred.
Al-Mamun: Al-Mamun (Arabesques).
Arabesques: Arabeski.
An Author's Confession: Avtorskaia ispoved'.
Bisavryuk, or St. John's Eve: Bisavriuk, ili Vecher nakanune Ivana Kupala.
The Bloody Bandore-Player: Krovavyi bandurist.
Boris Godunov: Boris Godunov.
The Brigands: Razboiniki.
The Brothers Tverdislavich: Brat'ia Tverdislavichi.
The Captive: Plennik.
The Carriage: Koliaska.
A Chapter from a Historical Novel: Glava iz istoricheskogo romana (The Hetman).
Christmas Eve: Noch' pered Rozhdestvom (Evenings on a Farm Near Dikanka).
Comedy. General Materials: Komediia. Materialy obshchie.
Dead Souls: Mertvye dushi.
The Denouement of *The Inspector General*: Razviazka "Revizora."
Diary of a Madman: Zapiski sumasshedshego.
The Dread Hand: Strashnaia ruka.
The Dread Wild Boar: Strashnyi kaban.
The Earth and Its Peoples: Zemlia i liudi.
Easter Sunday: Svetloe voskresenie (Selected Passages from Correspondence with
Friends).
An Enchanted Spot: Zakoldovannoe mesto (Evenings on a Farm Near Dikanka).
Evenings on a Farm Near Dikanka: Vechera na khutore bliz Dikan'ki.
Excerpt from a Letter Written by the Author to a Certain Man of Letters Shortly After
the First Performance of *The Inspector General*: Otryvok iz pis'ma, pisannogo
avtorom vskore posle pervogo predstavleniia "Revizora" k odnomu literatoru.
The Fair at Sorochintsy: Sorochinskaia iarmarka (Evenings on a Farm Near Dikanka).
The Fears and Terrors of Russia: Strakhi i uzhasy Rossii (Selected Passages from Correspondence with Friends).
A Few Thoughts on the Teaching of Geography to Children: Neskol'ko myslei o prepodavanii detiam geografii.
A Few Words About Pushkin: Neskol'ko slov o Pushkine (Arabesques).
Four Letters to Various Persons on *Dead Souls*: Chetyre pis'ma k raznym litsam po
povodu "Mertvykh dush" (Selected Passages from Correspondence with Friends).
A Fragment: Otryvok (The Order of St. Vladimir, Third Class).
From University Lectures on the History of the Middle Ages: Iz universitetskikh lektsii
po istorii srednikh vekov.
The Gamblers: Igroki.
Hanz Küchelgarten: Gants Kiukhel'garten.
The Hetman: Get'man.
The Inspector General: Revizor.
Italy: Italiia.
It Is Necessary to Travel Through Russia: Nuzhno proezdit'sia po Rossii (Selected Passages from Correspondence with Friends).
Ivan Fyodorovich Shponka and His Aunt: Ivan Fedorovich Shpon'ka i ego tetushka
(Evenings on a Farm Near Dikanka).
Landowners: Pomeshchiki.
The Last Day of Pompeii: Poslednii den' Pomei (Arabesques).
A Lawsuit: Tiazhba (The Order of St. Vladimir, Third Class).
Leaving the Theater after the Performance of a New Comedy: Teatral'nyi raz"ezd posle
predstavleniia novoi komedii.
Life: Zhizn' (Arabesques).
The Lost Letter: Propavshaia gramota (Evenings on a Farm Near Dikanka).
Marriage: Zhenit'ba.
Materials on Geography, Ethnography and Agriculture: Materialy po geografii, etnografii i sel'skomu khoziaistvu.

A May Night: Maiskaia noch' (Evenings on a Farm Near Dikanka).
Meditations on the Divine Liturgy: Razmyshleniia o Bozhestvennoi liturgii.
Mirgorod: Mirgorod.
Nesvky Prospect: Nevskii Prospekt (Arabesques).
A New Abode: Novosel'e.
Nights at a Villa: Nochi na ville.
The Nose: Nos.
(Notes) to the First Part (of *Dead Souls*): (Zametki) k pervoi chasti ("Mertvykh dush").
An Official's Morning: Utro delovogo cheloveka (The Order of St. Vladimir, Third Class).
Old-Fashioned Landowners: Starosvetskie pomeshchiki (Mirgorod).
On the Architecture of the Present Day: Ob arkhitekture nyneshnego vremeni (Arabesques).
On *The Contemporary*: O "Sovremennike."
On the Estates of Society in the State: O sosloviiakh v gosudarstve.
On Little Russian Songs: O malorossiiskikh pesniakh (Arabesques).
On the Love of God and the Nurturing of Self: O liubvi k Bogu i samovospitanii.
On the Lyricism of Our Poets: O lirizme nashikh poetov (Selected Passages from Correspondence with Friends).
On the Middle Ages: O srednikh vekakh (Arabesques).
On the Movement of Peoples at the End of the Fifth Century: O dvizhenii narodov v kontse V veka (Arabesques).
On *The Odyssey* as Translated by Zhukovsky: Ob Odisee, perevodimoi Zhukovskim (Selected Passages from Correspondence with Friends).
On the Poetry of Kozlov: O poezii Kozlova.
On the Teaching of World History: O prepodavanii vseobshchei istorii (Arabesques).
On the Theater, On a One-Sided View of the Theater, and On One-Sidedness in General: O teatre, ob odnostoronnem vzgliade na teatr i voobshche ob odnostoronnosti (Selected Passages from Correspondence with Friends).
The Order of St. Vladimir, Third Class: Vladimir tret'ei stepeni.
The Overcoat: Shinel'.
Parting Words: Naputstvie (Selected Passages from Correspondence with Friends).
Petersburg and Moscow: Peterburg i Moskva.
Petersburg Notes of 1836: Peterburgskie zapiski 1836 goda.
The Petersburg Stage in the 1835-36 Season: Peterburgskaia stsena v 1835-36 g.
The Portrait: Portret.
Preface to the Second Edition of *Dead Souls*: Predislovie ko vtoromu izdaniiu pervogo toma "Mertvykh dush."
Review of *The Dawn (Utrenniaia zaria)*.
Review of *The Dissatisfied Ones (Nedovol'nye)*, by M. N. Zagoskin.
Review of *A Journey to the Holy Places Made in the Seventeenth Century (Puteshestvie k sviatym mestam, sovershennoe v XVII v.)*.
Rome: Rim.
Rural Justice and Punishment: Sel'skii sud i rasprava (Selected Passages from Correspondence with Friends).
Russia Under the Yoke of the Tartars: Rossiia pod igom tatar.
The Russian Landowner: Russkii pomeshchik (Selected Passages from Correspondence with Friends).
St. John's Eve: Vecher nakanune Ivana Kupala (Evenings on a Farm Near Dikanka).
Scenes from Society Life: Stseny iz svetskoi zhizni.
Schloezer, Miller and Herder: Shletser, Miller i Gerder (Arabesques).
Sculpture, Painting and Music: Skul'ptura, zhivopis' i muzyka (Arabesques).
Selected Passages from Correspondence with Friends: Vybrannye mesta iz perepiski s druz'iami.
The Servants' Quarters: Lakeiskaia (The Order of St. Vladimir, Third Class).
Something About Nezhin, or, Fools Rush In Where Angels Fear to Tread: Nechto o Nezhine, ili durakam zakon ne pisan.
Subjects for the Lyric Poet at the Present Time: Predmety dlia liricheskogo poeta v nyneshnee vremia (Selected Passages from Correspondence with Friends).
The Success of a Mission: Uspekh posol'stva (The Dread Wild Boar).
The Suitors: Zhenikhi.
The Tale of a Clerk Who Stole Overcoats: Povest' o chinovnike, kradushchem shineli.
The Tale of How Ivan Ivanovich Quarrelled with Ivan Nikiforovich: Povest' o tom, kak possorilsia Ivan Ivanovich s Ivanom Nikiforovichem (Mirgorod).
Taras Bulba: Taras Bul'ba.

215

The Teacher: Uchitel' (The Dread Wild Boar).

A Terrible Vengeance: Strashnaia mest' (Evenings on a Farm Near Dikanka).

Textbook of Literature for Russian Youth: Uchebnaia kniga slovesnosti dlia russkogo iunoshestva.

Thoughts on Geography: Mysli o geografii (Arabesques).

To One Who Occupies an Important Place: Zanimaiushchemu vazhnoe mesto (Selected Passages from Correspondence with Friends).

Trends in Journal Literature in 1834 and 1835: O dvizhenii zhurnal'noi literatury v 1834 i 1835 g.

Two Fish: Dve ryby.

A View of the Formation of Little Russia: Vzgliad na sostavlenie Malorossii (Arabesques).

Viy: Vii (Mirgorod).

What a Wife Can Be for Her Husband in the Simple Domestic Life, Given the Present-Day Order of Things in Russia: Chem mozhet byt' zhena dlia muzha v prostom domashnem bytu, pri nyneshnem poriadke veshchei v Rossii (Selected Passages from Correspondence with Friends).

What Is the Wife of a Provincial Governor: Chto takoe gubernatorsha (Selected Passages from Correspondence with Friends).

What, Then, Constitutes the Essence of Russian Poetry, and What Is Its Special Nature: V chem zhe nakonets sushchestvo russkoi poezii i v chem ee osobennost' (Selected Passages from Correspondence with Friends).

Woman: Zhenshchina.

Woman in Society: Zhenshchina v svete (Selected Passages from Correspondence with Friends).

1834: 1834.